THE
HEALTHY
CUISINE
OF
INDIA

THE
HEALTHY
CUISINE
OF
INDIA
RECIPES FROM THE
BENGAL REGION

Bharti Kirchner

LOWELL HOUSE

Los Angeles

CONTEMPORARY BOOKS

Chicago

Library of Congress Cataloging-in-Publication Data

Kirchner, Bharti.
    The healthy cuisine of India : recipes from the Bengal
region / by Bharti Kirchner.
        p.   cm.
    Includes bibliographical references and index.
    ISBN 1-56565-009-3
    1. Cookery, India.   2. Cookery—India—Bengal.   I. Title.
TX724.5.I4K57   1992
641.5954 ' 14—dc20   92-4613
                                                         CIP

Lowell House
2029 Century Park East, Suite 3290
Los Angeles, CA 90067
Publisher: Jack Artenstein
Executive Vice-President: Nick Clemente
Vice-President/Editor-in-Chief: Janice Gallagher
Design: Carrington Design

Manufactured in the United States of America
10 9 8 7 6 5 4 3 2 1

Dedication

To my family in Bengal
You've given me more than I can say

Acknowledgments

To my husband Tom who, since the day he first tasted Bengali food, had asked me to write a book about it. He has read, tasted, and critiqued every recipe in this book.

To the critique group led by Dick Gibbons for reviewing my manuscript. To Lynn Bursten, Ph.D., for her suggestions and support.

To those who enthusiastically retested my recipes: Risa Laib, Natalie Ng, Lynn Bursten, Susan Wells, Sue Hamilton, Peter Holman, Didi White, and Joan Caine.

To those who answered my many questions: Gita Sirkar, Nivedita Dutta, Apu Dutta, Neelam Mukherjee, and Krishna Mukherjee.

To my photographer Ali Haider for his care and attention.

To my agent Doe Coover for her guidance, support, and humor.

And finally to my editor Janice Gallagher, who has been a pleasure to work with and who made this book possible.

I owe much to all of you.

✳

TABLE OF CONTENTS

I love you my golden Bengal
Your sky and your breezes play flute within my soul,
O Mother,
In spring among your forests of mangoes,
the fragrance intoxicates . . .

Rabindranath Tagore
(Nobel Prize–winning Bengali poet, 1861–1941)

THE
HEALTHY
CUISINE
OF
INDIA

THE RICHES OF BENGAL

The healthy, exciting cuisine of Bengal has a venerable history. Bengal is an ancient land whose people share a common language and cultural heritage. Many historians believe that the rich, luxuriant delta of *Ganga*, the river Ganges, was the site of one of our earliest civilizations. Impenetrable jungles to the east, massive Himalayas to the north, the lush jungles of Sunderban, "beautiful forest," and the Bay of Bengal to the south allowed Bengal to evolve in relative isolation. As the traditional invasion routes into the Indian subcontinent were from the northwest, Bengal was shielded from foreign invaders by the vastness of Western and Central India. The early Bengalis lived a life of relative ease and plenty. They developed traditions, rituals, and a language distinct from the rest of Northern India. They also produced a refined and extensive cuisine based on the bounty of their fertile land and its rivers.

Despite Bengal's protective geography, invaders did finally arrive. First Aryans ("tillers of the earth"), then Moslems, and later Mongols (called

In modern times Bengal has been divided into two political entities: Hindu West Bengal, a state in eastern India, and the independent Moslem nation of Bangladesh. West Bengal (88,752 sq. km) has slightly more than one-third the area of the United Kingdom and a population of nearly 60 million. Bangladesh concentrates a population of 105 million on 143,998 sq. km. Except in the North, the climate is hot and humid.

Moghuls in India) conquered the area, each in their turn, introducing fresh ideas to the Bengali culture. Starting in the 16th century, Portuguese, Dutch, French, and British traders came to Bengal, drawn by its thriving textile industry and agricultural bounty. In the ensuing struggle for control among the European powers, the British prevailed. Shortly thereafter, Bengal and the rest of India came under British rule and remained so until 1947. Calcutta, now the capital of West Bengal, functioned as the capital of British East India until the early part of the 20th century. During this period Bengal absorbed many new ideas, but the core of the culture remained true to the ancient traditions, especially in matters of food.

A HISTORY OF BENGALI CUISINE AND COOKERY

We know little about the food habits of Bengalis before their written history. It is believed that Bengalis adhered to the principles of cooking and eating described in *Bhagavad Gita*, "the Lord's song," the classic epic of ancient India. The *Gita* classified food into three categories: "pure," which some believe to be fruits, vegetables, grains, and dairy products; "passionate," possibly fresh fish, meat, and aromatics such as onion and garlic; "impure," fish and meat that were no longer fresh but edible nonetheless.

A distinct culinary tradition emerged based on the availability of local ingredients. The great river systems flowing through Bengal deposit vast quantities of rich silt from the Himalayas on its fertile lowland plains. Heat and humidity combine with the fertile soil to allow rice and an abundance of vegetables to thrive; these became the cornerstones of the diet. Mangoes, bananas, coconuts, and sugar cane grew in abundance; fish, milk, and meat were plentiful; yogurt and spices such as ginger and black mustard would season the dishes. According to an ancient Bengali poem, "Lucky is the man whose wife serves him rice, fish, and greens."

Even though fish and meat were generally popular, there was a predisposition to vegetarianism, based on religious principles, that has continued to the present. Even today some strict Bengali Hindus shun fish and meat based on the ancient dietary precept of *ahingsa*, or not taking life. These vegetarians also omit onion and garlic from their diet, foods that "heat rather than cool," preferring to substitute a garlicky-flavored spice called asafetida.

The taboo against the consumption of fish and meat became even stronger with the flowering of religions such as Jainism and Buddhism. Mahavira lived around 500 B.C. and his followers, known as Jains, practiced nonviolence. Jains today avoid not only flesh but also fermented food and vegetables that need to be uprooted such as onions, garlic, carrots, potatoes, and beets. It is their belief that harvesting these vegetables kills tiny insects living in the root systems.

Buddha was born around 566 B.C., and Buddhism, with its own principle of nonviolence, remained active in India until 1200 A.D. During this period, many Indians became Buddhists and stopped killing animals for food. Fa-hsien, a noted Chinese Buddhist monk, visited India in the fifth century A.D. and found many people to be vegetarians. With the decline of Buddhism in the ensuing centuries, fish and meat returned to the menu. However, a well-developed vegetarian cuisine, a legacy of the Hindus, Jains, and Buddhists, remained firmly established in Bengal.

Rice, the staple of Bengalis since ancient times, has been untouched by the currents of religious change and its preparation has held to a continuing high standard. An account from the 14th century describes rice this way: "still steaming, each grain unbroken and distinct; well-cooked, tasty, slender, and aromatic."

Ibn Batuta, a 14th-century Moroccan scholar and traveler, called Bengal a land "blessed with abundance." In the 16th century, the Dutch merchant Van Lincholen agreed with him, calling Bengal "the granary of the East." One crop a year was sufficient to sustain the people, providing ample leisure time for the Bengalis to pursue cultural ideals: oral literature, music, and the culinary arts.

The 16th-century Mongol kings left their mark on the cooking of Northern India, which to this day is known as *moghlai* (adjective of *Moghul*) cooking. With the introduction of Islam, Bengali Moslems adopted dishes such as kababs, skewered meat, koftas, spiced meatballs, and biriyani, a fragrant rice casserole, from their Moghul conquerors. But the major portion of Bengali Hindu cuisine retained its original characteristics both in predominantly Moslem East Bengal and Hindu West Bengal.

Eggs and milk (are) very cheap; butter dear; vegetables are plentiful and very fine, fruits of every kind (are) delightful— oranges, limes, lemons, bananas, (and) plantains.

—from a collection of letters written in Calcutta by Sophia Goldbourne, an Englishwoman, published in 1789 under the name of *Hartley House*

The European traders introduced food from the New World—potatoes, chilies, and tomatoes. Bengalis incorporated these items into their diet, combining them with a variety of native ingredients to create new dishes.

Then, as now, Bengali cooking is mostly confined to the home. Dishes are carefully prepared according to recipes handed down through generations. Thus, few restaurants serve Bengali food either in Bengal or in the rest of India. In the West, where there are relatively few Indians and even fewer Bengalis, Bengali cooking is practically unknown. Yet this is a superb cuisine, refined over thousands of years, to which those who have had the good fortune of being invited to a Bengali home will attest.

Menus in the Indian restaurants in the West bear little resemblance to Bengali food, as most such restaurants adhere to *moghlai* cooking. The rich, elaborate repast of the bygone royal court emphasized meat, prepared in *ghee* (clarified butter) and cream. The British, who ruled India after the Mongols, also favored such meals. So *moghlai* cooking has became the restaurant standard in India and abroad, and for non-Bengalis it is increasingly difficult to find Bengali food.

Also, in the latter part of the 20th century, Bengal has fallen upon hard times due to political upheaval and overpopulation. Rising prices and a more hurried lifestyle have forced many homemakers to reduce the number of dishes at each meal, and, to my dismay, some of my childhood favorites are no longer being made. I have tried to document this great but relatively little known cuisine with the hope that many more people outside of Bengali homes can enjoy it.

I find in each of my return visits to Bengal that the culture remains closely tied to food, as it was in the earlier days of plenty. Indeed, modern Bengalis have become culinary innovators. They search for, and experiment with, foreign culinary ideas, incorporating such new food items and dishes as soybeans, noodles, and caramel custard into an increasingly cosmopolitan bill of fare. But in their hearts, they still delight in such traditional dishes as *maacher chochori* (Country-style Fish and Vegetable Stew) and *rosgolla* (Milk Balls in Rose Syrup).

HOW DOES BENGALI CUISINE DIFFER FROM OTHER INDIAN CUISINES?

An abundant land provides for an abundant table. The nature and variety of dishes found in Bengali cooking are unique even in India. Fish cookery is one of its better-known features and distinguishes it from the cooking of the landlocked regions. Bengal's countless rivers, ponds, and lakes teem with many kinds of freshwater fish that closely resemble catfish, bass, shad, or mullet. Bengalis prepare fish in innumerable ways—steamed or braised, or stewed with greens or other vegetables, and with sauces that are mustard-based or thickened with poppyseeds. You will not find these types of fish dishes elsewhere in India.

Bengalis also excel in the cooking of vegetables. They prepare a variety of imaginative dishes using the many types of vegetables that grow here year-round. They can make ambrosial dishes out of the oftentimes rejected peels, stalks, and leaves of vegetables. They use fuel-efficient methods, such as steaming fish or vegetables in a small covered bowl nestled at the top of the rice cooker.

The use of spices for both fish and vegetable dishes is quite extensive and includes many combinations not found in other parts of India. Examples are the onion-flavored kalonji seeds and five-spice (a mixture of cumin, fennel, fenugreek, kalonji, and black mustard). Bengalis share a love of whole black mustard seeds with South Indians, but the use of freshly ground black mustard paste is unique to Bengal.

All of India clamors for Bengali sweets. Although grains, beans, and vegetables are used in preparing many desserts, as in other regions, the most delicious varieties are dairy-based and uniquely Bengali.

Finally, Bengalis share a universal love of good food. But the level of refinement to which they have carried this cuisine over thousands of years is equaled by few other cuisines, notably Chinese, Italian, and French in my experience. Bengalis will discuss food at length, serve an enormous number of dishes, and find every opportunity to throw a dinner party. This is the legacy I'd like to share with you.

DELIGHTING
THE SENSES

I feel fortunate to have been born into a Bengali family of good cooks. Bengali cooking is a regional cuisine with a genius for utilizing the wide variety of ingredients that is available. Even more important is the fact that the majority of Bengali dishes, which have evolved over several millennia, are inherently healthy.

As a child I ate rice, plenty of fresh fruits and vegetables, and many types of fish. My mother cooked these foods in vegetable oil, usually mustard; she formed savory sauces with ground seeds such as black mustard or white poppy; she further enhanced the sauces with fresh aromatics—onion, ginger, garlic, and chili, along with herbs and spices such as kalonji, cumin, coriander, turmeric, and cilantro. She used *ghee* rarely and in small quantities, and cream not at all.

These days I find that the Bengali diet of my youth, with its emphasis on rice and vegetables, is very much in agreement with the current Western recommendation that 55% of our daily calories come from carbohydrates. Fish, small quantities of meat, or various combinations of rice and legumes provide the Bengali with ample balanced protein. The large variety of vegetable dishes supplies necessary vitamins, minerals, and fiber.

The food on my family's table in Bengal was already low in fat. But in selecting and presenting these traditional recipes, I have chosen to reduce the use of salt, sugar, and fat even further—particularly animal fat, which is high in cholesterol. I have made *ghee,* which is occasionally used in Bengali dishes, an optional item because of its saturated fat content. I may sprinkle only a small amount of it on dishes to re-create the authentic flavor. Coconut, a flavorful ingredient often used in Bengali cooking, also contains saturated fat, and I have, therefore, limited its use.

7

I cook only with vegetable oil in the lowest possible amount. At the same time I keep in mind that a certain amount of oil is necessary to preserve the original flavors of the dishes. Many of the whole (and sometimes ground) spices will not release their flavor unless sautéed in hot oil. During recipe testing, I have tried to achieve a balance between the amount of fat used and the flavor of the dish. Using this approach, I have generally been able to produce results that are nearly indistinguishable from the original dishes with considerably less oil.

The recipes in this book will generally specify a variable amount of fat, typically ranging from 1 to 2½ tablespoons (15 to 37 ml). You obtain the most authentic flavor by using the greater amount of oil; you get a tasty, lower-fat, but less authentic result by using the smaller amount of oil. It's left to you.

I reduce the amount of salt but intensify its effect by adding it in earlier stages of cooking so that it blends better with the sauce. Souring ingredients like lemon juice, tamarind, mango powder, and vinegar also lessen the need for salt.

Throughout the book you will find additional tips for lowering fat, as well as suggestions for creating nutritionally sound menus. In recipes that call for deep-frying I provide fat-free baking alternatives. I include the use of nonfat and lowfat milk, yogurt, and dry milk as options. I suggest preparing fresh cheese, a protein source for vegetarians, with 2% lowfat milk. The dishes containing lowfat dairy products will taste similar to the original, but slightly less rich and creamy.

Your nonvegetarian guests will be satisfied with meat served in small portions, as is the custom in Bengal, since the sauces are so tasty. You can select from an endless array of balanced meals with a variety of flavors that come from fresh ingredients and combinations of spices.

Sweets are an intrinsic part of the Bengali food scene and are enjoyed during festive occasions. I have reduced their fat and sugar content and recommend serving them in small portions as a taste treat with fresh fruits.

Many of my recipes are cherished family favorites; others come from my travels in various parts of Bengal. But all of the recipes embody the centuries of refinement that this ancient cuisine has undergone, and healthy dietary habits that have sustained a people for thousands of years.

DINING BENGALI STYLE

A typical Bengali meal may begin with steamed, boiled, or fried vegetables or a *shukto*, a nutritious vegetable stew that is made with a variety of vegetables such as potatoes, green beans, and pumpkin, and is characterized by a mingling of flavors ranging from sweet to bitter. Aromatic, orange-red lentil stew, accented by ginger, might be the next course, perhaps followed by fragrant, roasted eggplant, or pungent, steamed fish in a shimmering mustard sauce. Rice (or sometimes flatbread) is eaten with all courses.

The meal usually includes a sharply flavored relish, such as a tart plum chutney, to stimulate the palate. Homemade yogurt—thick, smooth, cooling, and gently sweet—provides a perfect counterpoint to the intense flavors of the various dishes.

Each meal is a banquet, but variety and quality, not quantity, are the guiding principles. Since the portions are kept small, the entire meal doesn't seem excessive, yet tastebuds get a complete workout from the many complementary flavors. Diners leave the table satisfied, with no thought of food for hours.

EARLY FOOD MEMORIES

My earliest memories come from Kalimpong, a quaint market town located in the foothills of the Himalayas near Darjeeling. I recall the lively bazaar of Kalimpong, where colorfully dressed tribal merchants—Lepchas, Bhutias, Gorkhas, each speaking a different tongue—would come to sell a wide variety of goods. I was particularly drawn to the piles of red and green chilies, barrels of fruity tea leaves, and tins of fragrant spices such as cinnamon, cardamom, and coriander.

Every day my mother would prepare such Bengali specialties as Splendid Spinach, Butternut Squash in Rich Yogurt Sauce, and Onion-Fragrant Red Lentils. On weekends she would cook Tender Sweet Cheese Morsels in Creamy Sauce for the extended family.

I remember once when dear Uncle Harish, a distant relative, dropped by. My mother feigned a lack of appetite when she invited him to join us at the table to eat. She herself ate nothing at all in order that he could share in the meal. Such is the spirit of Bengali hospitality, which you will encounter in traditional homes even today.

I always enjoyed the visits to our ancestral home in the district of Comilla, now in Bangladesh. At joint family gatherings a hundred people would often appear, and, because of her culinary skills, my mother was usually elected chef for the day.

My Aunt Kona was no less a cook. As if to prove the point, during the harvest festival she once made 17 different types of *pithas*, sweet rice dumplings. She made them in different styles and varied the stuffing in each— cashew slivers, plump raisins, or thickened milk. To this day I remember how delightful they all were.

And I used to sit under the shade of a tamarind tree in our yard. The taste of the rich, brown pulp taken from the inside of a tamarind pod would be so tart that I had to sprinkle salt, not sugar, on it. We had a plum tree bordering a pond. Uncle Sukumar shook the tree and ripe plums would fall into the water and bob to the surface. Excited neighborhood children plunged into the water instantly, grabbing and eating as many as they could.

When I went to Calcutta to study, I experienced the city's vast culinary resources. New Market, a large covered market, sold everything from pickles to Viennese pastry. According to a popular saying, you could even find tiger's milk there.

Outside the market, food hawkers proudly offered their specialties, a tantalizing variety of hot and cold snacks. My mouth would water as I sniffed the fragrance wafting from a vendor's pot of aromatic, rich brown chickpea stew. Sometimes after school I would buy a piece of sugar cane stalk there, and savor its juicy sweetness as I walked home.

Another favorite place was the Coffee House in College Street. This café was a meeting ground for students from nearby Calcutta University, as well as the city's intelligentsia. Sitting under a portrait of Rabindranath Tagore, Bengal's Nobel laureate poet and philosopher, we sipped cups of golden tea and discussed topics ranging from the next political election to where to purchase the most savory lentil snacks.

ENTERTAINING BENGALI STYLE

During the years I studied and worked abroad I missed Bengali food. I returned home one autumn with my American husband Tom. Tom met my Uncle Sukumar and his wife Gouri on a day when Uncle Sukumar invited us for a midday meal. To mark the event, Uncle Sukumar had hand-printed a menu in his unique calligraphic writing style. It listed these nine courses:

Menu
Crisp Fried Eggplant
Bitter Melon with Many Flavors
Glorious Greens
Festive Chickpeas with Coconut and Whole Spices
Butternut Squash in Mustard Sauce
Fragrant Fish in Silky-thin Sauce
Fish in Aromatic Sauce
Sweet Yogurt "Custard"
Plain Boiled Rice

We spent the next several hours chatting and eating. We would mix one of the many dishes with rice, using the fingers of the right hand, then would make a small ball and deftly pop it into our mouths. Following Indian custom, we never used our left hand, and didn't let our palm touch the food on the plate. Tom quickly took to the custom. "It makes me feel more intimate with my food," he said.

Aunt Gouri served the meal in true Bengali fashion—bringing one course at a time. She brought the fried vegetables first, "to stimulate our appetite." Then she served the greens, "so full of vitamins." Later came the split chickpeas with the aroma of spices rising from the steaming sauce.

Announcing that "the meal is only getting started," Aunt Gouri then brought the stewed squash. The mustard-sauced vegetable was so flavorful that we applauded. After that, we were finally ready for the fish. Aunt Gouri first brought out a fragrant dish made with *pabda,* a silvery, foot-long fresh-water fish bearing a faint resemblance to catfish. She followed it with *rui,* a richly flavored member of the carp family, flavored with hot spices. The sauces were skillfully tailored to match the flavor and texture of each fish: light and delicate for the *pabda,* spicier and more complex for the *rui.* The meal ended on a cheery note with sweetened yogurt—dense, rich, and luscious. "Yogurt prolongs life," Uncle Sukumar told us.

Throughout the meal, Aunt Gouri replenished the rice on our plates and insisted that we eat more of each dish. By Bengali custom, she would not take her own meal until after her guests had finished every course. The expression on her face told me she enjoyed what we ate as much as we did.

Like Uncle Sukumar and Aunt Gouri, most Bengalis love to entertain. Any dinner may become a feast. The expression *atithi narayan* means that "a guest is godlike," and a visitor receives royal treatment. You need only the slightest excuse to throw a party. "My husband got a raise this summer," said one Bengali woman; "I must invite some friends over."

PLANNING A MENU AND SETTING THE TABLE

To me, putting together a meal, be it for a festive event or an everyday affair, is as important as the cooking of the individual dishes. Bengali meals are ideally suited for a wide variety of social situations, from elegant sit-down dinners to informal brunches and buffets. I have provided serving suggestions in the recipe chapters, as well as menus for various occasions in the Menu chapter. These suggestions are only guidelines. In Bengal, menus are flexible, and you can mix dishes according to your taste.

When planning a menu, I try to balance the nutrients with color, flavor, and texture. For example, Sweet and Tart Pumpkin and Glorious Greens appear together in one meal; Fish Braised in Light Mustard Sauce and Smoked Eggplant in Ginger-Yogurt Sauce in another. I refrain from serving two creamy dishes, each of which contains either milk or coconut milk, together. A vegetable dish with a dry gravy goes well with a fish or meat dish in plenty of sauce. A tender-textured dish balances one that is chewier. Chutneys accent a meal, and I serve one or more to round out the variety of tastes and colors.

If you're invited to a Bengali home, you'll notice that the table is simple. Elaborate decorations are not necessary, since food is the main attraction. You can serve the food on dinner plates or Bengali-style on a *thala,* a circular tray, which may be purchased in some Indian stores. A mound of fragrant, steaming rice (or flatbreads) is placed in the center. Meat, fish, and vegetables are placed in small bowls called *baatis.* These are arranged on the plate in a circle around the rice or bread. This is done so that the different sauces don't run together; each retains its distinct character and you can easily dip into them, according to your preference.

As in Bengal, you can put a scant teaspoon (5 ml) of salt, a wedge of lemon, and a whole fresh green chili on each plate. The salt and lemon are used to adjust the seasoning to taste. An occasional nip into a fiery green chili between mouthfuls of food excites the tastebuds and heightens the contrast between the dishes. Water is the only beverage served with a meal.

When the meal is over, a common custom in Bengal is to offer fennel seeds for the guests to chew. You can also serve a steaming cup of Fragrant Milk Tea spiced with ginger, cinnamon, and cardamom.

To set the mood, you might play *sitar* music, perhaps something recorded by Ravi Shankar, the renowned Bengali musician.

"THIRTEEN FESTIVALS IN TWELVE MONTHS"

I find that the Bengali love of elaborate dining and entertaining is nowhere more evident than during festivals. According to an old saying, there are "13 festivals in 12 months." In fact, nearly every day in the Bengali calendar is marked by some celebration.

My favorite seasons to visit my family are autumn and winter, as two of the biggest Bengali celebrations come during these periods. Durga puja, the worship of the goddess Durga and the biggest festival of the year, takes place in autumn. During this 10-day feast, everyone, young and old, rich and poor, mingles freely in a communal celebration that unites all Bengal.

Durga is the consort of Shiva, a god of the Hindu trinity. The Hindus worship her as the destroyer of evil. The story goes that at one time certain demons, possessed of boundless strength, decided to conquer the earth, the sky, and the sea. The demons fought the gods for a hundred years and dethroned all but Brahma, Vishnu, Shiva—the supreme triad—and their consorts. The demons caused so much suffering that the dethroned gods sought the help of Durga, the mighty 10-armed goddess. A fierce battle took place between her and an enemy army of millions, led by the formidable buffalo demon. In the end, Durga slew the army and captured and killed the demon. To this day, she represents the triumph of good over evil.

Thus once every year there comes a period when all minds are in a melting mood, fit for the springing forth of love and affection and sympathy. The songs of welcome and farewell to the goddess, the meeting of loved ones, the strains of the festive pipes, the limpid sky and molten gold of autumn, are all parts of a common mood of joy.

—Rabindranath Tagore, speaking of the festival of the goddess Durga

In Calcutta, during Durga puja, artists of distinction make life-size images of the goddess, depicting this victory. Durga has eyes shaped like lotus petals and an elaborate crown on her head. Poised on a lion, she carries weapons in her hands and strikes at the demon, lying at her feet, with a spear. In every neighborhood you will find one such image placed in a colorful tent.

For six days of Durga puja, Bengalis worship quietly and the priest performs small ceremonies. On the seventh day, large-scale communal festivities begin. In the morning, large platters of fruit and sweets are placed before the statue of Durga in the tent as *prasad*, food offerings. Bananas, fresh coconut, and uncooked rice are three sacred foods that are among the *prasad*. People bow their heads before the goddess, placing flowers at her feet. The community lunch that follows might feature Rice and Mung Beans Flavored with Whole Spices, sliced cucumbers, and fresh sugar cane cubes.

At dusk, the priest worships Durga in a beautiful ceremony with incense and a circle of small lamps. Bells are rung and traditional drums are played outside the temple. "People who hear these sounds are saved," murmurs the priest.

The worship of the goddess Durga is more than a religious festival; it is a cultural phenomenon. Literary and artistic activities flourish, new books are published, new drama productions open. After the evening ceremony, both adults and children sing and dance. They may perform plays for the community, late into the night.

THE FOOD OF THE GODS

During Durga puja, Bengali homemakers turn out their best dishes for family and friends. Calcuttans line up in front of Dwarik, a famous sweet and pastry shop. Here they buy *luchi*, Puffed Bread, and *cholar dal*, Festive Chickpeas with Coconut and Whole Spices, a mini-meal that is associated with this festivity. Many will celebrate the seventh day of the puja by indulging in an opulent dish such as Prawns in Coconut-Cream Sauce. For the nonvegetarians, mutton is a must on the eighth day; vegetarians will relish Fragrant Roasted Mung Bean Stew. Pan-raised Bread with Fiery Potatoes or Fresh Cheese and Mung Bean Delight might welcome the ninth day. On the tenth day, people exchange sweet delicacies such as *sandesh*, Silk and Satin Bars, and *chadrapuli*, Harvest Moon Cakes, while renewing social ties and forgiving past differences.

Other parts of India also celebrate Durga puja, but in Bengal the pomp and ceremony is the biggest I've seen. To Bengalis, Durga is not revered from a distance. She is looked upon as warmly as a member of the family— a married daughter who has returned home to visit her parents. At the end of the 10-day event, when the images of the goddess are immersed in the river, a feeling of sorrow lingers in the air, as if the daughter has left home. A simple snack afterward of yogurt and rice flakes, two of the most auspicious of all foods, will typically complete the observance.

If the reader be one who has never witnessed the magnificent spectacle of a Durga puja in Calcutta, we can only assure him that he will find the splendid fiction of the Arabian nights completely realized.

—an advertisement from *Calcutta Journal*,
September 22, 1819

When the holiday comes to a close, everyone returns to the daily routine, knowing that the next celebration is only weeks away.

Winter is another of my favorite seasons to visit Bengal, because in January comes Saraswati puja, the worship of the goddess of wisdom and learning. As schoolchildren we adored her, believing that Saraswati would help us pass the examinations. This was the only day of the year when we never touched a pen and were allowed to put our books away.

Ripe purple plums are in season at this time, but a classmate of mine would always resist the temptation of biting into one. She would wait until after she had offered a plum to the goddess on this special day.

Sculptors depict Saraswati sitting on a lotus—a picture of grace and beauty. For many Bengalis, who believe that the goddess loves vegetarian food, the meal on this day will customarily contain no meat. Others celebrate this occasion by preparing a pair of fish (usually the shad-type *eelish*), a symbol of prosperity. The fish will be steamed in a mustard sauce or cooked *korma*-style in a yogurt sauce.

A WEDDING FEAST

Another event that brings food, fun, and festivities together is a wedding. In the earlier part of this century, the host would present a fine handkerchief, imprinted with the menu, to each arriving guest. One of the rituals is *saptapadi,* taking seven steps together. The groom prays, "With the first step for food and sustenance; the second for strength; the third for keeping our vows; the fourth for a happy life," and so on. A high point of the ceremony occurs when the bride and groom exchange garlands. The bride's veil is lifted and the bride and groom see each other for the first time, the "auspicious first gaze." Afterward, the guests are feted with a grand repast, which will typically consist of Aromatic Rice with Peas and Whole Spices, mutton, Savory Sunday Chicken (or a mutton dish), Rich Roasted Eggplant, Cauliflower and Potatoes in Roasted Red Chili Sauce, Sweet Yogurt "Custard," Pleasure Boats, and Milk Puffs in Cardamom Syrup. The meal is traditionally served on large banana leaves.

BEGINNING THE JOURNEY

As you can see, food and culture are closely intertwined in Bengal. No matter what the activity, food and drink are never far away. This book, though primarily concerned with food, will endeavor to acquaint you with Bengal past and present, and its rhythms and ways of life. May I then open the door for you as we take a journey together to delight the senses. As Bengalis say when they meet, *namashkar,* "I bow to the divine in you."

When the belly is full, the back will bear burdens.
—Bengali proverb

THE MYSTERY OF SPICES

SPICES AND HERBS, FLAVORINGS, AND OTHER INGREDIENTS

Come with me to a bazaar in Bengal. Notice the alluring scents. See the open jute bags filled with spices, the lush colors ranging from coal-black to brilliant yellow.

"Chilies, very fresh," a shopkeeper scoops out a palmful of the slender green pods from an enormous straw basket. "*Mouri,* very sweet," he says, pointing to a jar of crescent-shaped fennel seeds.

On the opposite corner, a store owner weighs fresh ginger root using a hand-held scale, as vendors have done for centuries. A stray bullock wanders by, eyeing the edibles as if pondering how they taste.

Spice can be part of a flower such as saffron, seed such as cumin, or ripe berries such as coriander. Herbs are fragrant leaves of any of various annual and perennial plants, such as mint or cilantro, that don't have a woody stem. For millennia, people in India have used herbs and spices (hereafter referred to collectively as spices) not only for their color and flavor, but for their health-enhancing and medicinal properties.

For spices are the heart of this cuisine. A Bengali cook will not start the day's work until after selecting these vital ingredients at the morning market.

Spices are always used with a light hand; they should whisper to us rather than shout. The particular combination of seasonings and their art-ful blending with the major ingredients gives each dish its unique taste. Every cook is assumed to know how to use spices to transform the humblest ingredient into one of delight. I have heard women gossip, "Poor Mr. Sen

Gupta. You could smell the raw turmeric in his new wife's vegetables. She's never learned to cook."

How Spices Are Used

As mentioned earlier, spices are derived from flowers, seeds, leaves, bark, and roots. They may be used in their original form or chopped, powdered, or made into a paste. The volatile oil component, which is responsible for the character of a spice, releases its aroma when teased by heat or bathed in liquid. If used whole, a spice should be sautéed in hot oil or dry-roasted on a griddle, the intense heat drawing out its essence. When ground or grated, the cellular structure of a spice crumbles, dispersing its flavor. Ground spices merge more easily with other ingredients and enliven their taste.

Although powdered spices are gaining in popularity, many Bengalis insist on freshness and grind their own daily. They roast cumin seeds, then pulverize them to a powder. They crush ginger to make a paste. Although turmeric is bought as a powder all over the globe, many Bengalis still grind fresh turmeric root with water to make a smooth paste. The resulting spice preparation has a fresher and more intense flavor than its commercial counterpart.

How to Buy and Store Spices

Spices are best when bought whole and ground just before using. Light roasting before grinding will bring out their flavor. Since ground spices tend to lose their potency quickly, they should be bought in small quantities and used within a few weeks.

Heat, moisture, air, and light destroy spices. Store them in airtight containers and keep them in a cool, dark place.

Below is a list of the spices, flavorings, and other ingredients used in Bengali dishes. In the West, you can buy them in supermarkets or Indian groceries. Many of the spices will be familiar to Westerners although the way they're used may be new. Since a spice may be known by different names, I have included its botanical name. I also discuss how to make the spice powders and spice pastes so essential to this cuisine.

A number of other ingredients also impart the typical Bengali flavor. They could be a fruit like tamarind, a nut such as cashew, or a flavoring like rosewater, as well as some ingredients that are less known in the West. Unless otherwise noted, these items are available in Indian stores.

A Glossary of Spices and Other Ingredients

Asafetida — *Ferula asafetida* (*hing* in Hindi and Bengali):   The dried gum resin of a giant fennel plant that reaches a height of about 6 ft (1.8 m).

When the plant matures, the stems are trimmed close to the root and a pearly white juice flows out. This liquid quickly solidifies to a translucent, dark yellow mass, which becomes the spice. Asafetida can be bought in this original pure form as brown blocks and then ground to a powder. More commonly it is sold as an easy-to-use, pale yellow powder made by pulverizing the solid mass. The spice has a strong garliclike odor that disappears in cooking, leaving behind a delicate aroma. Many Hindus who shun onion and garlic use asafetida as a substitute. It is said to aid digestion.

In the recipes I specify asafetida in the powdered form, which may be adulterated with rice or wheat flour. The flavor is more concentrated in the lump form, so if you are grinding it at home, use half the amount specified in the recipe.

When asafetida powder is added to hot oil, it can form a lump. To prevent this from happening, I sprinkle it over other spices already frying in the pan or simply over the hot oil.

Basil — *Ocimum sanctum* (*tulsi* in Hindi and Bengali): The most sacred plant to the Hindus. In the courtyard of our family home, basil grew on an altarlike raised planter, as is a common custom. Each day family members bowed before the plant, uttering a prayer. Though native to India, basil leaves are never eaten in Bengal and are, therefore, not mentioned in the recipes.

Basmati rice — A fragrant, long, slender grain that has grown in the foothills of the Himalayas for centuries. It is exported to the West from India and Pakistan; a variety called Texmati is now grown in Texas. Basmati rice has a fine texture and a perfumy, nutlike aroma, and becomes elongated when cooked. It goes particularly well with Bengali dishes. (See "Rice" chapter for cooking instructions.) Brown Basmati rice, which is available in health food stores and specialty markets, has a similarly fine fragrance.

Black salt — (*kala nimak* in Hindi; *beet noon* in Bengali): This salt, imported from India, is not black in color but is sold either as a reddish-brown block with crystalline faces or as a brownish-gray powder. It is not a seasoned salt and is different from the rock salt available in health food stores and supermarkets in the West. Black salt is appreciated for its distinctive earthy flavor and is used in dishes such as chats, teatime salads, and Hot and Savory Party Mix. There is no substitute.

Breadcrumbs — Although you can buy breadcrumbs at Western supermarkets, with little effort you can make fresh, flavorful crumbs at home.

To prepare breadcrumbs:

For ½ cup (125 ml) breadcrumbs:
2 thin slices (¼ inch/6 mm thick) wholewheat or white bread

Cut bread into small cubes. Place on a baking sheet in a 300°F (150°C; gas mark 2) oven until dry and crumbly, 15 to 20 minutes; do not burn. Grind in a blender until reduced to small crumbs.

Cardamom — *Ellettaria cardamomum*: (*elaichi* in Hindi; *elaach* in Bengali): The dried ripe fruit of a perennial, bushy herb of the ginger family. This legendary spice, said to have existed in the hanging gardens of Babylon, grows abundantly in India.

The fruit, about ⅜ inch (9 mm) in diameter, is harvested when green and then sun-dried. It encloses numerous hard, round aromatic seeds that have a unique taste. The pods are brownish-green when raw and creamy white when bleached. Use the more flavorful green pods sold in Indian stores rather than the whitish Western supermarket variety.

Black cardamom, a larger variety (about 1 inch/2.5 cm long), has a brownish coat and contains seeds with an even stronger scent. Used whole in rice dishes, it emanates a full, warm flavor.

Powdered cardamom is used extensively in fish, meat, and vegetable dishes and also to enhance desserts. Bengalis sometimes chew seeds of green cardamom after dinner because of their clean, astringent taste, heady scent, and exotic flavor. You can serve the seeds on a small plate after a meal. This custom dates back to the Moghul period, when it was used to extend a royal welcome to guests.

Cashew nuts — *Anacardium occidentale* (*caju* in Hindi and Bengali): Anacard, a tropical tree, furnishes the cashew apple, a pear-shaped fruit. When roasted and cracked, the fruit reveals a soft seed, the cashew nut. The beige, crescent-shaped nut has a pleasant taste. Toasted, it is a garnish. Finely grated, it is used to thicken sauces and enrich the flavor of a dish. You can substitute almonds, which are more familiar in the West, though cashews have a richer flavor.

To toast cashews, pistachios, or almonds:

Place the nuts on an ungreased griddle or skillet over low heat. In a few minutes, when they are lightly browned on one side, turn them over. Remove from heat as soon as both sides have been lightly browned. These nuts, especially cashews, burn easily, so watch them carefully. If they burn, they will taste bitter and adversely affect the flavor of dishes.

Chilies, fresh — *Capsicum annum* (*mirch* in Hindi; *kancha lanka* in Bengali): The seed pods of the annual capsicum plant. Chilies are not native to India. Prior to the 16th century, black pepper accounted for the spicy heat in Indian dishes. Then the Portuguese arrived searching for ginger and cinnamon, and brought with them chili peppers from the New

World. The fiery fruit caught people's fancy and soon replaced black pepper in most recipes.

The hot taste of the pod comes from capsaicin, the volatile oil concentrated in the veins. Besides flavor, chilies add color and a refreshing taste and also stimulate the palate. Often whole fresh chilies or chili slivers garnish a dish but are not meant to be eaten.

When fresh, chilies are a shiny red or green. Red chilies are the fruits that have ripened on the plant. They are milder and sweeter than green chilies.

In the West, you can buy many varieties of fresh, green seasoning chilies, such as serrano, cayenne, and Thai chili. The size, shape, and hotness of different types vary. You can select any of them for the recipes in this book. (Jalapeño, readily available in many supermarkets, is inconsistently hot.) Don't use a larger cooking chili such as an Anaheim. For a mild effect, discard the hottest parts—the seeds and the white inner membrane—and use only the flesh. To get a more assertive flavor, either incorporate some of the seeds or increase the amount of the flesh. A whole fresh chili is sometimes added to a dish where, since it is uncut, it does not overpower the other spices. Although most recipes call for a teaspoon (5 ml) of chopped green chili, you can adjust that amount, depending on the hotness of the chili. To determine the hotness gently bite into the tip.

Do not let your eyes or other sensitive areas come in contact with this volatile spice. Wash your hands thoroughly after handling chilies; better yet, wear kitchen gloves. If you have eaten too much chili, drinking water won't help. Chew some rice or a piece of bread, or drink milk; it will absorb the volatile oil and reduce the discomfort.

Chilies red, dried and ground — *Capsicum annum* (*lal mirch* in Hindi; *shukno longka* in Bengali): Bengalis use chilies not only fresh but also dried and ground. Dried chilies have a dull, reddish color. They are generally roasted in their whole form in hot oil at the beginning of the cooking process. This turns their skin black and releases their distinctive flavor. The hotness of dried chilies varies. If the chili is too hot, you can remove and discard it in the early stages of cooking. For more hotness, chop a dried chili before sautéing. This will release its flavor more fully, exposing the seeds.

If I haven't achieved the desired hotness in a dish with green chili, I usually add a dash of ground red pepper. You can buy commercially prepared ground red pepper or red chili powder in Asian and Indian stores and in some Western supermarkets. Because of its hot, burning taste only a pinch of this spice should be used. You can also substitute the cayenne pepper available in Western supermarkets. Do not use supermarket chili powder, which is a mixture of several ingredients, as it will ruin the dish.

To prepare green chili paste:

Chop green chili coarsely, remove the seeds, and grind the flesh with a mortar and pestle or in a mini chopper to make a relatively smooth paste. For a hotter paste grind some of the seeds as well.

To prepare red chili paste:

Dried red chili, made into a paste, adds a rich, warm flavor and a mellow hotness to a dish. You can roast the chilies first to further enhance the sauce. Put 2 to 4 whole, dried red chilies on an ungreased griddle or skillet over low heat. Turn as soon as they start to darken on the bottom. Repeat for the other side. Soak the chilies (roasted or not) in hot water for about 15 minutes or until soft. You can remove the seeds to reduce hotness or leave them in if they are mild. Grind the flesh (and the optional seeds) with a mortar and a pestle or in a mini chopper using 2 teaspoons (10 ml) or so of the soaking water.

Do not substitute commercial red chili paste, available in Asian markets. This paste contains other ingredients and will alter the taste of a dish.

Cilantro (also called coriander leaves) — *Coriander sativum* (*dhania* in Hindi; *dhaney pata* in Bengali):   The bright green, lacy leaf of the coriander plant is pungent and agreeable, and has an entirely different flavor from the seeds (see "Coriander" in this section). The leaf resembles parsley and is indeed sometimes called Chinese parsley, but does not taste the same. In Western supermarkets, it is called by its Spanish name, cilantro. This is the name by which I have referred to it in this book. Cilantro, which complements chili, is used both in cooking and as a garnish. Even if you don't like its taste, don't omit or substitute it in recipes where it is an ingredient. When cooked, it loses its distinctive flavor but enhances the sauce.

Sold as a bunch, these perishable leaves keep for a week or two when you put their stems in a cup partly filled with water, as you would with a bouquet of flowers.

To prepare cilantro (or parsley) for garnish:

Wash and dry a bunch of cilantro. (I use a salad spinner for drying.) Slice off and discard the roots and the bottom ½ inch (1 cm) of the stems. Chop the stems and leaves finely. Start with 1 tablespoon (15 ml) or substitute parsley, preferably the Italian flat-leaf type. For a prettier effect, you can remove the leaves from the stems by hand and use them as garnish.

When garnishing rice or fish, I place a few sprigs of cilantro at the center or on one side of the serving platter. The delicate stems and the leaves enhance the appearance of the dish.

To prepare cilantro paste:

Grind chopped fresh cilantro with a mortar and pestle or in a mini chopper to produce a relatively smooth paste. A less desirable alternative is to mince the leaves very finely. Do not substitute parsley.

Cinnamon — *Cinnamomum zeylanicum* (*dalchini* in Hindi; *daruchini* in Bengali): The rust-colored bark of the cinnamon tree. It is used extensively in the form of sticks, an inch or two (2.5 cm or 5 cm) long, or powdered. It has a pleasing scent and an aromatic taste. The leaves, *tejpata* (in Hindi and Bengali), "foliage with a spirited aroma," are used in India like bay leaves in the West.

Clove — *Eugenia caryophyllata* (*lavang* in Hindi; *labongo* in Bengali): Unopened dried flower buds of the beautiful clove tree. The name comes from a French word, *clou*, meaning "nail," which the spice resembles. Clove was an expensive spice in medieval Europe, and men fought over control of its trade. It imparts a sharp, strong aroma to fish, meat, and vegetable dishes. After dining, Bengalis chew cloves to freshen their breath.

Coconut — *Cocos nucifera* (*nariyal* in Hindi; *narkol* in Bengali): The coconut is a large, graceful tropical palm tree that flourishes near Bengal's coastal regions; its nut is used at several stages of its growth cycle. The immature green fruit contains a deliciously sweet liquid, coconut water, a popular cooling beverage. The water is surrounded inside by a sweet, jelly-like substance that can be eaten with a spoon.

The shredded meat of a ripe coconut is used both as a flavoring agent and as a dessert ingredient. You can soak shredded coconut in hot water, then press it to derive a milky liquid called coconut milk. This is different from coconut water. Coconut milk is used to form a sauce for many fish, meat, and vegetable dishes. In the West, it is conveniently sold in cans in Asian markets and some supermarkets. Look for the unsweetened variety. For better flavor, however, buy a fresh coconut to make your own milk at home.

To prepare coconut milk from fresh coconut:

To open a coconut, use a corkscrew to make holes through two of the three eyes. Pour off the coconut water and save it. It can be served chilled as is or with a squeeze of lime for a refreshing drink.

It is often easier to remove the meat from the shell if you bake the coconut after draining it. This causes the meat to shrink away from the shell. Heat the coconut at 400°F (200°C; gas mark 6) for 18 to 20 minutes. On a hard surface, such as a concrete floor or a sink, hit the coconut with a hammer to crack the shell. Using a screwdriver or a knife, carefully pry the meat away from the shell. Make several slits across the coconut for easy removal of the meat. Peel the brown skin from the white meat using a vegetable peeler or knife.

To extract coconut milk, chop 1 cup (250 ml) of the meat into small pieces and put in a blender. Add 1 cup (250 ml) of boiling water. Blend for a few seconds. Let stand for 5 minutes to allow the hot water to absorb the coconut essence. Strain through layers of cheesecloth or a fine sieve. Makes 1 cup (250 ml); using less water will make a richer milk. Subsequent extracts using the leftover coconut will produce thinner milk.

To prepare coconut milk using dried coconut:

Use unsweetened dried (shredded) coconut, available in health food stores and Asian markets. Put in a blender 1½ cups (375 ml) dried coconut and 1½ cups (375 ml) hot water. Blend and strain as above. The coconut milk will be slightly thinner. Yields 1 cup (250 ml).

Coconut Tips

- *Reduced use of coconut and coconut milk:* Although coconut is a flavorful ingredient, I have minimized its use because of its saturated fat content. Coconut milk makes a rich, aromatic gravy that is usually reserved in Bengal for special occasions. You can replace ¼ cup (60 ml) of coconut milk in a recipe with water (or lowfat milk), as each recipe will indicate. When using dried coconut I usually grind it in a blender to a coarse powder. This disperses it better in a dish and heightens the flavor of the dish even when the amount used is small. You can serve small portions of those few sweets and chutney dishes where coconut is a main ingredient.

- How do you select a fresh coconut? Lift it. It should feel heavy for its size. Shake it. You should hear the liquid swishing inside.

- Should you choose not to make coconut milk at home, buy it in cans (the unsweetened variety) from Asian markets or Indian stores. I avoid buying coconut blocks, available in some Indian stores. These blocks are harder to use and can turn rancid rapidly.

- If using canned coconut milk (or the homemade version that has been refrigerated), stir to mix the thin and thick parts into which it separates during storage.

- The thinner the consistency of the coconut milk, the less rich and creamy the sauce will be.

- When cooking with coconut milk, keep heat very low and leave the pan uncovered; otherwise the milk will separate and can produce an unpleasant odor.

- Freshly grated coconut has a wonderful aroma. An alternative is to use frozen shredded (also called "crashed") coconut, which is available in some Asian markets (specifically Thai and Vietnamese) and is preferable to the packaged coconut available in Western supermarkets. In recipes where coconut is one of the main ingredients, I use freshly grated or the more convenient frozen shredded coconut for maximum flavor. If a recipe calls for coconut in small amounts, such as a few tablespoons, I use packaged coconut for convenience.

■ When frying coconut, watch carefully as it can burn very quickly.

The story goes that in ancient India a devout Hindu, on a walking pilgrimage, collapsed from hunger and exhaustion in a jungle. A coconut from a nearby tree fell, cracked in half, and woke him up. After eating the coconut, he regained his energy and resumed the journey. To this day, few festivities are complete without coconut, called "the tree of life."

Coriander — *Coriander sativum* (*dhaniya* in Hindi; *dhaney* in Bengali): The dried, round, ripe fruit of an annual herb. The yellowish seed resembles a pepper kernel in appearance and has a warm, fruity aroma. Of the two varieties, one tiny and the other somewhat larger (the size of black pepper), the smaller possesses a stronger flavor. Coriander is always used in Bengal in the powdered form and not as a seed.

Cumin — *Cuminum cyminum* (*jeera* in Hindi; *shada jeera* in Bengali): The dried ripe fruit of an annual, low-growing herb of the parsley family. The oblong, yellowish-brown seed resembles a caraway seed. It has a powerful aroma, which intensifies when roasted, and a slightly bitter taste. Cumin is versatile and appears often in Bengali dishes both as a seed and as a powder.

To prepare ground cumin, ground coriander, ground fennel, and ground fenugreek:
Place seeds in an ungreased skillet over low heat. In a minute or so they will start to darken and emit an aroma. Remove immediately from the skillet as otherwise they will turn bitter. (If the seeds begin to smoke, they have been overroasted.) Grind to a fine powder using a spice grinder or a mortar and pestle. The yield from 1½ teaspoons (7 ml) seeds is approximately 2 teaspoons (10 ml) powder, the amount needed in most

Overroasted spices, especially cumin, can spoil a dish. I usually taste a cumin seed after it has been roasted to test for excessive bitterness before grinding and adding it to a recipe.

Curry powder — As sold in the West, curry powder contains powdered cumin, coriander, cardamom, fenugreek, and turmeric. Traditionally Bengalis have preferred not to use a ready-ground spice mix such as curry powder. Instead they combine different spices for each dish to enhance the unique flavor of the ingredients. Also, if you use curry powder, all your curry dishes, whether chicken curry, beef curry, or potato curry, will taste alike. These are reasons why I don't use it. Buy the individual spices instead and use them as the recipes specify.

Dals (legumes) — See "Dals" chapter.

Eggplant — *Solanum melongena* **(*baigan* in Hindi; *begun* in Bengali):** This versatile vegetable blends well with many seasonings and ingredients. Different varieties are available in Bengal, such as the slender Japanese type and the small, round, and white Thai variety. In these recipes I have substituted the pear-shaped eggplant sold in the West with good results. To buy eggplant, look for smooth, firm, glossy, dark purple skin and fruit that feels heavy for its size. Do not store eggplant for more than a few days, as it doesn't keep well.

The spongy nature of eggplant can make it soak up an enormous amount of oil, so I prefer smoking (for some recipes) and roasting it before adding the seasonings. These steps also add a rich, complex character to the dish and an exquisite flavor. The exceptions are mixed vegetable dishes where eggplant cooks in water and the juice provided by other ingredients.

My mother occasionally removes the seeds of an eggplant after it has been roasted, as they can impart a bitter taste. But if you choose a young eggplant you can omit this step.

To smoke and roast an eggplant:

Some recipes call for smoking an eggplant. Depending on the method used, smoking may also soften the eggplant to its core; if not, you can achieve this by roasting (baking). If you don't want a smoky flavor or if the recipe calls for roasting the eggplant, you can simply roast it. The final steps necessary to prepare an eggplant for the recipes in this book are specified under "To prepare an eggplant after smoking or roasting," later in this section.

Smoke an eggplant over a gas flame, under the broiler, or on a barbecue grill.

Gas flame smoking:

Impale an eggplant on two forks, one in the stem end and one in the opposite end. Using the forks as handles, hold the eggplant over a medium high open gas flame. Rotate the eggplant about 90 degrees every half minute or so. The skin will gradually darken, the eggplant will start to sag, and you will notice a pleasant smoky smell. After about 10 to 15 minutes or when the skin is charred, remove eggplant from the flame and follow the steps specified in "To prepare an eggplant after smoking or roasting," later in this section.

This amount of cooking is sufficient to impart the desired smoky flavor. Depending on the size of the eggplant, it may also be sufficient to completely soften it. If not, you can finish cooking by roasting it in the oven (see instructions below).

Broiling:

Cut the eggplant in half lengthwise and place the halves on a cookie sheet or a piece of aluminum foil with the cut side down. Place under the broiler until the skin chars and gives out a smoky aroma, about 10 minutes; the time will vary with the size and thickness of the eggplant. Check often, as overbroiling will dry the flesh. With this method, the eggplant is usually thoroughly cooked and doesn't need to be roasted.

Barbecuing:

Lay the eggplant on a barbecue grill. When wisps of smoke start to come out and a smoky aroma is emitted, rotate the vegetable so that an un-cooked side now rests over the grill. Repeat until the skin is charred all over. This is closest to the original Indian method of roasting eggplant on the coals of the cooking fire.

If the middle of the eggplant is not cooked at this point, whichever method you use, you may complete the process by roasting it as follows.

Roasting:

Preheat oven to 450°F (230°C; gas mark 8). Cut eggplant in half length-wise and place on an ungreased baking sheet with the cut side down. (I place a sheet of aluminum foil under the halves to hold any escaping juice, which I later add to the dish along with the flesh.) Bake for 30 to 45 minutes or until the eggplant wrinkles and feels soft to the touch when pressed. (A toothpick inserted in the middle shows the inside to be soft and pulpy.) The timing will vary depending on the thickness of the eggplant and whether it was previously smoked or not.

To prepare an eggplant after smoking or roasting:

Allow the eggplant to cool. Discard the skin, finely chop the flesh, and mash it with a fork. Although I generally prefer unpeeled vegetables, I find the roasted eggplant skin has a rough texture and, if smoked pre-viously, a bitter taste. So make sure all of the skin has been removed, especially if the eggplant has been smoked first. The eggplant is now ready to be used in recipes.

Fennel — *Foeniculum vulgare miller* (*sonf* in Hindi; *mouri* in Bengali): The dried fruit of a perennial herb of the parsley family. The greenish-yellow seed, similar in appearance to cumin, has an agreeable scent and an aromatic, sweet taste like anise. (A fennel seed is larger and plumper than an anise seed.) Fennel is used whole or ground in meat and vegetable dishes. It is sometimes chewed after a meal because it freshens the mouth and leaves a pleasant aftertaste.

Fenugreek — *Trigonella foenum-graecum:* (*methi* in Hindi and Bengali): An annual plant of the pea family. The leaves are prized as a vegetable in Bengal. The rusty-brown seed, which is squarish in shape, has an agreeable bitter taste, with overtones of maple. When sautéing fenugreek seeds, do not allow them to burn; they will develop an unpleasantly bitter flavor. Fenugreek is said to stimulate the digestive system.

Five-spice (*panch phoron* in Hindi and Bengali): This spice combination, not to be confused with Chinese five-spice, is a mixture of black mustard, cumin, fennel, fenugreek, and kalonji seeds. (In some parts of Bengal a spice called *randhuni*, which resembles black mustard, is used. Since this spice is not available in the West, black mustard is substituted.) It is unique to Bengal and adds a distinctive taste to many fish and vegetable dishes. This mix appears so often in a dish that it is sometimes referred to as the "salt and pepper" of Bengal. Do not substitute Chinese five-spice.

Panch phoron is not always sold in Indian stores in the West; so I buy the spices individually and mix them together for use in the recipes.

To prepare five-spice:

In Bengal the five individual spices are sometimes combined in different proportions. For ease of use, I combine equal parts by weight—say, 1 ounce/30 grams each of the seeds of black mustard, cumin, fennel, fenugreek, and kalonji and store in a jar. You can reduce the amount of fenugreek, which has a hint of bitterness, by one third.

To prepare ground five-spice:

Roast the seed mixture on an ungreased griddle or skillet over low heat for a minute or so. (You may need to cover the griddle for a few seconds as some of the seeds will crackle.) Grind them in a spice grinder or with a mortar and pestle. Since they are used infrequently in powdered form, I grind them just before using.

Fresh cheese — (*channa* in Hindi and Bengali): Fresh sweet cheese, easily made at home, is the base for so many desserts that some call it the "dessert cheese." In appearance, though not in taste, it is similar to cottage cheese. As is the case with similar Western cheeses such as ricotta or farmer's cheese, this natural cheese doesn't keep for long. Therefore, it is best used the same day it's made, or within a day or two at most.

In addition to its primary use as a base for sweets, this cheese also appears in vegetarian dishes, providing protein as well as taste and texture.

To prepare fresh cheese:

8 cups (2 liters) whole milk (see "Fresh Cheese Tips" for lowfat options)
3 to 4 tablespoons (45 to 60 ml) lemon juice

1. Use a large, deep-sided, and preferably nonstick pan. Lightly oil the bottom and sides to prevent the milk from sticking. Heat milk over medium high heat, stirring occasionally to make sure it does not stick to the bottom and that a skin does not form on top. When milk comes to a rolling boil, lower the heat slightly and cook for about 1 more minute, stirring constantly. Stir in lemon juice, a little at a time, until milk separates into curds, known as channa, and the clear, thin, straw-colored whey. Remove from heat immediately so that the cheese does not harden. Do not add any more lemon juice than necessary, as it will make the cheese sour. (If you've added all the lemon juice and the liquid is still milky white, all the cheese has not separated yet. Keep the heat low and continue to stir.)

2. Line a colander or large strainer with several layers of cheesecloth or a thin piece of cloth. Place the colander inside a pan or bowl large enough to hold it. (You may do this prior to boiling the milk.) Strain the curdled milk through the cheesecloth so that all liquid drains into the bowl.

You can use this nutrient-rich whey for cooking rice or for preparing Frothy Whey Drink. (See Teatime chapter.) Whey is also used as a cooking liquid in place of water in some recipes that call for fresh cheese.

3. Gather up the sides of the cheesecloth and tie a knot on top to seal the cheese inside. Place the cheese bundle over a chopping board or other flat surface and top with a heavy object (such as a pot half-filled with water). This object should cover the surface of the bundle.

At this point the cheese is processed in one of two ways, depending on the consistency desired: (1) the "20-minute" routine for cheese to be used in all recipes except where it is to be cubed, or (2) the "1-hour" routine needed for cheese cubes.

4. "20-minute" routine: Let the cheese bundle rest under the weight for about 20 minutes. This compression forces out enough of the remaining liquid to produce a soft, doughy mass that may be kneaded into balls or patties. These will hold their shape when gently simmered. Remove

cheese from the cheesecloth and place it on a dry board. Knead it until smooth and pliable, about 10 minutes; kneading is important because it provides the proper texture to the cheese. The fresh cheese is now ready to be used in recipes. Makes 1 cup (250 ml).

5. "1-hour" routine: If the recipe calls for cheese cubes, either as an ingredient or as a garnish, make sure the weight is extra heavy (such as a cast iron skillet). Let the weight rest on the cheese bundle for about 1 hour. The heavier weight and the longer compression will press out even more water than the "20-minute" routine, and produce a denser cheese that will hold its shape when cut into cubes and subjected to more vigorous and lengthy cooking. Remove cheese from cheesecloth and cut with a knife into 1-inch (2.5 cm) cubes. The cheese is now ready to be used in recipes. Makes 1 cup (250 ml) of cubes.

Fresh Cheese Tips

- *Lowfat Options:* Fresh cheese made with whole milk has a rich flavor and tender texture, but you can substitute 2% lowfat milk, which also produces fine results. Do not use either 1% lowfat or nonfat milk, as the resulting cheese will have a dry, crumbly texture unsuitable for Bengali cooking.

- Use fresh cheese the same day it's made or within a day or so. As it sits it becomes drier and may turn sour, even in the refrigerator.

- Fresh cheese should be slightly moist but not watery. If too much liquid is left in it, it may not hold its shape during cooking.

   If you use a thick cloth, such as a kitchen towel, to drain the cheese, the whey will not be forced out. The resulting product will have the consistency of softened cream cheese, unsuitable for any recipe.

- *To use as a snack:* I dust fresh cheese, made by following the "20-minute" routine, lightly with brown sugar and top with slices of fresh mangoes, papayas, or bananas.

To prepare fried fresh cheese cubes:

Prepare fresh cheese cubes following the "1-hour" routine. Deep-fry them quickly just until lightly browned. (For directions on deep-frying, see Lentil Dumplings in the Dals chapter.) Drain on paper towels. You can also pan-fry them using about 1 tablespoon (15 ml) oil. You can serve these as an accompaniment to a vegetarian meal or as a garnish for rice dishes.

Garam Masala — (garam masala in Hindi and Bengali): Literally "hot spices," because they raise body heat. A mixture of fragrant, pulverized spices, which in Bengal consists of cinnamon, cardamom, and cloves.

(Variations in other parts of India may include black peppercorn, nutmeg, coriander, and so on.) This spice mix puts the finishing touch on many dishes. It is usually added at the last moment, after the heat has been turned off. Hot spices lose their aroma with high heat, and they turn bitter if overcooked. It is sometimes inaccurately referred to as "curry powder," but its content and use are entirely different.

Bengalis also use whole garam masala, a mixture of the hot spices in their whole form—cardamom pods, cinnamon sticks, and whole cloves. The spices are crushed lightly with a rolling pin to bruise them, then fried in hot oil at the start of cooking to release their fragrance. They impart a strong aroma to a dish.

You can buy ground garam masala at any Indian store or prepare it at home by roasting and pulverizing the whole spices. In some recipes I intensify the spiciness by frying whole garam masala in oil in the beginning, then add a small amount of ground garam masala at the end.

To prepare garam masala:

Grind a 2-inch (5 cm) cinnamon stick, the seeds of 6 cardamom pods, and 5 cloves in a spice grinder. You can pass the mixture through a sieve to remove any husks. Makes ½ teaspoon (2 ml), the amount needed in most recipes.

Garlic — *Allium sativum (lashan* in Hindi; *rasoon* in Bengali): A bulb belonging to the onion family, garlic has a penetrating flavor. It is sautéed in oil to reduce its sharpness and bring out its rich quality. Most recipes in this book call for 1 tablespoon (15 ml) or so of minced garlic, but the amount can be adjusted according to taste.

To prepare garlic paste:

Some recipes, especially meat marinades, call for garlic paste. Chop the garlic coarsely, then use a mortar and pestle, a mini chopper, or a garlic press to make a relatively smooth paste.

Ghee — clarified butter (*ghee* in Hindi and Bengali): A flavorful cooking medium that has been used since ancient times as it is believed to preserve food. It imparts a distinctive nutty fragrance to dishes. Ghee is made by removing the casein (protein) and other solids from butter. It requires no refrigeration, keeps indefinitely, and can be stored at room temperature, as was done in ancient times. It does not burn like butter as it has a higher smoking point.

Because of its saturated fat content, I specify ghee only as an optional flavoring in a few recipes. But for authenticity and because of its exquisite flavor, you may decide to sprinkle a small amount of ghee over some dishes (especially rice, dal, and vegetables) as a seasoning. You can buy it at Indian grocers and some supermarkets in the West, although the homemade version is more flavorful. I don't use vegetable ghee sold in Indian stores; this ghee contains hydrogenated fat and lacks flavor.

To prepare ghee (clarified butter):

For this purpose, butter is simmered over very low heat for up to an hour. This evaporates the water and separates the milk solids from the pure fat, producing a golden liquid called ghee. The distinctive nutty flavor of ghee results from the gentle browning of the milk solids in the fat during the cooking process.

Melt 1 pound (450 g) of unsalted butter in a heavy-bottomed pan over very low heat. Allow it to simmer undisturbed. A smooth, white foam will soon cover the surface as the milk solids begin to separate from the fat. The soft foam on the surface will gradually become crusty, turning yellowish initially and then light brown. As this occurs, some of the milk solids will start to settle to the bottom and shortly thereafter turn brown as they roast in the fat. Occasionally pull the crust back gently with a spoon and monitor the browning process.

In 45 to 60 minutes, when the butter has stopped foaming and the sediment at the bottom has turned golden brown, remove from heat. Pour the contents of the pan through 4 or more layers of dampened cheesecloth pressed into a strainer held over a container, making sure that none of the sediment gets through the cheesecloth. If it does, strain it again; the sediment, if left, could make the ghee turn rancid. Store the liquid, covered, in the refrigerator or indefinitely at room temperature. Ghee will solidify as it cools. Yields 1½ cups (375 ml).

Using ghee the lowfat way:

Because of its intense flavor you need only a few drops of ghee in a dish. To avoid adding more than necessary, I place the ghee in a bottle with a plastic sprinkling insert on the top (such as a soy sauce or Chinese sesame oil bottle). Since ghee solidifies when stored, I liquefy it by standing the closed bottle in a bowl of hot water for about 15 minutes.

In Bengal ghee is considered to be a sacred food. Rice, offered to a deity during a religious ceremony, is often mixed with ghee. Another ancient practice is to sprinkle ghee over an open fire during ceremonial occasions.

Sprinkle a few drops on a dish just before serving. Vegetables, legumes, and rice dishes are especially tasty this way.

Ginger — *Zingiber officinale* (*adrak* in Hindi; *ada* in Bengali): The fibrous root of a herbaceous perennial, related to bamboo. It has a light brown skin and is pale yellow inside. It possesses an aromatic, pungent, spicy-sweet flavor. Peeled fresh ginger is an indispensable ingredient in Bengali-style fish and vegetable dishes and is also used in chutneys.

How to buy and store fresh ginger:

Ginger is a key ingredient in most dishes in this book, and care must be taken to buy it. Select plump roots with smooth, unwrinkled skin. Snap off one of the "fingers" (blunt protrusions) on the side and look for a moist, crisp surface, a fresh fragrance, and few fibers. This type of ginger will be easy to mince. Avoid old ginger, which has a shriveled look. It is usually full of fibers and is hard to chop.

Asian markets sometimes sell "young" ginger, which has ivory-pink skin and is juicy and tender. Buy this ginger whenever possible. It can be used in cooking or slivered raw in fruit and vegetable salads.

Because ginger is perishable, it should be stored unwrapped in the refrigerator. In the West, ginger is often steeped in sherry or oil, both of which can dilute and alter its flavor. Simply kept as is, this aromatic will last for several weeks. For best results, buy in small quantities and use within a few weeks.

To prepare minced ginger:

Peel the ginger using a vegetable peeler. Do not a use a knife since you can lose some of the flesh. Chop the ginger *very finely*; the smaller it is chopped the better it will blend with the sauce. If the ginger is fibrous and difficult to mince, you can make a ginger paste.

To prepare ginger paste:

Some recipes, especially meat marinades, call for ginger paste. This is the form in which it is always used in Bengal. Pound the peeled, coarsely chopped ginger using a mortar and pestle or grind it in a mini chopper to make a relatively smooth paste.

To prepare ginger juice:

My sister Sheila sometimes extracts the juice from slivers of tender young ginger through a twist of cheesecloth. She uses this juice in a dish instead of minced or grated ginger to soften the effect of this aromatic. Young ginger is available occasionally in Asian markets in the West. You can also extract ginger juice from minced or grated ginger root.

"The great cure, the great medicine."
—referring to the status of ginger in ancient India.
From *Spices in Indian Life,* by S. N. Mahindru

Greens — In Bengal dark, leafy greens such as spinach, mustard, and amaranth (sold in Asian markets), as well as a host of others not readily available in the West, are eaten because of their nutritive properties. You can substitute collard, kale, or Swiss chard in these recipes.

To steam and puree fresh greens:

Bring 3 to 4 tablespoons (45 to 60 ml) water to a boil in a large, deep-sided pan. Add the slivered greens. (You can also chop the stems finely and add to the leaves, as they contain many nutrients.) Cover, turn heat to medium low, and steam until the greens are tender but still retain their color, 4 to 5 minutes. If using fresh spinach, you need only a minute or so of steaming. You can also blanch spinach instead of steaming.

To puree the greens: Do this in batches. Place about 2 tablespoons (30 ml) water and about 2 cups (500 ml) of cooked greens in a blender. Use the water left in the pan after the steaming (if any). In any case, don't use any more water than necessary to achieve a smooth puree. Blend until smooth.

Kalonji — *Nigella arvensis* (**kalonji** in Hindi; **kalo jeera** in Bengali):   The round black seed of a plant of the buttercup family; often mistaken for an onion seed. It has a sharp flavor and is highly valued by the Bengalis for its onionlike aroma. Kalonji enlivens fish and vegetable dishes and also provides a crunch and color accent to flatbreads.

"Five-spice with dried red chili and kalonji seeds with green chili" is a Bengali kitchen adage. That is, the flavor of dried red chili goes well in a dish that contains five-spice, whereas green chili improves a dish seasoned by kalonji seeds alone.

Kewra water — (*ruh kewra* in Hindi; *kewrar jol* in Bengali):   Essence of the large variety of screwpine, *pandanus odoratissimus.* The clear, fragrant fluid is distilled from the male flowers and is used to flavor dairy-based sweets. It has a stronger perfume than rosewater and you need only a few drops.

A thirsty visitor to a Bengali home in earlier times would be offered a white marble tumbler filled with chilled water that had been scented with kewra essence.

Mace — *Myristica fragrans* (*jaivtri* in Hindi; *jayatri* in Bengali): The red, lacy network that surrounds the brittle outer shell of nutmeg. This fiber is dried and then powdered. The orange-colored spice has a marvelous scent and is sweeter than nutmeg. It is used in some meat dishes and dessert recipes.

Mango — *Mangifera indica* (*aam* in Hindi and Bengali): This sensuously delicious tropical fruit, which is found throughout India, is one that enchants all Bengalis. It is oval-shaped, about the size of a large peach although occasionally larger. Green, firm, and sour when unripe, it turns a delicate yellowish-red and exudes an irresistible fragrance when ripe. To me and to most Bengalis, it is without doubt the most delicious of fruits. When speaking of summer, my mother would often call it the "mango season." Frequently on sultry summer afternoons, the entire family would sit down at the table and feast on a large basket of ripe mangoes.

A mango is used in all stages of ripeness. When green, it is used in chutneys or dried and powdered as a souring agent. The ripe fruit, in addition to being served fresh, is used in the preparation of chutneys and desserts. Its pulp is also sun-dried to form intensely flavored sheets akin to fruit leather, a much-favored snack during those times of the year when fresh mangoes are not available. Mangoes from Maldah district, located north of Calcutta, are considered especially flavorful. In the West, canned mangoes are available in Indian and Asian markets, but they are inferior to the fresh fruit. If buying canned mango pulp from Indian stores, look for "Alfonso" on the label (not a brand but the name of a fine variety of mango). Fresh mangoes are widely available in supermarkets.

How to buy mangoes: Choose ripe mangoes that have a fragrant, fruity aroma and whose skin is a rich yellowish-orange with red overtones. At their peak of ripeness they may have tiny, sticky beads of "perspiration" in the skin and will feel slightly soft to the touch. If you find too many wrinkles, brown spots, or soft spots on a mango skin, it is probably overripe and of inferior quality. Also avoid mangoes with skins predominantly green, as they often do not ripen well in the home.

To prepare fresh mango pulp and mango puree:

Remove the skin with a knife, and either sliver the pulp if the recipe calls for it or scrape the pulp and juice into a bowl. If mango puree is called for in the recipe, puree the pulp in a blender. Discard the large pit at the center.

Mango powder — (aamchoor in Hindi and Bengali): Unripe, green mango slices, dried and then crushed to form a light brown powder. It has an agreeable sour taste, reminiscent of lemon, though richer and more complex. Do not substitute.

Mint — Mentha spicata (pudina in Hindi and Bengali): The fresh leaves of a perennial herb that comes in many varieties. This herb has a strong, sweet, tangy flavor. Only fresh mint, not the dried variety, is used in Bengali cooking. Mint makes a fine chutney and blends well in raitas, or yogurt-based salads. I occasionally use mint sprigs or chopped fresh mint as a garnish.

Mustard — (rai sorson in Hindi; rai sorshe in Bengali): Brassica hirta, the yellow (or white) mustard, and Brassica juncea or brassica nigra, the black (or brown), are the two major mustard species. The seeds of either variety, though slightly bitter, are agreeable. When crushed they yield a strong, pungent flavor. Western supermarkets sell the yellow seeds. But it is the dark mustard seeds, half the size of the yellow but more pungent and flavorful, that are used in Bengali cooking. Whole or ground, they provide an authentic Bengali taste and are worth the extra effort required to visit an Indian store.

The mustard plant, an annual of the cruciferae family, has deep green leaves and yellow flowers. The leaves, flowers, and stems are used in vegetable preparations. Aromatic mustard oil, which is pressed from the seeds, is used for both sautéing and flavoring.

Mustard is a popular spice in Bengal. Many a recipe starts by sautéing black mustard seeds. Another favorite method of preparation is to make a mustard paste, then spread it on meat, fish, or vegetables for added pungency before steaming.

To prepare ground black mustard and black mustard paste:

Grind 1 teaspoon (5 ml) of black mustard seeds to a fine powder using a mortar and pestle or a spice grinder. Yields 2 teaspoons (10 ml) ground black mustard.

To make a paste, mix this powder with 1 tablespoon (15 ml) water.

Let stand for 30 minutes, during which time it will lose some of its sharpness and its flavor will develop. Adding a dash of salt while grinding will also remove its bitterness.

Keep the heat low when cooking with powdered mustard or mustard paste.

To "study a subject down to the mustard seeds" means to study something in great detail.

—phrase from the Buddhist period. From *Spices in Indian Life*, by S. N. Mahindru

Nutmeg — *Myristica fragrans houtt* (*jaiphal* in Hindi and Bengali): The seed of an exotic peachlike fruit of the beautiful nutmeg tree. Ground nutmeg has a warm, sweet flavor and appears in dessert recipes.

Onion — *Allium cepa* (*pyaz* in Hindi and Bengali): Bengalis use onion for flavoring and thickening sauces. An onion can be lightly sautéed, brown-fried, or used as a puree.

To brown-fry onion for sauces:

Many recipes call for frying onion until lightly or richly browned. This step is important. Onion turns sweet and mellow and acquires a "roasted" flavor when fried in this manner. When simmered slowly in a dish it adds a rich, exotic dimension and melts into the sauce, thereby thickening it as well.

I find that the more uniformly the onion is chopped the better is the result. Keep the heat medium low or else the onion will start to burn. For amounts exceeding 1 cup (250 ml), start with medium heat, then turn to medium low. Depending on the amount and how it is cut, the timing will vary, but should approximate the time specified in the recipe. All of the onion pieces should brown in about the same time if you stir them constantly and adjust the heat as specified above. Sprinkle with a few drops of water if the edges start to burn.

Reducing the amount of brown-fried onion in a dish: Since the brown-frying of onion requires oil, reducing the amount of onion in a recipe reduces the amount of fat required to brown it. For example, by reducing the amount of onion by ¼ cup (60 ml) you can eliminate nearly ½ tablespoon (7 ml) of oil. The sauce will not be quite as thick, but will still be tasty.

To brown-fry onion for garnish:

Heat 2 tablespoons (30 ml) vegetable oil in a skillet over medium low heat. Fry 1½ cups (375 ml) thinly slivered onion until it is richly browned but not burnt, about 10 to 15 minutes, stirring constantly. Drain on paper towels. Brown-fried onions are excellent as a garnish for rice, dal, and meat dishes.

To fry onion until translucent:

This is different from brown-frying. It only takes a minute or two for the onion to become translucent. In this case the onion will lose its sharpness and acquire a delicate sweet flavor, but will not have a "roasted" aroma. Onion cooked in this manner will disintegrate readily when simmered into a gravy and is often used as a thickening agent. Dishes where the onion flavor should be less noticeable call for onion fried this way.

To prepare and fry onion paste:

Some recipes call for pureeing onion (usually with ginger, garlic, and green chili). This paste makes for a smooth, thick, flavorful sauce. You puree the onion in a blender until liquefied; normally you will need no extra water to do this. If, however, the blender will not process the onion, add a tablespoon (15 ml) or so of water. Don't add any more water than necessary as this hampers frying.

The paste is fried and then simmered gently, usually for about 20 minutes. This step removes the raw taste of the onion, and other ingredients can now be cooked in the resulting sauce.

To prepare mild raw onion rings for garnish:

Mild onion is not always available in Western supermarkets. You can mellow the strong flavor of regular onion in the following way. Red onion looks especially pretty as a garnish.

Put ¼ cup (60 ml) of onion rings in a sieve or colander and sprinkle lightly with salt. Place the sieve over a bowl or in the sink and let the onion drain for 30 minutes. Remove the rings and soak in cold water for about 30 minutes to eliminate the salt. Drain and pat dry. These tender rings will have a mild flavor.

Peas — *Pisum sativum* (*matar* in Hindi; *matarsuti* in Bengali): For a discussion of dried peas, see Dals chapter. Fresh, cooked, or frozen peas are used not only as a vegetable but also as a seasoning in fish and vegetable dishes when pureed.

To make pea paste:

Place fresh, cooked, or thawed frozen peas in a mortar and grind with the pestle until a smooth paste results. This is best done ¼ cup (60 ml) at a time. If necessary, sprinkle with a little water. Alternatively, place the peas on a board and smash them with a flat, heavy object such as a skillet. A food mill will also produce acceptable results.

Pepper (black and white) — *Piper nigrum L.* (*kala mirch* in Hindi; *gol morich* in Bengali): The dried immature berries of a vine that originated in India. The fruits grow in clusters, green when young, then ripening to yellow and red shades. When the green berries are dried in the sun they turn brownish-black and become known as black pepper. White pepper comes from either the riper yellow berries or from black pepper berries that have had their dark outer shell removed.

The use of pepper in India can be traced back to 5000 B.C. Once it was called "the king of spices" and considered a precious commodity. With the arrival of chili in the 16th century, pepper's popularity declined. However, fresh ground pepper is still used in many fish and meat dishes. Whole black pepper is sometimes incorporated in rice dishes for fragrance.

Poppyseeds — *Papaver somniferum* (*khus khus* in Hindi; *posto* in Bengali): The tiny, dried, non-narcotic seed of the poppy plant, an annual herb, which is among the oldest cultivated plants. The seed has a pleasant, crunchy, nutlike flavor and also adds texture to a dish.

Only the cream-colored "white" poppyseeds, smaller in size and more common in Bengal than the blue-gray type, are used in cooking. They are available in Indian stores. Roasted, then ground, they make an intriguing sauce thickener and a flavoring ingredient. Fish, shellfish, and vegetables taste delicious when cooked in white poppyseed sauce. Do not substitute the blue-gray seeds. Bengalis also grind mustard and poppyseeds together to achieve yet another tantalizing flavor.

To prepare poppyseed paste:

The tiny white seeds are not easy to pulverize. I roast them first to bring out their flavor and also to ease the process of grinding. The smoother the paste, the better the sauce will look and taste.

Place the white poppyseeds on an ungreased griddle or skillet over low heat. Remove after 30 seconds to 1 minute and grind to a coarse powder. I use a mortar and pestle (since a blender doesn't grind them well) for this purpose. Add twice the amount of hot water—for 1 tablespoon (15 ml) poppyseeds add 2 tablespoons (30 ml) hot water—and grind until a relatively smooth paste results.

You can also soften the roasted seeds by soaking them first in double the amount of hot water for 30 minutes. Grind this mixture to a smooth paste using a mortar and pestle as above.

Potato — *Solanum tuberosum* (*alu* in Hindi and Bengali):   The Portuguese brought potatoes to India in the 16th century, and the vegetable has remained a favorite in the Bengali kitchen ever since. Bengalis prepare potatoes in many different ways and will even eat rice and potato in the same meal. When buying potatoes for the recipes in this book, use thin-skinned red, white, or yellow (boiling) potatoes. Do not use Idaho or russet (baking) potatoes unless the recipe specifically calls for it.

Brown-frying of potatoes:

In many recipes potatoes are brown-fried first, usually in 2 tablespoons (30 ml) of oil. This removes the flat, "boiled" taste from the potatoes, giving them a rich, nutty flavor and a pleasantly crunchy crust. To significantly lower the fat content of dishes using brown-fried potatoes, do the following: Heat 1 teaspoon (5 ml) oil in a 6- to 8-inch (15 to 20 cm) nonstick pan or skillet over medium to medium high heat. You can fry ½ pound (250 g) of potatoes to a medium brown color with this amount of oil. Turn them frequently to prevent burning. The potatoes may not brown as evenly as with a larger amount of oil, but the result will be quite acceptable. If the recipe calls for 1 pound (500 g) of potatoes, repeat this process with the second batch of potatoes and an additional 1 teaspoon (5 ml) oil. And so on for larger quantities of potatoes.

Rice flour — (*chawal atta* in Hindi; *chalen guro* in Bengali):   Also called ground rice or rice powder, this is made by pulverizing rice to a fine powder. The taste and texture added depend on the type of rice used: short grain, long-grain, brown, or organically grown. I generally buy the variety made from long-grain rice that is sold in Indian stores or the organically grown variety from health food stores. Both produce good results.

Rosewater — (*ruh gulab* in Hindi; *golaper jol* in Bengali):   The diluted essence of highly perfumed rose which flavors milk-based sweets. In my experience, Bengali Moslems use it more widely than Bengali Hindus. Rose petals are sometimes sprinkled on top of sweets such as rice pudding but are not eaten.

In the past, guests would ritually wash their hands in a bucket of water strewn with rose petals after a festive dinner.

Saffron — *Crocus sativus* (*jafran* in Hindi and Bengali):   The dried stigmas of the saffron crocus, a bulbous perennial. The purple flower, resembling the common crocus, blooms for a 10-day period in late autumn. Each of the three orange-red stigmas of the flower is laboriously plucked by hand and dried. It takes 75,000 to 100,000 stigmas to make a pound (about 500 g) of dried saffron—the world's most expensive spice.

Saffron has a powerful and exotic aroma and you need to use only a pinch. It can be used whole or ground. In desserts it's used whole, with the threads making a pattern through the sauce. In rice or meat dishes it is ground first. The spice, whole or ground, expands when immersed in liquid and imparts a brilliant yellow hue to a small amount of warm water or milk. This liquid flavors rice, meat, and dessert dishes and its intense color connotes a festive occasion.

Omit saffron if you must, but don't substitute it with either safflower (azafrán) available in Mexican stores or turmeric. Either of them will provide the color but not the flavor.

"Her skin had a saffron glow."

—description of a maiden from
an ancient Indian writing

Salt — (nimak in Hindi; noon in Bengali): I use sea salt, rather than common salt, in my cooking. When you add salt is important. Country-style Chunky Tomato Chutney is salted in the beginning so that the water from the tomatoes will be drawn out and a sauce will form. In a dal (legume) dish, salt is added after the dals have softened but before they have been spiced; otherwise it may toughen the dals. I don't usually add salt at the very end of cooking as the ingredients don't absorb it well.

"Not a taste of salt in the whole pan!"

—Bengali expression to describe
a worthless object or person

Sesame seeds — *Sesamum indicum* (til in Hindi and Bengali): The small, flat, creamy white or light brown hulled seeds of an ancient plant. The delicate, crunchy seeds are roasted and ground to enrich sauces. They also appear in many dessert recipes.

To toast sesame seeds:

Place the seeds on an ungreased griddle or skillet over low heat. Keep stirring for several minutes or until they are light brown in color. Transfer immediately to a bowl.

Silver leaf — (*chandi-ka-varaq* in Hindi; *rangta* or *rupali tabak* in Bengali): Pure silver is pounded until it forms tissue-thin, edible leaves that are used to decorate the tops of sweets such as Gold Bars and Silk and Satin Bars. Silver leaf does not have a taste of its own, does not alter the flavor of the sweet, and contains no calories.

Because the leaves are thin and fragile, they are sold encased between two layers of tissue paper. To use, remove the top layer of tissue paper, invert the leaf and the remaining layer of tissue over the sweet, and press gently. Discard the tissue. The leaf may wrinkle or break slightly; do not be concerned as this is quite normal. In the past, on special occasions, a few grains of cooked rice would be individually wrapped in a small piece of silver leaf and placed on top of pullao rice dishes for a striking presentation. Silver leaf (and sometimes gold leaf, which has a similar use) is available in Indian stores.

Tamarind — *Tamarindus indica* (*imli* in Hindi; *tetul* in Bengali): The fruit of a large tree also known for its beautiful wood. Both the English and the botanical names come from the Arabic word "tamr-hindi," Indian date (meaning the fruit, not a calendar date). Tamarind, a tan-colored pod about 5 inches (12.5 cm) in size, contains dark brown pulp and shiny seeds. The fibers and the seeds are discarded. The rich, tart pulp is a sauce ingredient for many dishes and makes a fine chutney. The complex, sensuous flavor of tamarind cannot be duplicated by any other ingredient.

Tamarind is still sold, as in centuries past, as a 1-pound (500 g) dried block. Some recipes in this book call for a puree made from a portion of this dried mass. For others, you can buy ready-to-use tamarind concentrate, which eliminates the need for further processing. For most of the recipes given in this book where the amount needed is small, I have used ready-made tamarind concentrate. For recipes where tamarind is a main ingredient, as in Tender Tamarind Chutney, I use the tamarind puree because of its richer taste.

To prepare tamarind puree:

When buying a block of tamarind, choose one that yields when you press it with your fingers. This type softens easily when soaked, making extraction of the pulp easier.

Chop off a 2½ x 1 x 1-inch (6 x 2.5 x 2.5 cm) piece from a block of dried tamarind and soak it in ½ cup (125 ml) of hot water in a nonmetallic bowl for 15 to 30 minutes. Press with a spoon to break the tamarind apart and mix with the soaking water. Remove the seeds and fibers, if any, and discard them. Puree the remainder in a blender, then strain it through a sieve. Use as much as is needed in a recipe, then store the rest covered in the refrigerator in a nonmetallic container. It will keep for several days. Yields ½ cup (125 ml).

Tamarind Tip

■ If tamarind does not soften even after it has soaked for 30 minutes, place it in a nonmetallic pan along with the soaking water over low heat. As soon as bubbles appear on the surface, turn off heat. Let stand covered until the mixture cools. The heat will soften the tamarind and make it easier to extract the pulp.

Thickened milk — (khoya in Hindi; khoa or kheer in Bengali): Made by slowly evaporating milk to a solid mass; has been used as the base for many desserts since ancient times. Milk, so reduced, kept well even at room temperature in the millennia prior to the invention of refrigeration.

In some parts of India, "kheer" refers to rice pudding made with thickened milk. To avoid confusion, I refer to thickened milk as "khoya" throughout this book.

The preparation is easy but time-consuming. I usually start it when cooking other dishes, so that I can watch over the milk.

To prepare khoya or thickened milk:

8 cups (2 liters) milk (whole or 2% lowfat)

1. Use a large, deep-sided, and preferably nonstick pan. Lightly oil the bottom and sides to prevent the milk from sticking. (A small piece of paper towel saturated with a few drops of oil may be used to rub the pan.) Bring milk to boil over medium high heat.

2. Turn heat to medium. Stir constantly until the boiling subsides. Cook for approximately 75 minutes, or until the mixture turns into a moist, doughy mass. Watch carefully, as the milk will rise every few minutes; when it does, stir with a spoon and the foaming will subside. Also scrape the sides and bottom every now and then and mix thickened bits of milk with the liquid milk. As the mixture becomes more doughy, lower the heat and stir very frequently to prevent it from burning. Let cool to room temperature.

This doughy mass, khoya, or thickened milk, is now ready to be used in recipes. Yields 1½ cups (375 ml).

Tomato — Lycopersicon esculentum: In Bengali cooking, tomato is used both as a vegetable and as a spice (in forming sauces). When used as a vegetable, tomato is treated like other ingredients. As a spice, chopped tomato is often simmered with various spices until it dissolves to produce a thick, tasty gravy. Other ingredients are then cooked in this tomato-based sauce.

I prefer to cook with Roma, also known as plum or Italian, tomatoes. This variety is more flavorful, less watery, and has a deeper color than regular tomatoes. Since fresh tomatoes are available year-round in the West, I never use canned.

To peel and seed tomatoes:

Lower the tomatoes into a pan of boiling water with a slotted spoon. Let cook for 30 seconds to 1 minute. Remove and allow to cool. Pull the skin off. Cut each tomato in half crosswise. Place a strainer over a bowl and gently squeeze the seeds out of each half while holding over the strainer to catch the juice. The juice may be used with the pulp in recipes; discard the seeds. You can save the tomato skins and sliver them to garnish raitas, yogurt-based salads.

Turmeric — *Curcuma longa* (*haldi* in Hindi; *halud* in Bengali): The dried root of the turmeric plant, a perennial herb of the ginger family. The orange-yellow root is often freshly ground in Bengal but is sun-dried and powdered before being sold in Western supermarkets. It is sometimes erroneously referred to as saffron because of the similarity of their colors. You cannot substitute turmeric for saffron.

Turmeric has a peppery scent and an aromatic, slightly bitter taste. Most Bengali dishes feature this flavoring and coloring ingredient, also prized because it preserves any dish that is cooked with it.

Be careful when cooking with turmeric since, if spilled, it can stain counter surfaces or clothing. This is especially true after turmeric has been mixed with oil. Wash the stains off immediately with soapy water.

Turmeric is more than a spice; it is a sacred object. One of the rituals of a Bengali wedding ceremony is called gaye halud, *"anointing the body with turmeric." Early on the wedding day the bride will bathe in turmeric-tinted water—a rite that announces her entrance into womanhood.*

Vegetable oils — (*tel* in Hindi and Bengali): Considered an important item in Bengali cuisine, these serve not only as a cooking medium but also as a flavor enhancer. Mustard oil, with its intensely pungent flavor, reigns as the top choice for fish and vegetable dishes. Do not substitute another oil when a recipe calls for mustard oil, which can be purchased in Indian stores. (Look first for "pure" mustard oil; if not available, buy mustard oil mixed with soybean or other oils.) I recommend keeping a bottle of it in your cupboard. "No mustard oil, no flavor," says my Aunt Gouri, always praised for her cooking.

In recipes that call for vegetable oil you can use peanut, safflower, or canola oil. I use canola, which is high in monounsaturated fats, low in saturated fats, and is one of the few vegetarian sources of omega-3 fatty acids. It is related to mustard oil, being derived from rapeseed, a member of the mustard family. Canola oil has a high smoking point and is suitable for deep-frying. Sesame oil, though common in some parts of India, is not used in Bengali cooking.

An oil that cannot be used in these recipes is olive oil, since its strong flavor clashes with Indian spices and flavorings.

Bengalis also sometimes add a small amount of oil at the end of the cooking process to achieve a unique flavor. A sprinkling of ghee or mustard oil may impart a sharp flavor to a dish just after it is removed from the heat. In such cases, you can enjoy the aromatic essence of the oil, which has not been mellowed by the cooking process.

Range of oil specified in a recipe: When a recipe specifies, for example, 1 to 2½ tablespoons (15 to 37 ml) oil, it means that you can produce a tasty dish with 1 tablespoon (15 ml) oil, but for best flavor use up to 2½ tablespoons (37 ml).

For those not particularly concerned with the fat content of a dish or for those special occasions when considerations of taste outweigh those of nutrition, use the maximum amount of oil called for in the recipe. A number of dishes are inherently lowfat and can be enjoyed by all without modification.

Also, when you cook a dish for the first time, consider using the largest amount of oil specified in the recipe to experience the authentic taste. Reduce the amount of oil progressively thereafter if you wish. Feel free to experiment.

Using a wok to reduce the amount of oil: Throughout the book I have offered many suggestions for lowering the fat content of a dish. The choice of utensil can also have an effect. A smaller amount of oil at the bottom of a wok or *karai* can sauté a relatively larger amount of ingredients. In the West, where cooking is done in flat-bottomed utensils, it takes a relatively larger amount of oil to form a thin layer at the bottom. For these reasons it is nearly impossible to make these dishes totally nonfat using Western utensils. For best results, consider experimenting with a wok.

Vegetable Oil Tips

■ I have used nonstick pans for testing these recipes and the amount of oil has been measured accordingly. If not using a nonstick pan, you may need to slightly increase the amount of oil (or liquid).

■ When you double a recipe, you generally double the amount of all ingredients. One exception to this rule is oil. If a dish calls for 2 table-spoons (30 ml) oil, in doubling the recipe you need not use 4 table-spoons (60 ml); 2½ to 3 tablespoons (30 to 45 ml) of oil may be suffi-cient.

COOKING STYLES, TECHNIQUES, AND EQUIPMENT

A Western friend watched me prepare a few dishes and, in amazement, said: "The flavors are so complex, but the cooking's so easy." Bengali cooking had to be. Its basic techniques were developed several millennia ago, when food was prepared over an open fire in a land where fuel was scarce and gadgets were unknown. Despite these limitations, Bengali cooking has evolved into a sophisticated cuisine. The dishes have been perfected over time—the right spices are added at the right moment, each harmonizing with the main ingredients. Many cooking styles have evolved, with distinct methods of spicing and even chopping the ingredients.

Practically anything can be curried.
—from *Anglo Indian Cuisine* by Constance E.
Gordon, published in 1913

STYLES OF COOKING

In Bengal, you frequently hear the names of various cooking styles during conversation. "Did you make a *pora* today?" meaning a roasted vegetable such as eggplant. Or, "I could barely taste the mustard in her *bhapa*," implying that the cook should have added more of the pungent spice when steaming fish.

Bengali cooking methods include a combination of steaming, sautéing, roasting, braising, and deep-frying. Since each family may vary the spicing somewhat to its own taste, standard recipes are difficult to find. Yet the flavor of a specific dish such as a *chochori* is identifiable. If you have a craving for a *chochori*, then a *kalia*, no matter how good, will fail to satisfy your palate.

You will find recipes using each of the following cooking styles in this book.

Bhaja:

Bhaja is the frying method and includes pan-fried and deep-fried food. Pan-fried browned onions serve as a garnish. Both deep-fried vegetables and deep-fried fish customarily accompany a lentil dish. You cut the vegetables in slices, optionally dust them with ground forms of coconut, black mustard, sesame, or chili and fry them in oil. Before frying, you can also dip the ingredients in a flavorful chickpea batter, which gives them a crunchy, fritterlike consistency. Quick-cooking at a high temperature is the key.

"Not all fish are fit for frying," a Bengali cook once told me. "The ones with scales are the best." The frying of fish is an art. Rub thick pieces of fish with ginger, turmeric, and ground red chili. "Keep the oil very hot or else the fish will break," reminds my mother. The result is fried fish that is crisp and fragrant outside and succulent inside.

Bhapa:

Bhapa or steaming is a technique that applies to both vegetable and fish dishes. For example, you can toss cauliflower pieces with oil and spices and then steam them until tender. You need not watch the pan during this stage. Bhapa is guaranteed to produce an aromatic dish.

Bengalis excel at the art of steaming fish. It proceeds with a fillet of fish marinated with spices and mustard oil, placed in a covered container over boiling water. A classic steaming technique is to wrap the fish in banana leaf to give it a faint musky, smoky scent. (In the West you can get by with heavy-duty aluminum foil—or buy banana leaves, which are increasingly available fresh or frozen at Asian markets.)

To save fuel, my mother puts the marinated fish in a covered bowl and cooks it along with rice. The steam infuses the fish with the unique fragrance of the native Indian rice.

Chechki:

Chechki, another frying method, is done with less oil than the bhaja technique. You can use fish, vegetables, or a combination of the two. Chop the ingredients and fry them with chili and whole spices until they become light brown in color. You then simmer them with water and ground spices, a step that also differentiates the method from bhaja.

Chochori:

This fascinating method was originally conceived to make use of rejected stalks, skins, and vegetable leaves. Down through the centuries, the tasty *chochori* has entered the mainstream of Bengali cooking, and homemakers now specifically shop for this dish.

This style of cooking produces a thick, clinging sauce. Both fish and vegetables can be cooked this way. Chop the fish and vegetables, or simply the vegetables—potato, eggplant, and cauliflower. Fry them first, then simmer them with spices. During frying you can raise the heat to char the bottom slightly, a characteristic of chochori. The ingredients will lose their identity and merge. The result is a melange of flavors, each bite bursting with taste.

Dom:

The word *dom* literally means "breath." In the "breathed-in" method, meat, fish, or vegetables cook in the flavorful steam produced by the moisture of the ingredients. It's similar to braising. In earlier times, a cook would make a paste of flour and water to seal the edges of the covered pan so that no steam would escape. A pot with a tight-fitting lid serves the same purpose today. Alternatively, you can press a piece of aluminum foil between the pot and the lid.

Ghanto:

A *ghanto* dish contains slivered fish or vegetables. This technique uses only one or two ingredients, stirred frequently during cooking. The name ghanto, "jumble," accurately describes the process.

Jhal:

The word *jhal* literally means "spicy hot." This style does not overuse chilies, but has an undertone of hotness due in part to freshly ground black pepper. Little liquid is used. The result is a thick, pungent gravy.

Jhol:

You rarely sit down to a meal in Bengal that doesn't include a plate of *jhol,* which literally means "gravy." This technique combines several aromatics with ample liquid to form a thin but robust sauce. You cut fish, meat, or vegetables in long strips or large cubes to expose maximum surface area to this light, flavorful gravy.

Kabab:

Kabab, or *shish-kabab,* is skewered food popularized by the Moghul kings. You marinate meat or fish in spices and yogurt and roast them over an open fire. A variation more common in Bengal is known as *haaree kabab,* "kabab in a kettle." Instead of roasting, you can simmer meat or fish cubes in a pot with excellent results.

Kalia:

A *kalia* is a richer, more elaborately seasoned version of *jhal.* You typically use onions and hot spices such as cardamom, cloves, and cinnamon in their whole form. Oftentimes yogurt or ground cashews enrich the gravy. An optional sprinkling of ghee at the very end enhances the flavor. The kalia style of cooking is most often used with fish. With the replacement of onion by ginger and garlic, a kalia becomes a *dalna,* which is used exclusively with vegetables or fresh cheese.

Koftas (or boras):

The Moghul kings loved *koftas,* also called *boras,* ground meat or vegetable croquettes bound together by spices and/or eggs. Many Bengali vegetarians, who omit eggs from their diet, use chickpea flour instead. You can serve these patties alone, with a chutney, or swimming in a thick, savory gravy.

Korma:

In the *korma* method, also inspired by the Moghul kings, fish or meat comes in contact with very little water. Instead, yogurt or tamarind puree enriches the sauce. In the past, a korma cook made liberal use of ghee or oil and garam masala. Although hot spices are still used, the amount of oil has been reduced to cut down the fat content of the dish.

Malai:

Malai is a smooth, creamy sauce made with milk or coconut milk. You can transform everyday meat, fish, or vegetables into an elegant dish by cooking in this manner.

Pora:

You can *pora,* or roast, vegetables over direct heat both to soften them and to develop a smoky flavor. The best result is achieved with eggplant roasted under a broiler, over a gas flame, or on a barbecue grill. (Or you can bake it in an oven. This will not, however, develop a smoky flavor.) Once it's tender, you can remove the charred skin and spice the fleshy part in many ways.

Sambara:

The spicing method called *sambara* or *tarka* is most commonly applied to legumes after they have been simmered to tenderness, and also to chutneys and other dishes. Heat a tablespoon (15 ml) or so of oil, usually mustard oil, in a pan. Then fry bay leaves, whole dried red chilies, five-spice, black mustard seeds, or kalonji seeds for a few seconds. Sambara is the pouring of this aromatic mixture over the cooked ingredients. Since it is done in the last few minutes, the fragrance of the spices remains at its peak.

BASIC COOKING PRINCIPLES AND PREPARATION

Regardless of the style chosen, some basic principles are followed for those styles of food preparation that take place in multiple stages. To start the cooking, fry five-spice and whole dried red chili in hot oil. This releases the aroma of the seasonings into the oil. Next, fry onion and garlic; this process softens the vegetables and mellows their flavor. With further cooking, they begin to disintegrate and help thicken the gravy.

Once the oil has been prepared, add the chief ingredient, fish, meat, or vegetable, which is sautéed for a minute or so. This step is done quickly to retain the moistness of the ingredients. Then simmer the ingredients in their accumulated juices or add a small amount of water. Ground spices such as cumin or coriander, and optional pastes such as one made with ginger, mustard, or poppyseeds, may be added at this stage.

When the ingredients have reached the desired degree of doneness, garam masala, a mixture of hot and fragrant spices, is sprinkled over them. This announces the end of cooking. Just before serving, scatter a handful of chopped cilantro leaves on top to enliven the dish and enhance its visual appeal.

COOKING TECHNIQUES

Frying (also called sautéing, pan-frying, or shallow-frying):

This technique involves cooking ingredients in small amounts of moderately hot oil. In most recipes, spices are sautéed first in this manner to release their flavor; aromatics such as onion and garlic are fried so that their flavors are mellowed and enhanced; other ingredients such as meat and potatoes are fried to brown them and seal in their juices. The ingredients are seldom completely cooked in this manner. Frying is followed by other techniques, such as braising or simmering to complete the cooking process. The words "frying" and "sautéing" are used interchangeably in this book.

Tips on Frying

■ I usually heat a pan or skillet for a few minutes before adding oil to it. Make sure the oil is very hot (but not smoky) before frying spices or other ingredients; otherwise they will absorb oil but not fry properly, and will take a longer time than specified in the recipe. A piece of raw potato dipped into the oil should sizzle immediately and start to turn brown.

■ Many pans and skillets have a slightly curved bottom. When frying spices you will find that oil usually accumulates around the sides, especially if the amount used is small. I usually put the spices where the oil has accumulated. They are better sautéed when drenched in oil this way.

■ "When the oil floats on top": When frying ground spices and aromatics, the traditional test to check when they are ready is to see whether or not the oil has formed a layer on top of the spice mixture. Since I have reduced the amount of fat in these recipes, the oil rarely forms a separate layer on the top; rather, it will tend to collect in little depressions and irregularities.

Deep-frying:

Often a small amount of deep-fried food accompanies a Bengali dinner. Deep-frying involves frying food quickly at a high temperature in plenty of oil. Properly done, deep-fried food absorbs little oil and retains its natural juices. If the heat is too high, the food will brown quickly but may not cook properly at the center. You need to regulate the heat so that the surface is sealed but the food is barely tender inside.

■ In order to deep-fry, you must have sufficient oil (about 2 inches/5 cm deep) to cover the food. Use a pan large enough so that it is not more than half full.

■ Do not use either mustard oil or olive oil for deep-frying as they will impart their own flavors to the ingredients. Use oil with a lighter flavor such as peanut, safflower, or canola.

■ When you deep-fry, make sure the oil is very hot. To test, drop in a piece of bread or a slice of raw potato, which should sizzle immediately. (One exception is the recipe for Milk Puffs in Cardamom Syrup, in which case deep-frying is done over slightly lower heat and for a longer period of time.)

■ If the food is coated with batter, remove any excess before frying. Use slotted spoons both for removing food from the batter and for lifting it out of the oil.

■ Once food is deep-fried, do not cover it; it will become soggy. You can place a paper towel on top (and bottom) to absorb any excess oil.

■ An Indian karai or a Chinese wok requires less oil for deep-frying due to its rounded shape. An electric deep-fat fryer requires more oil but allows you to adjust the temperature more readily.

■ Do not deep-fry too many items at a time; this will cause the temperature to fall. More oil will seep into the food, making it soggy and fat-laden, and a brown crust may not form.

Simmering:

This technique involves cooking gently at or below the boiling point. When simmering a dish make sure that the liquid in the pan is moving but not boiling vigorously. The heat adjustment will depend on the amount of liquid and solid ingredients and the size and shape of the pan. With too little heat, the dish will not finish cooking in the specified amount of time. Too much heat will overcook the ingredients and affect their texture.

Steaming:

Fish, shellfish, or vegetables can be steamed—that is, cooked over indirect moist heat—with excellent results.

To steam fish or shellfish: Place the seafood and the marinade (see "Marinating" in this section) on a piece of heavy-duty aluminum foil large enough to make a steaming pouch. Draw the edges of the foil over the seafood and seal them together tightly so that no water can seep in during the cooking process. Place this pouch in a steamer basket (for this purpose, you need a basket without a vertical rod in the center). Pour water, ½ inch (1 cm) deep, in a pan that has a tight-fitting lid and that can hold the steamer basket. Bring water to boil. Turn heat to medium low or low. Place the steamer basket with the fish in the pan and cover with the lid.

Seafood cooking time will vary with its thickness. For fish less than an inch (2.5 cm) thick, 10 to 15 minutes is sufficient. For thicker fish, you will need 15 to 20 minutes or longer. For medium-sized prawns (large shrimp), 8 to 10 minutes may be sufficient. Remove the pouch from the steamer and open it carefully. Pierce the seafood with a fork and twist gently to expose the flesh inside. If the inside is opaque, the seafood is done. Do not cook any longer than necessary to achieve this, as the texture of the seafood will deteriorate with overcooking.

To steam vegetables: Place the vegetables in a steamer basket. (You can use a basket with a vertical rod at the center.) Insert the basket in the pan and steam as described for fish or shellfish. The timing for steaming various vegetables will vary. Steam until they are tender but still firm.

Marinating:

In many fish and meat recipes, the ingredients are marinated, that is, rubbed with spices or steeped in a flavored liquid medium (called a marinade) for a period of time. If you use this technique, the marinade will penetrate fish or meat more deeply than if the ingredients are simply cooked in a sauce. A marinade containing yogurt will also tenderize the meat somewhat.

GENERAL COOKING TIPS

Following are some general tips that will help you get started. Refer to the recipe chapters for additional tips.

- Do not let the long list of ingredients for some recipes deter you from trying them. Many of the ingredients are simply spices. But do not substitute or omit items.

- Measure all ingredients. I have kept fat (and salt) in these recipes to a minimum and the ingredients will cook adequately in the amount of oil specified. Larger quantities of ingredients may not produce the desired results.

- Before beginning to cook, prepare the ingredients and arrange them on a counter near the stove in the order they will be used. Since spices turn bitter when overcooked, the ingredients are added in a rapid-fire fashion and must be readily available.

- Although I have specified lemon juice as a substitute for lime juice in these recipes, the effect is not the same. Use lime whenever possible to make use of its distinctive flavor.

- The dimensions of fish, meat, and vegetables, as specified in these recipes, are approximate. Raw materials often come in irregular shapes.

- Whenever a recipe calls for milk, yogurt, or dry milk, you can use the lowfat or nonfat variety except where noted.

- In converting to metric measurements I have rounded the numbers, whenever necessary, for ease of use. For example, 1 pound has been rounded to 500 g and ½ inch to 1 cm.

- When cooking with yogurt, bring it to room temperature first, whenever possible. Also keep the heat low or else the yogurt might curdle. An alternative is to add a little flour to the yogurt—½ teaspoon (2 ml) or so per 2 tablespoons (30 ml) of yogurt.

- A teaspoon (5 ml) or less of sugar enlivens many fish, meat, and vegetable dishes. The purpose is not to sweeten the dish, but to bring out the flavor of the ingredients.

- The word "dash" as applied to a spice measure means "less than ⅛ teaspoon (.5 ml)," or roughly a pinch.

- Vegetables should be chopped uniformly for eye appeal. As an example, in a *jhol*-style dish, both potatoes and eggplant are cut in long strips, but in a *korma*-style meat dish, the vegetables are cubed to resemble the meat pieces.

- You can remove the whole spices, bay leaf, and whole red and green chilies from a dish before serving, or simply warn your guests. Like a nutshell, the husks of these spices are inedible (or fiery hot, in the case of a chili). And whole spices, when bitten into, produce an intense flavor that interferes with a diner's appreciation of the dish.

- Leftover Bengali-style meat, fish, and vegetable dishes are excellent when warmed up the next day. The spices develop their flavors more fully when refrigerated overnight.

- Cilantro is the garnish of choice for all meat, fish, and vegetable dishes. I specify only the additional garnishes (if any) in the recipes.

- Finally, your dishes are as good as the quality of the ingredients. Shop for the freshest fish, meat, and produce. Whenever possible, grind spices just before cooking. If you follow the steps exactly and buy only high-quality ingredients, you'll soon savor authentic Bengali dishes.

Even the least thing well done brings marvellous results; therefore let everyone do what little he can. If the fisherman thinks he is the spirit, he will be a better fisherman.

—Swami Vivekananda, from "Vedanta in Its Application to Indian Life" in *Letters from Colombo to Almora*

EQUIPMENT

You need little special equipment or gadgets to cook the Bengali way. The traditional utensil for cooking is the *karai,* a woklike iron pan that requires little oil and disperses heat easily. A deep pot or pan works nearly as well.

I prefer pans and skillets with a nonstick surface. I use 2 large, deep-sided nonstick pans, one 12 inches (30 cm) and another 10 inches (25 cm) in diameter and both 4½ inches (11 cm) deep; several nonstick skillets 10 inches (25 cm) in diameter; and several small nonstick saucepans, 6 to 8 inches (15 to 20 cm) in diameter. Many Bengali dishes require more than one pan.

An electric blender is convenient for grinding chutneys, blending legumes, and pureeing vegetables. To mince ginger, garlic, or cilantro, I turn to a mini food processor (also called a mini chopper). You can use an electric coffee grinder for this purpose, but if you do, you cannot grind coffee beans in it any longer. I pulverize black mustard seeds or white poppyseeds with a mortar and pestle. Then I pour the water needed to make a paste into the mortar, making it an easy operation.

In Bengal we use a *tawa,* an iron griddle that retains heat well, for preparing flatbreads and toasting spices. You can use a flat nonstick griddle or, better yet, an iron skillet.

For stirring, I prefer spoons made of synthetic material rather than metal ones; the latter may scratch the bottom of the pan and impart a metallic flavor to the dish. Wooden spoons tend to harbor bacteria in their porous surface, so I don't use them. I use slotted spoons and slotted spatulas when I want to lift food out of oil or liquid, as when deep-frying or simmering.

Finally, a few miscellaneous items. In my kitchen I keep a scale that is especially useful for weighing potatoes. For rolling flatbreads, you need a cutting board and a rolling pin; I prefer the slender, smooth rolling pins sold in Indian stores. A steamer basket is indispensable for steaming fish and vegetables. I prefer one without a vertical rod at the center for steaming fish. A few layers of cheesecloth come in handy when making *channa*, fresh cheese, or for draining the liquid out of yogurt.

Other than the above, use the same pots, pans, bowls, spoons, and skillets that you employ in everyday Western cooking.

Control of heat during cooking is important, so I prefer cooking with a gas stove on which you can switch promptly from one heat intensity to another. If using an electric stove, heat one burner to medium low and another to low. After the spices have been fried at medium to medium low heat and the recipe instruction calls for a lower heat, simply remove the pan from the first burner and place it over the second.

DALS

"Should dal be eaten first?" I crouched in my hiding place under the stairs as my Uncle Sukumar and his guest from Burdwan district debated the issue.

"I always start my meal with a sip from a bowl of dal," insisted Uncle Sukumar. "It's the only proper way to eat."

He has no salt for the vegetables, but he can find ghee for the lentils.

—Bengali proverb describing a person
who lives beyond his means

"Preposterous!" huffed his guest. "How else to finish a meal but with dal?"

And I learned that the art of eating dal is as important as the dals themselves.

In India "dal" is a generic name for legumes—lentils, peas, and beans that come in a variety of colors, sizes, and tastes. They can be olive green like *mung*, salmon pink like *masur*, or black like *urad*. When left whole in their jackets they are round; when shelled and split in half, they closely resemble the split peas used in Western cooking. In their whole state *chhola* (chickpeas, garbanzo beans, or ceci beans) taste different than split chickpeas, which are called *chana dal*. But both forms are treated as food items belonging to the dal category.

Regardless of the type, each variety has a unique taste and is loaded

with carbohydrates, B vitamins, and iron. Another English name for legumes is "pulse," and indeed these nutritious legumes pulsate with life.

I remember as a child peeking into a neighbor's kitchen on the occasion
of her daughter's wedding. Two pots of dal were simmering on the stove.

"Isn't one enough?" I asked.

The woman shook her head. "When I was growing up," she said, "my
family offered at least four types of dal during a ceremony. Plain dal would
start the meal. Vegetable-flavored dal would be served next, followed by dal
made with fish, or shrimp. Finally came tart dal or one with a sweet and
sour taste."

Legumes have been grown in India for many thousands of years. Exactly
when they first appeared in Bengali kitchens is not known, but they have
long been an integral part of the cuisine. Bengali vegetarians eat them with
bhat, rice in countless forms. Rice and dal are two food items now recognized in the West as excellent sources of complementary protein. Meat and
fish eaters in Bengal, who do not need it for dietary reasons, consume
several servings of dal every day with pleasure.

Imagine my surprise when a Bengali parent I met in the U.S. confided
to me, "You see, my two children were both born in the U.S. But they love
dal-bhat." Bengalis show great reverence for legumes even when living away
from their homeland.

Although Westerners think of peas, beans, and lentils as soup or stew
ingredients, the versatile legumes appear in the Bengali cuisine in many
forms—whole, powdered, mashed, and pureed. Legumes, finely ground,
form inner layers in savory breads such as Pea-filled Puffed Buns. One might
suspect the delicious dessert Gold Bars to be laced with almonds when, in
fact, it is made with ground beans.

Rice and lentils make a Bengali.

—Bengali expression

A popular legume derivative is *bori,* a meat substitute, which is as
crunchy as a crouton and comes in a variety of flavors. Although these tiny
dumplings can be bought in stores, Bengali women have traditionally fash-
ioned them at home. The women first combine powdered lentils with spices
and water, then divide the mixture into bite-sized pieces and shape them
like chocolate kisses. The boris are then dried in the sun—the secret to
their robust fresh air fragrance.

The weight of the peas flattens the tiny red lentil seeds.

—Bengali proverb, said when a person
of power intimidates other people

In some small towns women make boris to earn a living. Even children may playfully dip their fingers in the lentil powder to make a few boris before going to school.

You can buy boris in Indian stores or prepare them at home (see "Lentil Dumplings" in this section). They are delicious simply fried, or use them to enhance vegetable and fish dishes. During the monsoon season, when fresh vegetables are in short supply, boris are in even greater demand. They add protein, textural contrast, and a rich taste to any meal.

Because legumes are a daily staple, Bengali cooks vary their preparation in a thousand different ways. (This is why I have dedicated a separate chapter to them rather than include them in the "Vegetarian Dishes" chapter.) A dal with a thick consistency is served with bread, whereas a thinner dal moistens rice. Bengalis will introduce such items as raisins, shredded coconut, or tamarind puree, transforming the character of the dish. Or they may designate dal as a sauce base.

Chickpea Lamb Treasure, lamb cubes simmered in a rich chickpea sauce, is popular home fare. Mung beans are often dry roasted before simmering to impart a nutlike aroma to the final dish. A wedge of lime is simmered with pigeon peas to add a citrusy flavor.

Regardless of how they are cooked, dals are always appreciated and frequently discussed. The debate as to when to eat them continues.

A GLOSSARY OF LEGUMES

Of the many varieties of legumes, the following are commonly used in a Bengali kitchen. Indian grocers who supply these products generally designate them by their Hindi names.

Many health food stores in the West also sell a variety of dals. The greenish-brown lentils sold in Western supermarkets are not used in Bengal and do not substitute well in these recipes. Shop instead for the variety named in the recipe, as each dal has a unique flavor and the cooking time varies.

Bengal gram (*chana dal* in Hindi; *chholar dal* in Bengali):   These split Indian chickpeas resemble yellow split peas but are smaller, nuttier, and more flavorful. Do not substitute yellow split peas. Spiced and roasted, split chickpeas are a popular snack, as described in the recipe Hot and Savory Party Mix in the "Teatime" chapter.

Black gram (*urad dal* in Hindi; *kalai dal* in Bengali): A black-jacketed legume that is white inside. These are not to be confused with black-eyed peas or black beans. They are sold either whole (the black variety) or split (the off-white variety). Split *urad* is used to prepare boris (lentil dumplings) and *urad dal* flour in making *papad* (lentil wafers).

Chickpeas, garbanzo beans, or ceci beans (*chana* in Hindi; *chhola* in Bengali): Round, beige, fat beans with a sproutlike pointy edge on one side. The Indian variety, called *kalo chana* or black chickpea, is smaller and has a brownish coat. Chickpeas are used both whole and split. The split varieties are called Bengal gram and have been described separately in this section.

To cook chickpeas:

Soak 1 cup (250 ml) chickpeas overnight in 4 cups (1 liter) of water. Next day, add more water, if needed, to cover the chickpeas by an inch (2.5 cm). Bring to boil. Simmer covered 1 hour or until they are tender. (The smaller, darker, more intensely flavored Indian chickpeas, *kalo chana*, will take 1½ hours or longer.) Chickpeas will not disintegrate but will turn tender to the bite. I usually taste one to test for doneness. During this period, if the water level falls below that of the chickpeas, add boiling water to cover them again. Yields about 2 cups (500 ml).

Chickpea flour (*besan* in Hindi and Bengali): A pale yellow, high-protein flour with a distinctive flavor, made by grinding chickpeas. This flour is sold at Indian groceries in the West. It is perishable and should be refrigerated. Do not substitute wheat flour.

Dried peas (*matar dal* in Hindi and Bengali): In their whole form they are light green in color. In their hulled, split form they can be either green or yellow. The yellow split peas closely resemble *chana dal*, split chickpeas, but are slightly more opaque. They also taste different and lack the flavor of *chana dal*.

Mung beans or green gram (*moong dal* in Hindi; *muger dal* in Bengali): Small round beans with an olive green exterior and pale yellow flesh. These are the same beans that produce bean sprouts, used occasionally in salads in Bengal. The beans themselves are sold whole, or split and hulled. The yellow hulled variety, also called yellow gram, is commonly used in Bengali recipes. The smaller variety (about ⅛ inch/3 mm in diameter) is preferable to the larger variety (¼ inch/6 mm in diameter).

To roast mung beans:

Place the split mung beans on an ungreased griddle or skillet over medium to medium low heat. Stir often. In 8 to 10 minutes the beans will acquire a light brown color and emit a pleasant nutty aroma. Don't let them turn dark brown. Transfer immediately to a bowl. You can now wash the beans, if desired, before using them in a recipe.

Red lentils or Egyptian lentils (*masur dal* in Hindi; *musurir dal* in Bengali): In its whole form this lentil is dull olive-brown in color. In its split form it varies in color from reddish-orange to salmon pink. The smaller reddish-orange variety is more flavorful. Said to have the highest protein content of all lentils, this legume cooks quickly.

Split pigeon peas (*toor dal* in Hindi; *arhar dal* in Bengali): These yellow peas resemble *chana dal* but are slightly bigger. Because of their unique taste they cannot be substituted in a recipe. Sometimes they are sold coated in castor oil, which gives them a shiny appearance. If you purchase them in this form, wash them thoroughly with hot water before using.

Dal Tips

- Always scan dals for pebbles or other debris, then rinse them until the water runs clear. The exception is when they are to be roasted before simmering. In that case, wash them after roasting.

- As noted in some recipes, dals can be presoaked to reduce their cooking time.

- Remove and discard foam from the top of dal as it comes to a boil, or let it subside in the liquid.

- A slow simmer is the best way to cook dals. If the heat is too high, they won't soften. Dals should be thoroughly cooked to make them digestible.

- Spices such as cumin, ginger, and turmeric also help make the dals easily digestible. In Bengal, dals are served in small amounts.

- A whole fresh green chili is sometimes added to a dal dish while it simmers. Since the chili is uncut, it adds a refreshing taste but not undue hotness. As with other whole spices, you can remove the chili before serving.

- In the *sambara*, or final spice frying phase, a few spices are fried in a little oil in a small pan and poured over the cooked lentils. Since spices and oil may stick to this small pan, a ladleful of dal may be poured into it and swished to extract all the spices. The dal, which will sizzle immediately, is then returned to the pot.

  This spiced oil is part of the flavoring for the dal. A few drops of ghee, sprinkled on just before serving, will also make the dal more tasty. Ghee especially enhances the taste of strongly flavored dals, such as split pigeon peas and split chickpeas.

- Fresh lime or lemon juice, added just before serving, enlivens the dal and reduces the amount of salt needed.

- Lime or lemon wedges and finely chopped fresh cilantro are the garnish for all dal dishes. I have specified additional garnish for some of the dishes.

- If dals are not served immediately, they will thicken. Add a little hot water and reheat gently before serving.

Musurir Dal
ONION-FRAGRANT RED LENTILS

The fastest-cooking of all lentils, the hulled orange-red variety is served in Bengal nearly every day. These lentils turn pale yellow as they soften. Caramelized onions add an exquisite sweetness to this dish, the texture of which is as smooth as velvet.

3 cups (750 ml) water
1 cup (250 ml) red lentils
¼ tsp. (1 ml) turmeric
½ tsp. (2 ml) salt
1 tsp. (5 ml) sugar
2 Tbs. (30 ml) vegetable oil (mustard oil preferred)
2 bay leaves
2 whole dried red chilies
½ tsp. (2 ml) kalonji seeds
1 cup (250 ml) thinly slivered onion
1 tsp (5 ml) seeded, chopped fresh green chili (or to taste)
1 tsp. (5 ml) garam masala
2 Tbs. (30 ml) fresh lime or lemon juice
1 Tbs. (15 ml) finely chopped fresh cilantro

1. Bring water to boil in a pan over medium heat. Add lentils. Add turmeric and simmer, covered, until lentils are tender, about 15 minutes. They should break easily when pressed between thumb and index finger.
2. Add salt and sugar. Puree the mixture in a blender until smooth. Return to the pan and keep warm.
3. Heat oil in a skillet over medium low heat. Fry bay leaves and red chilies until the chilies darken. Add kalonji seeds and fry for a few seconds. Fry onion until richly browned but not burnt, 15 to 18 minutes, stirring constantly. Stir in green chili. Pour this mixture over the pureed lentils. Simmer for 2 to 3 more minutes.
4. Remove from heat. Stir in garam masala, lime juice, and cilantro. Garnish with lemon wedges and serve immediately.

4 servings.

Serving suggestions: One of my favorite meals is this light lentil dish served with rice, Peanut Cucumber Salad with Chili-Lime Dressing, and Splendid Cilantro Chutney. Also try with rice (or Pan-raised Bread), Crisp Fried Fish (or Spicy Home Fries), and Mellow Tomato Chutney for another taste excursion.

Toker Dal
TART RED LENTILS

Take a spoonful and enjoy the complex flavors. The tart taste predominates, giving it the nickname of "Lentil Chutney." In Bengal this is served during the summer, but you may try it whenever you desire a new taste treat.

3 cups (750 ml) water
1 cup (250 ml) red lentils
1 Tbs. (15 ml) peeled, minced fresh ginger
1 tsp. (5 ml) seeded, chopped fresh green chili (or to taste)
½ tsp. (2 ml) salt
1 tsp. (5 ml) sugar
½ tsp. (2 ml) tamarind concentrate (see note below)
1 tsp. (5 ml) vegetable oil (mustard oil preferred)
¼ tsp. (1 ml) black mustard seeds
½ tsp. (2 ml) five-spice, roasted and ground

1. Bring water to boil in a pan over medium heat. Add lentils. Reduce heat and simmer, covered, until lentils are tender, about 15 minutes. They should break easily when pressed between thumb and index finger. Remove from heat.
2. Puree this mixture with the ginger and green chili in a blender until smooth. Return to pan and bring to simmer. Add salt, sugar, and tamarind and stir to dissolve the tamarind. Remove from heat.
3. Heat oil in a 6-inch (15 cm) skillet over medium low heat. Fry black mustard seeds for a few seconds. As soon as the seeds start popping, remove from heat and pour contents of pan over the lentil mixture. Simmer 2 to 3 more minutes. Stir in five-spice. Cover and let stand for a few minutes to help develop the flavors. Garnish with lemon wedges and cilantro and serve.

4 servings.

Serving suggestions: Pack in a lunchbox with Soft Bread. For a grand meal, accompany with Vegetable Pullao, Mustard-drenched Chicken (or Egg and Cauliflower in Savory Cumin Sauce), and Joyous Ginger-Raisin Chutney.

Note: Alternatively, use tamarind puree, which will make the dish more flavorful. You will need 6 to 8 tablespoons (90 to 120 ml) puree, adjusted according to taste. To extract this amount of puree, break off a 5 × 5 × 1 inch (12.5 × 12.5 × 2.5 cm) piece of dried tamarind block. Soak it in ½ cup (120 ml) of water. (See "A Glossary of Spices and Ingredients.")

Bhaja Muger Dal
FRAGRANT ROASTED MUNG BEAN STEW

"A man is a king twice in his life—the day he is born, and the day he weds," they say in Bengal. This delectable dish, sometimes served at weddings, is a royal treat.

Golden split mung beans, toasted until they turn light brown, mingle with aromatic spices. Fresh whole chilies add flavor and heat but do not overpower the dish.

1 cup (250 ml) yellow split mung beans
5 cups (1 liter 250 ml) water
¼ tsp. (1 ml) turmeric
1 to 2 whole fresh green chilies
¾ tsp. (3 ml) salt
1 tsp. (5 ml) sugar
2 tsp. (10 ml) ground cumin
2 tsp. (10 ml) ground coriander
1½ Tbs. (22 ml) vegetable oil (mustard oil preferred)
1 bay leaf
½ tsp. (2 ml) kalonji seeds
3 Tbs. (45 ml) peeled, minced fresh ginger
1 tsp. (5 ml) seeded, chopped fresh green chili (or to taste)
¼ tsp. (1 ml) garam masala
2 Tbs. (30 ml) fresh lime or lemon juice
A sprinkling of ghee (optional)
Garnish: slivered mild fresh green chili

1. Roast the mung beans (see "A Glossary of Legumes" in this chapter).
2. Bring water to boil in a pan. Stir in the roasted beans, turmeric, and the whole chilies. Simmer, covered, until the beans are very tender, 35 to

45 minutes. Uncover occasionally and stir, adding a tablespoon (15 ml) or so of water, if the mixture sticks to the bottom. (The beans are ready when they are tender to the bite and break easily when pressed between thumb and index finger.) Add salt, sugar, cumin, and coriander. Keep warm.

3. Heat oil in a skillet over medium low heat. Add bay leaf and kalonji and fry for a few seconds. Add ginger and chopped green chili and fry until ginger is lightly browned, about 2 minutes, stirring constantly. Pour contents of skillet over the bean mixture and mix well. Simmer 2 to 3 minutes, then remove from heat. Blend in garam masala, lime juice, and ghee. Cover and let stand for a few minutes to help develop the flavors. Serve hot.

4 to 5 servings.

Serving suggestions: Accompanied by rice (or Carrot-filled Pan Bread), Vegetables in a Mingling Mood, and Yogurt Coconut Dip, this stew makes a festive meal.

Chhaner Tarkari
FRESH CHEESE AND MUNG BEAN DELIGHT

Mung bean is an ancient food, referred to in Indian scriptures 3,000 years old. During religious ceremonies, mung beans, softened by overnight soaking, are often combined with other salad vegetables and offered to the deity.

Here ground mung beans and tender natural cheese are combined to form savory croquettes. These croquettes are then cooked in an attractive yellowish-red tomato sauce, prettier still when garnished with fresh cilantro. Black mustard aromatizes this protein-packed dish.

For the croquettes:
Fresh cheese (see "A Glossary of Spices and Ingredients")
2 Tbs. (30 ml) mung bean flour, available in Indian shops
1 tsp. (5 ml) regular Cream of Wheat

For the sauce:
1½ Tbs. (22 ml) vegetable oil
¼ tsp. (1 ml) five-spice
1 Tbs. (15 ml) minced, peeled fresh ginger
1 tsp. (5 ml) seeded, chopped fresh green chili (or to taste)
1 tsp. (5 ml) black mustard seeds, ground to a powder, mixed with 2 tsp. (10 ml) water, and allowed to stand for 30 minutes

½ cup (125 ml) chopped tomatoes (2 Roma or 1 regular tomato)
¼ tsp. (1 ml) salt
½ tsp. (2 ml) sugar
1 cup (250 ml) hot water

1. To make the croquettes: Prepare fresh cheese following the "20-minute" routine. While cheese is still slightly warm, combine it with mung flour and Cream of Wheat® to form a dough. Knead for at least 5 minutes to make the dough smooth. Pinch off portions of the dough and roll into balls about an inch (2.5 cm) in diameter. Flatten into croquettes about 1¾ inches (4 cm) in diameter. Set aside. Yields 12 to 14 croquettes.

2. Heat oil in a skillet over medium low heat. Fry five-spice until it starts popping. Add ginger and green chili and stir for a few more seconds. Stir in black mustard paste. (Cover the pan partially if the mixture starts to splatter the cooking area.) Add tomatoes, salt, sugar, and water and bring to boil.

3. Lower the heat slightly and simmer, covered, for a minute or so. Uncover and mash the tomatoes with the back of a spoon, mixing them in with the sauce. Gently add the reserved croquettes and simmer, tightly covered, for 25 to 30 minutes, turning the croquettes a few times so they don't stick to the bottom of the skillet. Add a tablespoon (15 ml) or so of hot water if necessary. The croquettes will absorb the sauce and will slightly expand in size.

4. If the sauce is still a little watery, carefully remove the croquettes with a slotted spatula and set aside in a plate. Turn heat to medium and cook the sauce uncovered for 2 to 5 minutes. As soon as the sauce thickens, remove from heat (overcooking will destroy the pretty color of this sauce). Return the croquettes to the skillet. Scatter cilantro on top. Serve immediately.

3 to 4 servings.

Serving suggestions: Delight your vegetarian guests by serving these croquettes with rice, Steamed Spicy Cauliflower, and Splendid Cilantro Chutney.

Matar Dal Shorshe Diyea
GREEN SPLIT PEAS IN ZESTY MUSTARD SAUCE

Chili, coconut, and black mustard form a powerful spice mix that turns many a dish into a culinary delight. In this case the lowly split pea is so transformed.

You can substitute yellow split peas, although the color of the dish is more attractive when made with green peas.

You can reduce the cooking time to 30 minutes or less by soaking the peas in the same amount of water for 6 hours or overnight.

4 cups (1 liter) water
1 cup (250 ml) green split peas
1 bay leaf
¼ tsp. (1 ml) turmeric
½ tsp. (2 ml) salt
1½ Tbs. (22 ml) vegetable oil (mustard oil preferred)
1 Tbs. (15 ml) peeled, minced fresh ginger
1 tsp. (5 ml) seeded, chopped fresh green chili (or to taste)
2 tsp. (10 ml) black mustard seeds, ground to a powder, mixed with 4 tsp. (20 ml) water and allowed to stand for 30 minutes
3 Tbs. (45 ml) dried shredded or flaked sweetened coconut, ground in a blender to a coarse powder (or freshly grated or shredded coconut mixed with ½ tsp./2 ml sugar)
A sprinkling of ghee (optional)

1. Bring water to boil. Lower the heat slightly. Add split peas, bay leaf, and turmeric and simmer, covered, until peas are tender, 40 to 45 minutes. (They should break easily when pressed between thumb and index finger.) During this period, uncover occasionally and stir, adding a tablespoon (15 ml) or so of hot water if the mixture sticks to the bottom of the pan. Add salt. Keep warm.
2. Heat oil in a 6-inch (15 cm) skillet over medium low heat. Fry ginger and green chili until ginger is lightly browned, 1 to 2 minutes. Add mustard paste and fry for another minute, stirring constantly. (You may need to keep the skillet partially covered for a few seconds if the spices start to splatter the cooking area.) Add coconut and stir several times. Remove from heat. Pour over the pea mixture and stir. Cover and let stand for 15 minutes to help develop the flavors. Garnish with cilantro, sprinkle with ghee, and serve.

4 servings.

Serving suggestions: My dinner guests savor this dish. Rice (or Soft Bread), Golden Potatoes in Poppyseed Sauce, and Sweet and Sour Tomato-Mustard Chutney are the perfect accompaniments.

Tarkari Diyea Arhar Dal

FRAGRANT PIGEON PEAS AND SWEET
SQUASH WITH A HINT OF LIME

Throughout the 10-day autumnal festival of Durga puja, sumptuous preparations of fish, meat, and vegetables stream forth from the kitchens of
Bengal. Split pigeon peas are a Bengali favorite during this time of merri-
ment and feasting. This strongly flavored dal requires spicing with a bold
hand.

Tender squash cubes, kalonji seeds with their nutty and yet onionlike
aroma, and a wedge of lime make this an unforgettable dish. Whole green
chilies impart a gentle background warmth but don't make the dish over-
whelmingly hot.

1 cup (250 ml) toor dal (split pigeon peas), soaked overnight in 4¼ cups
    (1 liter plus 60 ml) water
¼ tsp. (1 ml) turmeric
1 to 2 whole fresh green chilies
A wedge of lime or lemon, seeded
1 tsp. (5 ml) ground cumin
1 tsp. (5 ml) ground coriander
½ tsp. (2 ml) salt
½ tsp. (2 ml) sugar
1 cup (250 ml) peeled butternut squash or sweet potatoes, cut into 1-inch
    (2.5 cm) cubes
¾ cup (175 ml) green beans, cut crosswise into 2-inch (5 cm) pieces
2 Tbs. (30 ml) vegetable oil
1 bay leaf
¼ tsp. (1 ml) kalonji seeds
1 cup (250 ml) finely chopped onion
1 Tbs. (15 ml) peeled, minced fresh ginger
1 tsp. (5 ml) seeded, chopped fresh green chili (or to taste)
¼ tsp. (1 ml) garam masala
2 Tbs. (30 ml) fresh lime or lemon juice
A sprinkling of ghee (optional)

1. Bring toor dal and the soaking water to boil in a pan. Add turmeric,
   whole green chilies, and the lime wedge. Simmer, covered, for 20 minutes. Add cumin, coriander, salt, sugar, and butternut squash. Simmer
   for 5 more minutes. Add green beans and simmer for another 10 to 15
   minutes or until the dal, squash, and green beans are tender. (When
   pressed between thumb and index finger the dal should break easily; the
   green beans should retain a little crunch.) During this period, stir

often and add 1 to 2 tablespoons (15 to 30 ml) hot water if the dal starts to stick to the bottom.

2. Heat oil in a skillet over medium low heat. Fry bay leaf and kalonji for a few seconds. Add onion and fry until richly browned but not burnt, 10 to 15 minutes, stirring constantly. Add ginger and chopped green chili and stir several times. Pour contents of skillet over the dal and mix well. Simmer 2 to 3 more minutes. Remove from heat. Add garam masala. Cover and let stand for a few minutes to help develop the flavors. Discard lime wedge. Blend in lime juice and ghee. Garnish with cilantro and serve hot.

5 to 6 servings.

Serving suggestions: I ladle this hearty dal over rice and serve Tempting Mint Chutney on the side for a nutritious family meal. Since flatbread provides a contrast in texture, I also serve this dal with Banquet Bread, Glorious Greens, and Ginger Yogurt Chutney for a pleasant luncheon or dinner.

Chholar Ghughni–I
DOWN-HOME CHICKPEA STEW

During a visit to Bengal, I went to see a film by Satyajit Ray, the renowned Bengali filmmaker. After the show I saw the moviegoers gather around a street vendor outside the cinema house. The vendor was simmering a large pan of rich brown chickpeas on a portable stove in his cart. He would ladle some into a small plate, top it with a flatbread, and hand it to a customer. The aroma of cumin and coriander filled the sidewalk. The garnish of tomato, fresh cilantro, and onion drew bold color patterns. I knew I had come home.

My guests often mistake this rich sauce to be that of meat or eggplant. The secret is the slow browning of the onions. Do not omit the garnishes, as they not only make the dish pretty but balance its texture as well.

2½ Tbs. (37 ml) vegetable oil (mustard oil preferred)
1 bay leaf
2½ cups (625 ml) finely chopped onion
1 Tbs. (15 ml) minced garlic
1 Tbs. (15 ml) peeled, minced fresh ginger
½ tsp. (2 ml) turmeric
2 tsp. (10 ml) ground cumin
2 tsp. (10 ml) ground coriander
1 tsp. (5 ml) seeded, chopped fresh green chili (or to taste)

½ cup (125 ml) chopped tomatoes (2 Roma or 1 regular tomato)
¼ tsp. (1 ml) salt
1½ cups (375 ml) cooked chickpeas (see "A Glossary of Legumes" in this chapter), or a 16-oz (450 g) can of chickpeas, drained
Garnish: mild raw onion rings (see "A Glossary of Spices and Ingredients"), chopped Roma tomatoes, and finely chopped fresh cilantro

1. Heat oil in a skillet over medium heat. Add bay leaf and onion. Fry onion until richly browned but not burnt, 15 to 20 minutes, stirring often and reducing heat to medium low halfway through cooking.
2. Stir in ginger and garlic and cook several minutes. Add turmeric, cumin, coriander, and green chili and mix well. Add tomatoes and salt. Lower the heat slightly, cover and cook until tomatoes disintegrate and a thick sauce forms, about 10 minutes. Stir occasionally to prevent sticking, adding a tablespoon (15 ml) of water if necessary. Add chickpeas, cover and cook 5 more minutes. Remove from heat and let stand, covered, for a few minutes to help develop the flavors. Garnish with onion, tomatoes, and cilantro. Serve piping hot.

4 servings.

Serving suggestions: This tasty, pretty dish is a hit at potlucks. Try with rice, Fiery Potatoes, and Splendid Cilantro Chutney for a memorable meal.

Chholar Ghughni–II
CHIC TART CHICKPEAS

Although chickpeas have a character of their own, they absorb other flavors well. Laced with tamarind, they acquire a subtle sour taste, and beg to be dipped into with a piece of flatbread.

2 Tbs. (30 ml) vegetable oil
1 bay leaf
1 Tbs. (15 ml) peeled, minced fresh ginger
1 tsp. (5 ml) seeded, chopped fresh green chili (or to taste)
¼ tsp. (1 ml) turmeric
1 tsp. (5 ml) ground cumin
1 tsp. (5 ml) ground coriander
¼ tsp. (1 ml) salt
1½ cups (365 ml) cooked chickpeas (see "A Glossary of Legumes" in this chapter), or a 16-oz. (450 g) can of chickpeas, drained
¼ cup (60 ml) water
1 tsp. (5 ml) tamarind concentrate

1. Heat oil in a skillet over medium low heat. Fry bay leaf and ginger until ginger is lightly browned. Stir in green chili, turmeric, cumin, coriander, and salt. Add chickpeas and water and bring to boil. Lower the heat slightly and simmer, covered, 10 minutes.
2. Add tamarind. Uncover and cook 3 to 5 minutes to allow the sauce to thicken, stirring often. Garnish with cilantro and serve.

3 to 4 servings.

Serving suggestions: When accompanied by Soft Bread (or Vegetable Pullao), Red Chard and Eggplant Medley, and Ginger Yogurt Chutney, these tart chickpeas make a splendid vegetarian dinner.

Chholar Dal
FESTIVE CHICKPEAS WITH COCONUT AND WHOLE SPICES

This heavenly dish is often served after a puja, a worship ceremony in honor of a particular god or goddess. Raisins gently sweeten the sauce and combine surprisingly well with the dal. A touch of coconut gives this dish an extra special flavor.

1 cup (250 ml) chana dal (split chickpeas), soaked overnight in 5 cups (1 liter 250 ml) of water
¼ tsp. (1 ml) turmeric
1 whole fresh green chili
½ tsp. (2 ml) salt
2 tsp. (10 ml) ground cumin
2 Tbs. (30 ml) raisins
1½ Tbs. (22 ml) vegetable oil (mustard oil preferred)
1 bay leaf
1 whole dried red chili
5 whole cardamom pods
2-inch (5 cm) cinnamon stick
2 whole cloves
¼ tsp. (1 ml) kalonji seeds
1 Tbs. (15 ml) seeded, chopped fresh green chili (or to taste)
2 Tbs. (30 ml) dried flaked or shredded sweetened coconut (or freshly grated or shredded coconut mixed with 1 tsp./5 ml sugar)
¼ tsp. (1 ml) garam masala
A sprinkling of ghee (optional)

1. Bring chana dal and the soaking water to boil in a large pan over medium heat. Add turmeric and whole chili. Simmer, covered, 1 hour

or until the dal is very tender and breaks easily when pressed between thumb and index finger. During this period, uncover and stir often, adding 1 to 2 tablespoons (15 to 30 ml) of hot water if the dal starts to stick to the bottom. Discard whole chili. Add salt and cumin. Remove from heat.

2. Puree 1 cup (250 ml) of the dal mixture in a blender, adding a little water if necessary. Return to the pan. Add raisins. Bring to simmer, then keep warm.

3. Heat oil in a 6-inch (15 cm) pan over medium low heat. Fry bay leaf and red chili until the chili darkens. Fry cardamom, cinnamon, and cloves for 5 seconds. Add kalonji and fry another few seconds. Turn heat to low. Add chopped green chili and coconut and cook for a few seconds, stirring constantly. Remove from heat. Add this spice mixture to the dal. Simmer 2 to 3 more minutes. Remove dal from heat. Blend in garam masala. Garnish with lemon wedges, sprinkle with whole cilantro leaves and ghee, and serve.

4 to 5 servings.

Serving suggestions: Entertain your guests with these savory chickpeas, rice (or Banquet Bread), Cabbage and Potatoes in Browned Onion Sauce, and Tender Tamarind Chutney.

Chingri Maach Diyea Chholar Dal
PRAWNS IN A POT OF GOLD

When you serve this dish, the pink prawns float alluringly in a golden gravy and whole spices delight guests with their fragrance. The onion is not minced as in most dishes, but cut into wide slivers like a vegetable, to provide a contrast in texture. All in all, a most delightful dish.

1 cup (250 ml) chana dal (split chickpeas), soaked overnight in 5 cups (1 liter 250 ml) water
¼ tsp. (1 ml) turmeric
1 whole fresh green chili
¾ cup (175 ml) slivered onion (about ¼ inch/6 mm wide)
½ lb. (¼ kg) peeled potatoes, about 2 medium, cut into 1-inch (2.5 cm) cubes
1 tsp. (5 ml) ground coriander
½ tsp. (2 ml) salt
1½ tsp. (7 ml) sugar
2 Tbs. (30 ml) mustard oil

1 bay leaf
1 whole dried red chili
5 whole cardamom pods
2-inch (5 cm) cinnamon stick
2 whole cloves
½ lb. (¼ kg) raw prawns or shrimp, shelled and deveined
¼ tsp. (1 ml) garam masala
1 Tbs. (15 ml) finely chopped fresh cilantro
A sprinkling of ghee (optional)

1. Bring chana dal and the soaking water to boil in a pan. Add turmeric, green chili, and onion. Simmer, covered, 30 to 40 minutes or until dal is somewhat soft, stirring often and adding 1 to 2 tablespoons (15 to 30 ml) hot water if the dal starts to stick to the bottom of the pan. Add potatoes and simmer, covered, for another 20 to 25 minutes or until both dal and potatoes are tender. (The dal should break easily when pressed between thumb and index finger.) Stir in coriander, salt, and sugar. Keep dal at a low simmer.

2. Heat oil in a skillet over medium low heat. Fry bay leaf and red chili until the chili blackens. Fry cardamom, cinnamon, and cloves for a few seconds. Add prawns and cook just until they turn pink, about a minute, stirring often. Pour the contents of this skillet over the dal.

3. Cook, covered, 3 to 5 minutes or just until the prawns are done. (See "Test for doneness" under "Fish and Seafood Tips" in the "Fish and Seafood" chapter.) Remove from heat. Stir in garam masala, cilantro, and ghee gently so as not to break the prawns. Cover and let stand for a few minutes to help develop the flavors. Garnish with lemon wedges. Serve piping hot.

5 to 6 servings.

Serving suggestions: I find that this unusual combination of legumes and shellfish excites many diners. Accompany with rice and Green and White Coconut Chutney for a family meal. Serve with rice, Potatoes Braised in Rich Tart Sauce, and "Happy Heart" Chutney when entertaining.

Chholar Dal Manghsha Diyea
CHICKPEA LAMB TREASURE

In this dish the characteristic fine flavor of chickpeas is elevated to the sublime when stewed in a thick gravy enriched by lamb and tomatoes. The combination may seem unusual, but the final result, which is a Moslem specialty, is truly a treasure of a dish.

For the dal:

1 cup (250 ml) chana dal (split chickpeas), soaked overnight in 5 cups
    (1 liter, 250 ml) water
¼ tsp. (1 ml) turmeric
½ tsp. (2 ml) salt

For the meat:

2½ to 3 Tbs. (37 to 45 ml) vegetable oil (mustard oil preferred)
2 cups (500 ml) thinly sliced onion
5 whole cardamom pods
2-inch (5 cm) cinnamon stick
2 whole cloves
2 Tbs. (30 ml) minced garlic
2 Tbs. (30 ml) peeled, minced fresh ginger
1 tsp. (5 ml) seeded, chopped fresh green chili (or to taste)
2 tsp. (10 ml) ground cumin
¾ lb. (375 g) leg of lamb, cut into 2 × 2 × 1-inch (5 × 5 × 2.5 cm) pieces
½ cup (125 ml) chopped tomatoes (2 Roma or 1 regular tomato)
¼ cup (60 ml) water

1. Prepare the dal: Bring dal and the soaking water to boil in a pan. Add
   turmeric and simmer, covered, 1 hour or until dal is very tender and
   breaks easily when pressed between thumb and index finger, stirring
   occasionally and adding a tablespoon (15 ml) or so of hot water if the
   mixture sticks to the bottom of the pan. Add salt and keep warm.
2. Prepare the meat: You can start the meat preparation midway through
   the dal preparation in step 1 above. Heat 2 tablespoons (30 ml) oil in a
   large, deep pot or Dutch oven over medium heat. Fry onion until it is
   richly browned but not burnt, 10 to 15 minutes, stirring constantly and
   reducing heat to medium low halfway through cooking. Remove with a
   slotted spoon and set aside.
3. Add ½ tablespoon (7 ml) oil to the pot and heat over medium low heat.
   (Add ½ tablespoon/7 ml more oil for fuller flavor and to prevent sticking.) Fry cardamom, cinnamon, and cloves for a few seconds. Add
   garlic, ginger, and green chili and fry until garlic and ginger are lightly
   browned, 1 to 2 minutes. Add cumin. Lower heat and add lamb,
   tomatoes, and water. Lower heat slightly and simmer, covered, 45 minutes, stirring occasionally adding a tablespoon (15 ml) or so of water if
   the meat sticks to the bottom.
4. Add the reserved dal to the meat and mix well. Simmer, covered, until
   meat is tender, another 20 to 30 minutes, stirring occasionally and
   adding a tablespoon (15 ml) or so of water if the dal sticks.

5. Remove from heat. Mix in the reserved onions. Garnish with cilantro and serve (see note).

4 to 5 servings.

Serving suggestions: This saucy meat dish is a favorite of many Bengalis when served with rice and Spicy Home Fries or another potato dish. For a more elaborate meal serve with Rice (or Banquet Bread), Wedding Day Greens, and Yogurt Coconut Dip.

Note: If allowed to stand, the sauce will thicken. You may need to add a little water before reheating.

Boris
LENTIL DUMPLINGS

You can buy these tiny dumplings at Indian groceries in the West. But the homemade version is fresher and more flavorful, and keeps for a few weeks when refrigerated. They are easy to make. Red lentils require a lesser amount of presoaking. Boris made with urad dal take longer to bake, but are especially tasty. I use split urad dal rather than urad dal flour for better flavor.

For making boris with red lentils:

1 cup (250 ml) red lentils soaked in 3 cups (750 ml) water for 6 to 8 hours
  or overnight
¼ tsp. (1 ml) asafetida powder
½ tsp. (2 ml) salt
2 tsp. (10 ml) ground cumin
Dash ground red chili or cayenne pepper (or to taste)
1½ Tbs. (22 ml) besan (chickpea flour)

For making boris with urad dal:

1 cup (250 ml) split, hulled urad dal (black gram), soaked in 3 cups
  (750 ml) water overnight
½ tsp. (2 ml) salt
1 tsp. (5 ml) fennel seeds, roasted and ground
2 tsp. (10 ml) ground cumin
2 tsp. (10 ml) ground coriander
1 tsp. (5 ml) black pepper, preferably freshly ground
¼ tsp. (1 ml) ground cardamom
1½ Tbs. (22 ml) besan (chickpea flour)

To make the boris with either type of dal:

1. Drain dal. (You can use the drained water for cooking dal, rice, or vegetable dishes.) Preheat oven to 200°F (110°C; gas mark ¼). Puree the dal in a food mill, processor, or a blender 1 cup (250 ml) at a time until smooth, scraping the sides often. If needed, add water 1 teaspoon (5 ml) at a time. (With urad dal you will need about 3 tablespoons/45 ml water per batch.)

2. In a bowl combine the dal mixture with the remaining ingredients. Stir 5 minutes with an electric mixer or 6 to 8 minutes with a fork. This will give the boris a lighter texture. Let stand for a few minutes.

3. On one or more greased baking sheets, place ½-teaspoon (2 ml) mounds of the mixture about an inch (2.5 cm) apart. The boris should have a slightly pointy top, like a chocolate kiss; the smaller, more compact, and more thoroughly dried they are, the better they hold their shape during cooking. You can either sun-dry, bake, or dry in a dehydrator.

To sun-dry:

During summer I sun-dry the boris in a room with western exposure and large windows. Simply leave the baking sheet(s) for about two full days in hot sun. At night I cover the sheets with plastic wrap and refrigerate them. I continue to sun-dry them until they are dry to the touch.

To bake:

Bake at 200°F (110°C; gas mark ¼) for 1 to 1½ hours (for urad dal boris, about 2½ hours) or until the boris are dry to the touch. (After 45 minutes or when they are dry on top, you should turn them upside down.) The length of time varies with the size of the boris and the amount of water used in the dough.

You can also dry boris overnight in a food dehydrator. Follow the manufacturer's directions, making sure to open the top and bottom vents as much as possible.

Gently remove the boris and allow to cool. They are now ready to be used in recipes. Or place in a covered container and store in the refrigerator. Makes about 50 boris.

To prepare boris for use as a garnish or an appetizer:

The traditional way is to deep-fry them. The boris become moist and flavorful this way. I find that baking without the addition of any oil also yields acceptable results.

To bake:

Place the boris on an ungreased cookie sheet. Bake at 350°F (180°C; gas mark 4) for 15 to 20 minutes or until the boris are warm and crisp. Homemade boris are especially fragrant when baked this way.

To deep-fry:

½ cup (125 ml) boris

Vegetable oil for deep-frying, at least 2 inches (5 cm) deep

Heat oil in a deep-fat fryer or pan to 375°F (190°C). Fry the dumplings, three or four at a time, until they turn medium brown all over. Drain on paper towels.

For garnishing, crush the baked or deep-fried boris to small pieces using a mortar and pestle. Alternatively, place them over a board and smash them with a rolling pin or some other heavy object. Boris add a delightful crunch when sprinkled over vegetable dishes.

You can also serve the baked or deep-fried boris as an appetizer with cherry tomato halves and Tender Tamarind Chutney.

To prepare boris for cooking:

In Bengal, boris are deep-fried first and then soaked in water before they are added to fish or vegetable dishes. I simply soak the boris for several seconds in water. The harder, store-bought boris may need to soak a little longer. Don't soak too long as boris might break.

VEGETARIAN DISHES

In Bengali vegetarian cuisine the concept of a main dish does not exist. Several dishes, each equally important, and condiments form a meal. In a vegetarian dinner, a dal (legume) dish combines with rice or a flatbread to provide a totally balanced diet. Abundant carbohydrates as well as additional protein are supplied by such typical accompaniments as lentil dumplings, raita (yogurt-based salads), or an egg or fresh cheese dish. The accompanying vegetable dishes provide the majority of the meal's vitamin and mineral content as well as dietary fiber.

Roasting eggplant over another's fire.
—Bengali proverb meaning to
take advantage of someone

As a child, ignorant of the sound nutritional basis of a vegetarian diet, I nonetheless loved vegetables. And the credit goes to my grandmother. She didn't need to cajole or lecture. The aroma of her cooking alone persuaded me.

My widowed grandmother, a staunch vegetarian, lived with my family. She had a separate kitchen in our house, and late in the afternoon she would prepare her only meal of the day. In her hands, everyday vegetables were transformed into culinary splendors that would make a king beg for more. When the large courtyard where I played began to fill with the enticing scent of spices such as cardamom, kalonji, and cloves, I knew my grandmother was cooking. My heart would dance with joy as I rushed over to her side.

Sitting on a raised stool, I would gaze at the *thala,* a large, circular tray with a mound of fragrant, steaming rice at the center. Around it were several small bowls brimming with variegated vegetarian delights. A typical meal would consist of crisp fried eggplant; a zesty sauté of stalks, leaves, and peels of assorted vegetables; cabbage made fragrant by whole hot spices; hearty greens simmered in a sauce flavored with black mustard; and seasoned potatoes steamed in their own juice.

The radish seedling is recognized by its leaves.
> —Bengali proverb meaning "as
> the child is, so is the man"

Depending on the number of vegetables, my grandmother would call the meal a "five-" or "seven-delights" dinner. Each was a dazzling concert of color, texture, and taste.

Many years later I learned how wonderfully varied and nutritionally sound the Bengali vegetarian cuisine really is. Many vegetarian Bengalis live long and healthy lives without so much as touching meat or eggs, in spite of the difficult living conditions that prevail in modern Bengal. And mealtime for them is a pleasurable event.

The numbers five, seven, and nine were considered sacred in ancient India. Five because of five moral precepts and five major rivers. Seven because of seven heavens, seven seas, and the constellation of seven stars. Nine because of nine planets, nine gems, and nine islands of the Ganges.

Bengali widows, such as my grandmother, who take a vow of vegetarianism after their husband's death, are credited with developing an extensive vegetarian cookery. Millions of them choose to live an austere life, leaving the choicest morsels for other members of the family and using only leftovers and scraps for themselves. As a result of their ingenuity down through the centuries, their pinchpenny recipes became as coveted as any meat, fish, or fowl dishes due to their variety and flavor. Living in this wholesome vegetarian fashion, my grandmother maintained excellent health late into her life.

Many of the vegetables my grandmother used are not available in the West. Some items, such as banana blossom, bottle gourd, and bitter melon, can be found only in Asian markets. Still, the number of vegetable dishes seems endless. I cook them with great delight, frequently finding ways to vary them.

And this I owe to my grandmother.

Vegetable Tips

- For best flavor and nutrition, use fresh vegetables whenever possible.

- Cauliflower is used in a number of these recipes. Look for a creamy white, dense head and fresh stems. Avoid those with brownish smudges on top.

- In some recipes, a bit of sugar is caramelized before frying other spices. This technique imparts a rich, mellow flavor and a warm brown hue to a dish.

- I don't generally peel vegetables, because many nutrients are located close to the surface. The exceptions have been noted. In such cases the skin is removed because it is not edible or interferes with the smoothness of the sauce or the absorption of spices.

- I have included a few deep-fried vegetable recipes in this chapter as they are a part of Bengali dining tradition. Properly fried, the vegetables absorb little oil. They are meant to provide a contrast in flavor and texture to other dishes and are usually served in very small amounts.

- A few recipes call for cooked potatoes. When boiling potatoes that will later be sautéed, it is best to allow them to cool first. They acquire a firmer, drier texture this way, are less likely to crumble, and will brown more easily.

- *Reusing cooking water*: Consider saving the water that is used to boil potatoes (or other vegetables) for the preparation of rice or vegetable dishes.

- *When cooking with mixed vegetables*: The practice of combining vegetables (oftentimes as many as 10) in one dish comes from ancient times when a cook simply went to the garden and harvested whatever produce was available. When mixed with spices, the result is an intricate taste that you cannot achieve by cooking a single vegetable. These dishes are also nutritionally rich.

Since the quantity is initially large, I use a 12-inch (30 cm), deep-sided skillet. This allows the vegetables to lie in a single layer, which results in more even cooking and a rich roasted flavor. Also, the vegetables hold their shape better. A smaller pan will tend to produce soft, boiled vegetables at the bottom and raw, uncooked vegetables on top.

■ *Brown-frying of potatoes*: In many recipes potatoes are brown-fried first, usually in 2 tablespoons (30 ml) of oil. This removes the flat, "boiled" taste from the potatoes, giving them a rich, nutty flavor and a pleasantly crunchy crust. To significantly lower the fat content of dishes using brown-fried potatoes, do the following: Heat 1 teaspoon (5 ml) oil in a 6- to 8-inch (15 to 20 cm) nonstick pan or skillet over medium to medium high heat. You can fry ½ pound (¼ kg) of potatoes to a medium brown color with this amount of oil. Turn them frequently to prevent burning. The potatoes may not brown as evenly as with a larger amount of oil, but the result will be quite acceptable. If the recipe calls for 1 pound (½ kg) of potatoes, repeat this process with the second batch of potatoes and an additional 1 teaspoon (5 ml) oil. And so on for larger quantities of potatoes.

Jhal Alu
FIERY POTATOES

Potatoes are much appreciated in Bengal because, in addition to being filling and nutritious, they absorb the flavor of other ingredients so well. Here they acquire a melange of flavors, highlighted by the faint maple taste of fenugreek, the sweetness of coconut, and the heat of chili.

2 Tbs. (30 ml) vegetable oil (mustard oil preferred)
½ tsp. (2 ml) black mustard seeds
¼ tsp. (1 ml) fenugreek seeds
1 Tbs. (15 ml) peeled, minced fresh ginger
1 tsp. (5 ml) seeded, chopped fresh green chili (or to taste)
¼ tsp. (1 ml) turmeric
½ tsp. (2 ml) salt
Dash ground red chili or cayenne pepper (or to taste)
1½ lb. (750 g) peeled or unpeeled cooked potatoes (about 5 medium),
    cut into 1-inch (2.5 cm) cubes, at room temperature
¼ cup (60 ml) dried flaked or shredded sweetened coconut, ground in a
    blender to a coarse powder, or freshly grated or shredded coconut mixed
    with ½ tsp. (2 ml) sugar
1 Tbs. (15 ml) finely chopped fresh cilantro

1. Heat oil in a skillet over medium low heat. Add mustard seeds. As soon as the seeds start popping, add fenugreek, ginger, green chili, and turmeric and fry for about 1 minute, stirring often. Keep the skillet partially covered to prevent the mustard seeds from flying out.
2. Add salt, red pepper, and potatoes and fry for a minute or so, stirring constantly. Turn heat to low. Add coconut and cilantro and mix well. Remove from heat. Serve hot or at room temperature.

4 to 5 servings.

Serving suggestions: Pack with Soft Bread in a lunch box. For a family meal, lay the table with rice, Onion-fragrant Red Lentils, and Ginger Yogurt Chutney.

Siddha Alur Bhaja
SPICY HOME FRIES

This simple dish draws rave reviews. A variation using *aamchoor*, or dry mango powder, has a pleasantly tart taste, especially welcome during summer heat or any time your tastebuds hunger for a change. In the United States, the best potato varieties for this dish are Yellow Finn and Yukon Gold.

1½ lb. (750 g) unpeeled potatoes (about 5 medium), cut into 1-inch (2.4 cm) cubes
Water for boiling potatoes (see "Reusing cooking water" in "Vegetable Tips")
½ tsp. (2 ml) salt
2½ Tbs. (37 ml) vegetable oil (mustard oil preferred)
1 bay leaf
1 whole dried red chili
½ tsp. (2 ml) asafetida powder
½ tsp. (2 ml) salt
1 tsp. (5 ml) sugar
1 Tbs. (15 ml) ground cumin
Dash ground red chili or cayenne pepper (or to taste)
½ tsp. (2 ml) garam masala

1. Boil the potatoes with water to cover and salt until the potatoes are tender but still hold their shape, 15 to 20 minutes. Drain. Let cool to room temperature.

2. Heat 2 tablespoons (30 ml) oil in a skillet, at least 10 inches (25 cm) wide, over medium heat. Fry the potatoes until they turn medium brown, 5 to 6 minutes, turning often. Remove with a slotted spoon and set aside.

3. Add remaining ½ tablespoon (7 ml) oil to the same skillet and heat over medium low heat. Fry bay leaf and red chili until the chili darkens. Sprinkle asafetida over the spices. Add salt, sugar, potatoes, cumin, and red pepper. Fry for 2 to 5 minutes to blend flavors, stirring often. Remove from heat. Stir in garam masala. Serve hot or at room temperature.

4 servings.

Serving suggestions: Excellent as an appetizer or a side dish. Serve with Pan-raised Bread for breakfast or brunch. Accompanied by Lemon-laced Rice, Down-home Chickpea Stew, and Mint Yogurt Sauce, these spicy potatoes make a filling meal.

VARIATION

SOUR SPICY FRIES

Add ¼ teaspoon (1 ml) mango powder along with the reserved potatoes in step 2. Just before serving, sprinkle 2 tablespoons (30 ml) fresh lemon juice.

Serving suggestions: Ginger-scented Yogurt Rice and Splendid Cilantro Chutney complement these pleasantly sour potatoes.

Alu Posto
GOLDEN POTATOES IN POPPYSEED SAUCE

With a handful of potatoes and a few spices, a Bengali cook can create a masterpiece. The crispy chunks of potato are immersed in a rich, nutty sauce to produce a dish that is equally at home in a picnic basket or on a banquet table.

2 to 3 Tbs. (30 to 45 ml) vegetable oil (mustard oil preferred)
1½ lb. (750 g) peeled potatoes (about 5 medium), cut into ½-inch (1.2 cm) cubes
1 whole dried red chili

¼ tsp. (1 ml) five-spice
¼ tsp. (1 ml) turmeric
1 tsp. (5 ml) seeded, chopped fresh green chili (or to taste)
½ tsp. (2 ml) salt
1 tsp. (5 ml) sugar
½ cup (125 ml) water
2 Tbs. (30 ml) white poppyseeds, made into a paste (see "A Glossary of
   Spices and Ingredients")
2 Tbs. (30 ml) fresh lemon juice
Garnish: A few sprigs of fresh mint

1. Heat 2 tablespoons (30 ml) oil in a pan over medium heat. Fry potatoes
   until they turn medium brown, about 5 minutes, turning often. Remove
   with a slotted spoon and set aside. (Or fry in 1 tablespoon/15 ml oil. See
   "Brown-frying of potatoes" in "A Glossary of Spices and Ingredients.")
2. Add 1 tablespoon (15 ml) oil to the same pan and heat over medium low
   heat. Fry red chili until it darkens. Add five-spice. As soon as the five-
   spice starts to crackle, stir in turmeric, green chili, salt, and sugar. Add
   water and potatoes and simmer, covered, for 10 minutes.
3. Add poppyseed paste and simmer, covered, until potatoes are tender,
   another 10 minutes. Stir occasionally to prevent sticking, adding 1 tablespoon (15 ml) or so water if necessary. Remove from heat. Let stand
   covered for a few minutes to help develop flavors. Sprinkle with lemon
   juice and place the mint sprigs at the center. Serve immediately.

4 servings.

Serving suggestions: Fragrant Roasted Mung Bean Stew provides a contrast
in flavor and texture. Follow with rice and Tempting Mint Chutney for a
full meal.

Alu Matarer Dalna
TENDER GARDEN PEAS AND POTATOES

While you cook this dish, the green peas, red ripe tomatoes, and turmeric-
dusted yellow potatoes will remind you of a summer garden. Made fragrant
by the addition of hot and mellow spices, this tangy dish is good party fare.

1½ to 3 Tbs. (22 to 45 ml) vegetable oil (mustard oil preferred)
1½ lb. (750 g) peeled potatoes (about 5 medium), cut into 1-inch (2.5 cm)
   cubes (see Note)

1 bay leaf
5 whole cardamom pods
2 whole cloves
½ tsp. (2 ml) turmeric
2 tsp. (10 ml) ground cumin
2 tsp. (10 ml) ground coriander
1 tsp. (5 ml) sugar
½ cup (125 ml) chopped tomatoes (2 Roma or 1 regular tomato)
½ tsp. (2 ml) salt
½ cup (125 ml) water
½ cup (125 ml) fresh or thawed frozen peas
2 Tbs. (30 ml) plain yogurt, lightly beaten until smooth
¼ tsp. (1 ml) garam masala

1. Heat 2 tablespoons (30 ml) oil in a large skillet (at least 10 inches/
   25 cm in diameter) over medium heat. Fry potatoes until they turn
   medium brown, about 5 minutes, turning often. Remove with a slotted
   spoon and set aside. (Or fry in 1 tablespoon/15 ml oil. See "Brown-
   frying of potatoes" in "A Glossary of Spices and Ingredients.")
2. Add ½ tablespoon (7 ml) oil to the skillet and heat over medium low
   heat. (Or add 1 tablespoon/15 ml oil for richer flavor.) Fry bay leaf, cardamom, and cloves for 5 seconds. Add turmeric, cumin, coriander, and
   sugar and stir several times. Stir in the potatoes, tomatoes, and salt. Add
   water and lower the heat slightly.
3. Simmer, covered, until potatoes are tender, 15 to 20 minutes. Stir
   occasionally to prevent sticking, adding a tablespoon (15 ml) water if
   necessary. Add fresh peas halfway through cooking time, frozen peas
   2 minutes before end of cooking. Remove from heat. Gently blend in
   yogurt and garam masala without breaking the potatoes. Let stand covered for a few minutes to help develop flavors. Garnish with cilantro.
   Serve piping hot.

5 to 6 servings.

Serving suggestions: I often serve this dish at buffet dinners. For a main
meal, try with rice (and/or Puffed Bread), Rich Roasted Eggplant, and
Sweet and Sour Tomato-Mustard Chutney.

Note: The potatoes in this dish are kept in large chunks for eye appeal. You
can lightly prick them with a toothpick before cooking so that the sauce can
penetrate better.

Alu Matarshuti

POTATOES IN PIQUANT PEA PUREE

Here peas are used to produce an attractive green sauce as well as to impart a delicate flavor. Tender cubes of potato add a contrast of color and texture to the jade-green sauce. "What is this made of?" your guests will ask, as they urge you to make it more often.

1½ cups (375 ml) cooked fresh or thawed frozen peas, made into a paste
   (see "A Glossary of Spices and Ingredients")
¼ cup (60 ml) plain yogurt, lightly beaten until smooth
½ tsp. (2 ml) salt
Dash ground red chili or cayenne pepper (or to taste)
2 to 3 Tbs. (30 to 45 ml) vegetable oil (mustard oil preferred)
1¼ lb. (625 g) unpeeled potatoes (about 4½ medium), cut into 1-inch
   (2.5 cm) cubes
1 whole dried red chili
¼ tsp. (1 ml) asafetida powder
¼ tsp. (1 ml) black mustard seeds
½ tsp. (2 ml) turmeric
1 tsp. (5 ml) seeded, chopped fresh green chili (or to taste)
¾ cup (175 ml) water

1. In a bowl combine the pea paste, yogurt, salt, and red pepper. Set aside.
2. Heat 2 tablespoons (30 ml) of the oil in a deep-sided pan or Dutch oven, at least 10 inches (25 cm) in diameter, over medium heat. Fry potatoes until they turn medium brown, 5 to 10 minutes, turning often. Remove with a slotted spoon and set aside. (Or fry in 1 tablespoon/ 15 ml oil. See "Brown-frying of potatoes" in "A Glossary of Spices and Ingredients.")
2. Add 1 tablespoon (15 ml) oil to the skillet and heat over medium low heat. Fry red chili till it darkens. Sprinkle asafetida over the red chili. Add mustard seeds. As soon as the seeds start to crackle, stir in turmeric and green chili. Lower heat slightly and add the pea mixture; excessive heat will lighten the green color of the sauce, so watch it carefully. Add water. As soon as the mixture comes to a simmer, add the potatoes.
3. Simmer, covered, until the potatoes are tender, 15 to 20 minutes. Stir occasionally to prevent sticking, adding 1 tablespoon (15 ml) or so of

water if necessary. Remove from heat. Let stand covered for a few minutes to help develop the flavors. Garnish with cilantro. Serve hot.
4 servings.

Serving suggestions: Butternut Squash in Mustard Sauce provides a contrast
in color and texture. Add rice (or Soft Bread) and Peanut Cucumber Salad
with Chili–Lime Dressing for a meal with many flavors.

Alur Dom

POTATOES BRAISED IN RICH TART SAUCE

In my grandmother's time, the dom or "breath" style of cooking entailed
placing live coals on top of a covered pan, whose lid was sealed with a flour
paste and which sat on a charcoal stove. The heat came from both top and
bottom, and food cooked in its own steam.

Modern stoves and pans with tightly fitted lids eliminate the need for
such an elaborate method, but dom cooking, which is similar to braising,
enjoys immense popularity in Bengal to this day. Every cook has a recipe for
potatoes prepared this way. After experimenting with many I settled on this
version, which is simple but elegant.

1 Tbs. plus 2 tsp. to 3 Tbs. (25 to 45 ml) vegetable oil (mustard oil
    preferred)
1 lb. (½ kg) peeled or unpeeled potatoes (about 4 medium), cut into 1-inch
    (2.5 cm) cubes
2 whole dried red chilies
½ tsp. (2 ml) asafetida powder
3 Tbs. (45 ml) peeled, minced fresh ginger
1 tsp. (5 ml) seeded, chopped, fresh green hot chili (or to taste)
2 tsp. (10 ml) ground cumin
Dash ground red chili or cayenne pepper (or to taste)
½ (2 ml) tsp. salt
½ tsp. (2 ml) sugar
½ cup (125 ml) water
1 tsp. (5 ml) tamarind concentrate

1. Heat 2 tablespoons (30 ml) oil in a skillet over medium heat. Fry
   potatoes until they turn medium brown, 6 to 7 minutes, turning often.
   Remove with a slotted spoon and set aside. (Or fry in 2 teaspoons/10 ml
   oil. See "Brown-frying of potatoes" in "A Glossary of Spices and
   Ingredients.")

2. Add 1 tablespoon (15 ml) oil to the skillet and heat over medium low heat. Fry red chilies until they darken. Sprinkle asafetida onto the chilies. Add ginger, green chili, cumin, red pepper, salt, and sugar and stir a few times. Stir in the potatoes. Add water and simmer, covered, until potatoes are tender but still hold their shape, 15 to 20 minutes.
3. Add tamarind and stir gently to mix in with the potatoes. Remove from heat. Let stand covered for 10 minutes to help develop the flavors. Garnish with cilantro and serve.

4 servings.

Serving suggestions: These potatoes can be served alone as an appetizer or a snack. As part of a main meal, accompany them with rice (or Flaky Bread with Zippy Egg Filling), Fragrant Roasted Mung Bean Stew, and Splendid Cilantro Chutney.

Alur Khosha Bhaja
POTATO SKIN FRY

The potato skin is not only nutritious but tasty. Since many recipes require that potatoes be peeled, you often end up with a pile of potato skins. Rather than waste this nutritious food, try this delicious and unusual recipe. The aroma of chickpea flour and the crunch of poppyseeds make the fried peels a sensory delight.

1 Tbs. (15 ml) besan (chickpea flour)
1 cup (250 ml) firmly packed potato peels, cut into 1½-inch (4 cm) lengths
1 Tbs. (15 ml) vegetable oil (mustard oil preferred)
1 Tbs. (15 ml) white poppyseeds
⅛ tsp. (.5 ml) salt
Dash ground red chili or cayenne pepper (or to taste)

1. Put besan in a paper bag and add the potato peels. Close the bag tightly and shake 8 or 10 times until peels are evenly coated.
2. Heat oil in a nonstick skillet over medium low flame. Add poppyseeds and sauté until lightly browned, a few seconds. Add salt and red pepper. Add the peels and fry until medium brown and crisp, 10 to 15 minutes, stirring constantly. (The peels will absorb the oil quickly, but continue to fry them.) Remove from heat. Serve hot or at room temperature.

2 servings.

Serving suggestions: I enjoy snacking on these fried peels when they are just off the stove, served alone or with Soft Bread. They make an excellent light meal when eaten with rice and Tart Red Lentils.

Begun Pora
RICH ROASTED EGGPLANT

A popular vegetable, eggplant appears frequently on the Bengali menu. Roasting gives depth to its flavor; bits of red tomato and green cilantro leaves accentuate the bright yellow color of this dish.

1 medium eggplant, about 1 lb. (½ kg)
2 Tbs. (30 ml) vegetable oil (mustard oil preferred)
¼ tsp. (1 ml) kalonji seeds
1 to 2 whole green chilies
1 cup (250 ml) finely chopped onion
1 Tbs. (15 ml) minced garlic
1 Tbs. (15 ml) peeled, minced fresh ginger
1 tsp. (5 ml) seeded, chopped fresh green chili (or to taste)
¼ tsp. (1 ml) turmeric
½ tsp. (2 ml) salt
½ tsp. (2 ml) sugar
½ cup (125 ml) chopped tomatoes (2 Roma or 1 medium tomato)
1 Tbs. (15 ml) finely chopped cilantro
Garnish: chopped green onions

1. Smoke or roast the eggplant (see "A Glossary of Spices and Ingredients"). Set aside.
2. Heat oil in a skillet over medium low heat. Fry kalonji seeds and whole green chilies for a few seconds. Add onion and fry until it is richly browned but not burnt, 8 to 10 minutes. Add garlic and ginger and stir several times. Add chopped green chili, turmeric, salt, sugar, and tomatoes. Simmer, covered, until tomatoes disintegrate into a sauce, about 10 minutes. Discard whole green chiles, if desired.
3. Add the eggplant and simmer, covered, 10 minutes to blend flavors, stirring occasionally to prevent sticking. Remove from heat. Let stand covered for 15 minutes to help develop the flavors. Add cilantro and mix well. Garnish with green onions and serve.

4 servings.

Serving suggestions: You can serve this spicy eggplant puree either as a dip for papad or as part of a full meal. I often choose it as a side dish, as its meaty texture harmonizes with meat or fish. Accompany with rice (or Soft

Bread), Down-home Chickpea Stew, and Potatoes in Yogurt-Mustard Sauce for a well-balanced vegetarian dinner.

Variation: My mother makes a simpler version of this dish by thoroughly mixing the smoked eggplant after step 1 in a bowl with the mustard oil, chopped green chili, and salt. Serve it hot or at room temperature with rice and papad.

Dudh Diyea Begun
SMOKED EGGPLANT IN CREAMY SAUCE

The opulent smoky flavor of the eggplant, simmered in a milk sauce, transports you to a faraway place. The complex flavors of this exotic dish belie the simplicity of its ingredients. A fine dish for entertaining.

1 medium eggplant, about 1 lb. (½ kg)
2 Tbs. (30 ml) vegetable oil (mustard oil preferred)
1½ cups (375 ml) finely chopped onion
¼ tsp. (1 ml) turmeric
1 tsp. (5 ml) seeded, chopped fresh green chili (or to taste)
½ tsp. (2 ml) salt
½ tsp. (2 ml) sugar
Dash ground red chili or cayenne pepper (or to taste)
1 cup (250 ml) milk
Garnish: chopped green onions and a sprig of fresh mint

1. Smoke and roast the eggplant (see "A Glossary of Spices and Ingredients"). Set aside.
2. Heat oil in a skillet over medium low heat. Fry onion until it is richly browned but not burnt, 15 to 20 minutes, stirring often. Stir in turmeric, green chili, salt, sugar, and red pepper. Add milk.
3. As soon as the milk is heated through but not boiling, turn heat to low. Blend in the eggplant and cook uncovered until all milk is absorbed and the sauce is thick, 10 to 12 minutes, stirring often. Remove from heat. Let stand covered for a few minutes to help develop the flavors. Scatter green onions on top and place a sprig of mint at the center. Serve piping hot.

4 servings.

Serving suggestions: For an elegant seafood meal, try with rice and Steamed Fish in Chili-Mustard Sauce. Or dazzle your vegetarian friends by serving with rice (or Pan-raised Bread), Tart Red Lentils, and Tempting Mint Chutney.

Pyajkalir Chochori
SMOKED EGGPLANT AND GREEN ONIONS
IN ROASTED RED CHILI SAUCE

This simply spiced dish is hard to resist. The latent hotness comes from the roasted red chili puree and the meaty texture from the eggplant. A generous sprinkling of scallion tops adds a fresh green contrast to the yellowish-brown chunks of eggplant.

1 medium eggplant, about 1 lb. (½ kg)
1½ Tbs. (22 ml) vegetable oil (mustard oil preferred)
2 whole dried red chilies
¼ tsp. (1 ml) five-spice
¼ tsp. (1 ml) turmeric
½ tsp. (2 ml) salt
1 to 2 tsp. (5 to 10 ml) roasted red chili paste (see "A Glossary of Spices and Ingredients")
1 Tbs. (15 ml) water
1 cup (250 ml) green onions (green part only), cut into 1-inch (2.5 cm) lengths

1. Smoke and roast the eggplant (see "A Glossary of Spices and Ingredients").
2. Heat oil in a skillet over medium low heat. Fry red chilies until they darken. Add five-spice and fry until it starts to crackle. Stir in turmeric and salt. Add red chili paste and the water and mix well. Add the eggplant and simmer, covered, 10 to 15 minutes to blend the flavors. Add green onions and simmer, covered, another 2 minutes. Serve at once or the green onions will lose their color; this will not, however, affect their flavor.

4 servings.

Serving suggestions: This springtime dish goes well with seafood dinners. Or serve with rice, Fragrant Pigeon Peas and Sweet Squash with a Hint of Lime, and Ginger Yogurt Chutney for a fine meatless meal.

Dim Begun
EGGPLANT SCRAMBLE

Egg and eggplant make an unbeatable combination, especially when seasoned with lime and cilantro. This hearty dish is ideal for potlucks, picnics, or parties. It is also good on those cold, rainy days when you crave a nourishing, home-cooked meal.

1 medium eggplant, about 1 lb. (½ kg)
2 Tbs. (30 ml) vegetable oil (mustard oil preferred)
1 bay leaf
5 whole cardamom pods
2-inch (5 cm) cinnamon stick
2 whole cloves
1 cup (250 ml) finely chopped onion
1 Tbs. (15 ml) minced garlic
1 Tbs. (15 ml) peeled, minced fresh ginger
1 tsp. (5 ml) seeded, chopped fresh green chili (or to taste)
¼ tsp. (1 ml) turmeric
¼ tsp. (1 ml) salt
3 Tbs. (45 ml) water
2 eggs or 4 egg whites, lightly beaten
2 Tbs. (30 ml) finely chopped fresh cilantro
2 Tbs. (30 ml) fresh lime or lemon juice
Garnish: toasted sesame seeds and lime or lemon wedges

1. Roast the eggplant (see "A Glossary of Spices and Ingredients"). Set aside.
2. Heat oil in a pan over medium low heat. Fry bay leaf, cardamom, cinnamon, and cloves for a few seconds. Add onion and fry until it is richly browned but not burnt, 8 to 10 minutes, stirring constantly. Add garlic, ginger, and green chili and stir a few times. Add turmeric, salt, and water. Lower the heat slightly. Add the reserved eggplant and simmer, covered, 5 minutes, stirring occasionally to prevent sticking.
3. Stir in eggs. When they are beginning to set but still soft, remove from heat. (They will be cooked from the remaining heat in the pan.) Let stand covered for a few minutes. Blend in cilantro and lime juice. Sprinkle sesame seeds on top. Garnish with lime wedges and serve.

4 servings.

Serving suggestions: Since eggs provide the protein, I omit a legume dish from the menu. For a light family meal, rice and Spinach in Spiced Yogurt will make an appropriate accompaniment. For a dress-up dinner, serve with Aromatic Rice with Peas and Whole Spices and Mellow Tomato Chutney.

Begun Posto
SMOKED EGGPLANT IN GARLIC-POPPYSEED SAUCE

For those who love eggplant, here's another taste treat. Fenugreek, green chili, and white poppyseeds impart a complex, intriguing flavor to the tender roasted eggplant. Both oil and spices are used with a light hand.

1 medium eggplant, about 1 lb. (½ kg)
2 Tbs. (30 ml) vegetable oil
2 whole dried red chilies
¼ tsp. (1 ml) fenugreek seeds
1½ Tbs. (22 ml) minced garlic (or to taste)
1 tsp. (5 ml) seeded, chopped fresh green chili (or to taste)
¼ tsp. (1 ml) turmeric
¼ cup (60 ml) water
2 Tbs. (30 ml) white poppyseeds, made into a paste (see "A Glossary of
   Spices and Ingredients")
½ tsp. (2 ml) salt
½ tsp. (2 ml) sugar
Garnish: chopped green onions

1. Smoke and roast the eggplant (see "A Glossary of Spices and Ingredients"). Set aside.
3. Heat oil in a skillet over medium low heat. Fry red chilies until they
   darken. Add fenugreek, garlic, and green chili and stir until garlic turns
   light brown. Add turmeric and water and bring to boil. Lower the heat
   slightly and stir in the eggplant. Add poppy paste, salt, and sugar and
   mix well. Simmer covered for 20 minutes, stirring occasionally to prevent sticking. Remove from heat. Let stand covered for a few minutes to
   help develop the flavors. Garnish with green onions and serve.

4 servings.

Serving suggestions: This eggplant dish marries well with legume or potato
dishes. Accompanied by rice (or Pan-raised Bread), Chic Tart Chickpeas,
and Pleasing Plum Chutney, it makes a gorgeous vegetarian meal.

Begun Bhaja
CRISP FRIED EGGPLANT

This simple dish, which is typically served during festivals and religious ceremonies, nonetheless is a pleasant addition to any meal. A crunchy spiced
batter surrounds tender slices of eggplant. A seedless young eggplant is preferred for this dish.

1 cup (250 ml) besan (chickpea flour)
½ tsp. (2 ml) baking powder
2 tsp. (10 ml) ground cumin
¼ tsp. (1 ml) salt

½ tsp. (2 ml) sugar
2 tsp. (10 ml) vegetable oil
½ cup (125 ml) plain yogurt, lightly beaten until smooth
1 cup (250 ml) water
1 small to medium eggplant, up to 1 lb. (½ kg), cut into 2½ × ½ × ¼-inch
    (6 cm × 1 cm × 6 mm) pieces
Vegetable oil for deep-frying (at least 2 inches/5 cm deep)

> My most favorite food is hot rice, lentils, and fried eggplant.
> —Sunil Gangopadhay, from The Land
> of Pictures, The Land of Poems

1. In a bowl, combine besan, baking powder, cumin, salt, and sugar. Mix
   in oil and yogurt. Gradually add water, stirring with a spoon, so that a
   smooth batter forms. Place a few pieces of eggplant in the batter.
   Remove with a slotted spoon.
2. Heat oil in a saucepan or deep-fat fryer to 375°F (190°C). Heat oven to
   200°F (110°C; gas mark ¼). Fry a few eggplant pieces at a time until
   they turn golden brown all over, about a minute on each side, turning
   once. (Cut one fried piece in half to see if the inside is cooked properly.) Drain on paper towels. Serve immediately or keep them warm in
   the oven until all have been fried.

8 small servings.

Serving suggestions: Serve as an appetizer with Tender Tamarind Chutney
or Sweet and Sour Tomato-Mustard Chutney. Or serve as part of a main
meal with any dal dish.

Lowfat Variation: Instead of frying, you can broil the eggplant pieces. Use
the following light marinade for this.

1 Tbs. (15 ml) vegetable oil
⅛ tsp. (.5 ml) turmeric
1 tsp. (5 ml) ground cumin
Dash ground red chili or cayenne pepper (or to taste)
⅛ tsp. (.5 ml) black salt

⅛ tsp. (.5 ml) salt
1 cup (250 ml) eggplant cut into 2½ × ¼ × ¼-inch (6 cm × 6 mm × 6 mm) pieces

Combine all ingredients except eggplant in a bowl. Dip the eggplant pieces in this marinade until well coated. Broil until browned but not burnt.
3 to 4 small servings.

Kumror Korma
BUTTERNUT SQUASH IN RICH YOGURT SAUCE

The tartness of yogurt contrasts with the sweet taste of butternut squash. A sprinkling of five-spice and bits of green cilantro dot the yellowish-orange cubes.

2 Tbs. (30 ml) vegetable oil (mustard oil preferred)
1 whole dried red chili
¼ tsp. (1 ml) five-spice
2 Tbs. (30 ml) peeled, minced fresh ginger
¼ tsp. (1 ml) turmeric
½ tsp. (2 ml) sugar
4 cups (1 liter) peeled butternut squash or fresh pumpkin cut into 1-inch (2.5 cm) cubes
½ cup (125 ml) water
½ tsp. (2 ml) salt
3 Tbs. (45 ml) plain yogurt, lightly beaten until smooth
½ tsp. (2 ml) garam masala

1. Heat oil in a skillet at least 10 inches (25 cm) wide, over medium low heat. Fry red chili until it darkens. Add five-spice and fry until the spices start popping. Stir in ginger, turmeric, and sugar. Add squash and mix well. Add water and salt. Bring to a boil, then lower the heat.
2. Simmer, covered, until squash is tender but not mushy, 15 to 18 minutes. Remove from heat. Carefully blend in yogurt and garam masala so as not to break the squash cubes. Sprinkle with cilantro and serve.
4 to 6 servings.

Serving suggestions: This autumn dish excites diners who are unaccustomed to having butternut squash in a spicy sauce. Accompanied by rice, Cabbage Smothered in Spicy Chickpea Puree, and Pleasing Plum Chutney, it makes a filling vegetarian dinner.

Kumror Ghanto

BUTTERNUT SQUASH IN MUSTARD SAUCE

Here the squash cubes are simmered in a piquant black mustard sauce with subtle overtones of onion-scented kalonji seeds. Coconut adds a hint of background sweetness. I often entertain with this exotic dish.

2 Tbs. (30 ml) vegetable oil (mustard oil preferred)
1 bay leaf
1 whole dried red chili
¼ tsp. (1 ml) kalonji seeds
1 tsp. (5 ml) seeded, chopped fresh green chili, or to taste
   (see Note)
¼ tsp. (1 ml) turmeric
4 cups (1 liter) butternut squash cut into 1-inch (2.5 cm) cubes
½ tsp. (2 ml) salt
½ tsp. (2 ml) sugar
¼ cup (60 ml) water
1 tsp. (5 ml) black mustard seeds ground to a powder, mixed with 2 tsp.
   (10 ml) water and allowed to stand for 30 minutes
¼ cup (60 ml) dried flaked or shredded sweetened coconut or freshly grated
   or shredded coconut mixed with ½ tsp. (2 ml) sugar

1. Heat oil over medium low heat in a skillet. Fry bay leaf and red chili until the chili blackens. Fry kalonji seeds for a few seconds. Add green chili and turmeric and stir a few times. Stir in butternut squash, salt, sugar, and water.
2. Simmer, covered, 10 minutes. Add mustard paste and stir gently to mix with sauce. Simmer, covered, until the vegetables are tender but not mushy, 5 to 13 minutes. Carefully stir in coconut. Remove from heat. Scatter cilantro on top and serve.

4 to 5 servings.

Serving suggestions: To contrast with the yellowish-orange color of the squash, I serve a leafy dish such as Glorious Greens or green-hued Splendid Cilantro Chutney. Vegetable Pullao and Fragrant Roasted Mung Bean Stew round out the meal.

Note: This dish tastes best when slightly chili-hot. So use a larger amount of green chili than usual or incorporate some of the seeds.

Kumror Dalna
SWEET AND TART PUMPKIN

Bengalis love the contrast of sweet and tart flavors in the same meal and often in the same dish. Even those who find pumpkin or squash too sweet delight in this dish tempered with the tartness of tamarind.

In the United States, the smaller and sweeter "sugar pie" pumpkin is preferable to the larger, relatively tasteless "field pumpkins" sold around Halloween. You can substitute butternut or other sweet winter squashes.

2 Tbs. (30 ml) vegetable oil (mustard oil preferred)
½ tsp. (2 ml) asafetida powder
¼ tsp. (1 ml) kalonji seeds
½ tsp. (2 ml) turmeric
1 tsp. (5 ml) seeded, chopped fresh green chili (or to taste)
¾ tsp. (3 ml) salt
3½ tsp. (17 ml) sugar
¾ cup (175 ml) water
5 cups (1 liter 250 ml) peeled fresh pumpkin or butternut squash cut into
    ½-inch (1 cm) cubes
1¼ tsp. (6 ml) tamarind concentrate

1. Heat oil in a skillet over medium low heat. Sprinkle asafetida over the oil. Add kalonji and fry for a few seconds. Add turmeric, green chili, salt, and sugar. Add water and pumpkin. Simmer, covered, until vegetables are tender but not mushy, 18 to 25 minutes.
2. Stir in tamarind gently so as not to break the squash cubes. Cook uncovered for a minute or so to allow the sauce to thicken. If the sauce is still a little watery, mash a few of the vegetable cubes with the back of a spoon and mix in with the sauce. Remove from heat. Let stand covered for a few minutes to help develop the flavors. Scatter cilantro on top.

4 to 6 servings.

Serving suggestions: The gentle sweetness of Green and White Coconut Chutney accentuates the flavor of this pumpkin dish. Chickpeas have an affinity for pumpkin, so I add rice and Down-home Chickpea Stew to make the meal exciting.

Lau Ghanto
YELLOW CROOKNECK SQUASH IN
CORIANDER-RED CHILI SAUCE

This classic dish is made with bottle gourd, a large, pale green vegetable that is similar in shape to cucumber and whose flavor resembles summer squashes. Since it is not readily available in the West, I have substituted yellow crookneck squash, which yields similar results and tastes delectable when simmered in milk and water. Dried red chili paste imparts a warm, rich flavor, while coriander powder flavors and thickens the sauce.

2 Tbs. (30 ml) vegetable oil (mustard oil preferred)
1 bay leaf
¼ tsp. (1 ml) cumin seeds
1 Tbs. (15 ml) peeled fresh ginger, grated or made into a paste (see "A Glossary of Spices and Ingredients")
1 tsp. (5 ml) seeded, chopped fresh green chili (or to taste)
½ tsp. (2 ml) turmeric
2 tsp. (10 ml) ground coriander
1 lb. (½ kg) unpeeled yellow crookneck squash (about 4 medium), cut into matchstick pieces
1 to 2 tsp. (5 to 10 ml) red chili paste (see "A Glossary of Spices and Ingredients")
2 Tbs. (30 ml) milk
2 Tbs. (30 ml) water
½ tsp. (2 ml) salt
½ tsp. (2 ml) sugar
1 Tbs. (15 ml) dried flaked or shredded sweetened coconut, ground in a blender to a coarse powder
Garnish: Crushed boris (see "Dals" chapter) or toasted cashews

1. Heat oil in a skillet over medium low heat. Fry bay leaf and cumin seeds for a few seconds until the seeds darken. Add ginger and green chili and fry until ginger is lightly browned, stirring constantly. Add turmeric and coriander.
2. Add squash and red chili paste. Add milk, water, salt, and sugar. Simmer, covered, until the vegetables are tender but not mushy, 8 to 12 minutes, stirring occasionally. Gently stir in coconut, taking care not to break the squash pieces. Remove from heat. Let stand covered for a few minutes to help develop the flavors. Garnish with crushed boris. Serve piping hot.

4 to 5 servings.

Serving suggestions: I look forward to the sight of yellow crookneck squash in the market during summer so I can prepare this dish. I arrange a meal in which rice, Fresh Cheese and Mung Bean Delight, and Tender Tamarind Chutney are the accompaniments.

VARIATION

SHRIMP AND YELLOW CROOKNECK SQUASH IN CORIANDER-RED CHILI SAUCE

For a nonvegetarian variation, add shrimp to the above dish. Fry ⅓ pound (150 g) of fresh or thawed frozen shrimp in 1 tablespoon (15 ml) oil until the shrimp changes color. Add to the above dish during the last 2 to 3 minutes of cooking.

Shorsher Chochori
WEDDING-DAY GREENS

Dark, leafy green vegetables have occupied a prominent place in Bengali cooking since ancient times, especially in the villages. Greens are highly valued for both nutritional content and flavor and are used to symbolize any feast. A wedding invitation in earlier times often asked guests to come for *sakanna*, "greens and rice," even though many more dishes would be served.

The yellow potato chunks, orange sweet potato cubes, and deep green leaves make this dish so attractive that additional garnish is unnecessary. You can, optionally, sprinkle brown-fried onions on top for added flavor and texture (see "A Glossary of Spices and Ingredients").

3½ cups (875 ml) firmly packed, coarsely chopped mustard greens or other
    hearty greens, such as collards, kale, or chard
2 to 4 Tbs. (30 to 60 ml) vegetable oil (mustard oil preferred)
1 lb. (½ kg) peeled or unpeeled potatoes (about 3 medium), cut into 1-inch
    (2.5 cm) cubes
¼ tsp. (1 ml) five-spice
1 cup (250 ml) finely chopped onion
1 tsp. (5 ml) seeded, chopped fresh green chili (or to taste)
¼ tsp. (1 ml) turmeric
1 tsp. (5 ml) black mustard seeds, ground to a powder
2 tsp. (10 ml) ground cumin
2 tsp. (10 ml) ground coriander
¾ cup (175 ml) water
1 tsp. (5 ml) sugar
½ tsp. (2 ml) salt
2 cups (500 ml) peeled sweet potatoes cut into 1-inch (2.5 cm) cubes
½ tsp. (2 ml) garam masala

Young greens and ripe old fish.

—Bengali proverb meaning that some things are
better young and some things improve with age

1. Steam the greens and puree in a blender (See "A Glossary of Spices and Ingredients"). Set aside.
2. Heat 2 Tbs. (30 ml) oil in a large pan over medium heat. Fry potatoes until they turn medium brown, about 5 minutes, turning often. Remove with a slotted spoon and set aside. (Omit this step for a lower-fat dish; they will be cooked in step 3.)
3. Add 2 Tbs. (30 ml) oil to the pan and heat over medium low heat. Fry five-spice until it starts popping. Add onion and green chili and fry until onion is translucent, about 2 minutes, stirring constantly. Blend in turmeric, mustard powder, cumin, and coriander and fry for a few seconds. Add water, sugar, salt, potatoes, and sweet potatoes. Bring to boil, then lower the heat.
4. Simmer, covered, until the vegetables are tender, 18 to 20 minutes, adding a tablespoon (15 ml) or so of water if the bottom is dry. Mash a few of the sweet potatoes with the back of a spoon and mix into the gravy. Stir in the pureed greens. Cook uncovered for a minute or so to heat the mixture through. Remove from heat and blend in garam masala. Serve immediately. If allowed to stand, the greens may lose their attractive bright green color; this will not, however, affect their flavor.

4 to 6 servings.

Serving suggestions: I often include these festive greens as side dishes with fish or meat dinners. Leafy greens also go well with dal dishes. Select Tart Red Lentils, Lime-splashed Butternut Squash over rice (or Soft Bread), and Ginger Yogurt Chutney in your menu for a memorable evening.

Lal Saaker Ghanto
RED CHARD AND EGGPLANT MEDLEY

This dish is prepared with the tender red leaves of a hearty green that grows in Bengal. In the West, you can substitute red Swiss chard or beet greens. Bengalis prefer to cook with a whole vegetable, wasting no part of it whenever possible. So I buy beets with leaves still on and use the fleshy root for salads. I may cook the nutritious beet greens in a dish such as this, where the eggplant turns mellow and acquires a buttery consistency in the sauce.

8 cups (2 liters) firmly packed, coarsely chopped greens, preferably red
   Swiss chard or beet greens (include the stems, finely chopped, if desired)
2 Tbs. (30 ml) vegetable oil (mustard oil preferred)
1 whole dried red chili
¼ tsp. (1 ml) five-spice
1 cup (250 ml) finely chopped onion
1 tsp. (5 ml) seeded, chopped fresh green chili (or to taste)
¼ tsp. (1 ml) turmeric
½ tsp. (2 ml) salt
1 tsp. (5 ml) sugar
1 cup (250 ml) water
3½ cups (875 ml) eggplant cut into 1-inch (2.5 cm) cubes (about
   ½ medium eggplant)
¼ tsp. (1 ml) garam masala
Garnish: Raw mild onion rings (see "A Glossary of Spices and
   Ingredients")

1. Steam the greens and puree in a blender (see "A Glossary of Spices and Ingredients"). Set aside.
2. Heat oil in a skillet over medium low heat. Fry red chili until it darkens. Add five-spice and fry until the spices start crackling. Add onion and fry until it is richly browned but not burnt, 10 to 12 minutes, stirring constantly. Stir in green chili, turmeric, salt, and sugar. Add water and bring to boil. Add eggplant. Lower the heat slightly and simmer, covered, until eggplant is soft, 20 or so minutes.
3. Add the pureed greens. Cook uncovered for a minute or so to heat the mixture through, stirring constantly. Remove from heat and blend in garam masala. Garnish with onion rings and serve at once. If allowed to stand, the greens may darken; this will not, however, affect their flavor.

4 to 5 servings.

Serving suggestions: For a light brunch, serve these fragrant greens with Pan-raised Bread. For a vegetarian meal, delight your guests with rice (or Soft Bread), Fragrant Pigeon Peas and Sweet Squash with a Hint of Lime, and Mint Yogurt Sauce.

Saak Bhaja
GLORIOUS GREENS

Diwali is a spectacular affair in India and in Bengal. The Sanskrit word *Deepavali* means a garland of light. On this day, every home is decorated with tiny earthen lamps, *diwas* or *dipas,* fueled by ghee. On the night before Diwali, tradition dictates that a mixture of 14 different types of greens be eaten in the same dish. The elaborate family meal typically begins with a pretty plate such as this, in which slivers of onion, rendered golden by turmeric, peek through the dark leafy greens. In my American kitchen, for the sake of convenience, I use only three types of greens, such as chard, collards, and kale.

2 Tbs. (30 ml) vegetable oil (mustard oil preferred)
¼ tsp. (1 ml) five-spice
2 cups (500 ml) thinly sliced onion
½ tsp. (2 ml) turmeric
¼ tsp. (1 ml) salt
3 cups (750 ml) firmly packed slivered mustard greens and/or collards, kale, and chard (see Note)

1. Heat oil in a pan over medium low heat. Add five-spice and fry until it starts popping, a few seconds. Add onion and fry until translucent, 2 to 3 minutes, stirring constantly. Stir in turmeric and salt.
2. Add greens. Turn heat to low. Cook, covered, just until the greens are tender and limp but still retain their color, 5 to 10 minutes. (If the greens are young and tender, this will barely take 5 minutes.) Remove from heat and serve at once.

3 to 4 servings.

Serving suggestions: This simple but elegant leafy green dish balances rich meat and poultry dishes such as Beef in Rich Ginger-Poppyseed Sauce or Mustard-drenched Chicken. For a gala vegetarian menu, serve with rice, Fragrant Roasted Mung Bean Stew, and Smoked Eggplant in Ginger-Yogurt Sauce.

Note: Mustard greens, which are not widely used in the West, are considered nutritious in Bengal, and the young leaves are prepared in many delicious ways. In the West, tender mizuna mustard, available in Asian (particularly Japanese) markets, is the best choice. The younger the greens the better.

Palong Saak Bhaja
PEANUT-TOPPED GREENS

Spinach is so popular in Bengal that we find many ways of serving it. One of my favorites is this recipe, in which roasted peanuts bring a crunchy contrast to the tender greens. Besides, the nuts provide protein to a vegetarian meal.

6 cups (1 liter 500 ml) firmly packed, coarsely chopped hearty greens, such
   as fresh spinach, chard, collards, kale, and/or mustard greens
2 Tbs. (30 ml) vegetable oil (mustard oil preferred)
1 bay leaf
1 whole dried red chili
¼ tsp. (1 ml) asafetida powder
1 tsp. (5 ml) seeded, chopped fresh green chili (or to taste)
1 Tbs. (15 ml) peeled, minced fresh ginger
¼ tsp. (1 ml) turmeric
⅛ tsp. (.5 ml) black pepper, preferably freshly ground
2 tsp. (10 ml) ground cumin
¼ tsp. (1 ml) salt
½ cup (125 ml) milk
¼ cup (60 ml) unsalted dry roasted peanuts, coarsely chopped

1. Steam the greens until tender and puree in a blender (see "A Glossary
   of Spices and Ingredients"). Set aside.
2. Heat oil in a large skillet over medium low heat. Fry bay leaf and red
   chili until the chili darkens. Sprinkle asafetida on top of red chili. Stir
   in green chili, ginger, turmeric, black pepper, cumin, and salt. Add
   milk and cook until reduced to about half its volume, 3 to 5 minutes,
   stirring often.
3. Add the pureed greens. Cover and place over low heat for 3 to 5 minutes
   to blend the flavors and heat the mixture through. Remove from heat.
   Sprinkle peanuts on top.

3 to 4 servings.

Serving suggestions: For a vegetarian dinner that tempts even the meat-
eaters, serve with rice, Festive Chickpeas with Coconut and Whole Spices,
and Sweet and Sour Vegetable Chutney.

Palong Saaker Ghanto
SPLENDID SPINACH

Here mellow browned potatoes and crunchy lentil dumplings swim in a
dense spicy stew of tender spinach. Very Bengali and very good.

1 Tbs. plus 1 tsp. to 3 Tbs. (20 to 45 ml) vegetable oil (mustard oil
   preferred)
½ lb. (¼ kg) peeled potatoes (about 2 medium), cut into 1½-inch
   (4 cm) cubes

1 bay leaf
1 whole dried red chili
¼ tsp. (1 ml) five-spice
¼ tsp. (1 ml) turmeric
⅛ tsp. (.5 ml) black pepper, preferably freshly ground
2 tsp. (10 ml) ground cumin
1 Tbs. (15 ml) peeled, minced fresh ginger
1 tsp. (5 ml) seeded, chopped fresh green chili (or to taste)
½ tsp. (2 ml) salt
1 tsp. (5 ml) sugar
½ cup (125 ml) water
8 to 10 boris (see "Dals" chapter)
3½ cups (875 ml) firmly packed slivered fresh spinach, collards, kale,
    or other hearty greens
¼ cup (60 ml) thawed frozen peas
Garnish: toasted cashews or slivered almonds

*Author Bibhutibhusan Bandopadhaya depicts the Bengali love
of greens in a short story titled* The Trellis. *A humble peasant girl
is surprised to find* pui, *the choicest of all hearty greens, on her
lunch plate. The happy expression on her face fills her mother's
heart with joy.*

1. Heat 2 tablespoons (30 ml) oil in a skillet over medium heat. Fry
   potatoes until they turn medium brown, 4 to 5 minutes, turning often.
   Remove with a slotted spoon and set aside. (Or fry in 1 teaspoon/5 ml
   oil. See "Brown-frying of potatoes" in "A Glossary of Spices and
   Ingredients.")
2. Add the remaining 1 tablespoon (15 ml) oil and heat over medium low
   heat. Fry bay leaf and red chili until the chili blackens. Fry five-spice
   until it starts crackling. Stir in turmeric, black pepper, cumin, ginger,
   green chili, salt, and sugar and fry for a few seconds. Add water and
   bring to boil. Add the potatoes and boris. Simmer, covered, until
   potatoes and boris are tender, 15 to 20 minutes, stirring occasionally
   and adding 1 tablespoon (15 ml) or so of water if the mixture starts to
   stick to the bottom of the skillet.
3. Gently stir in greens so as not to break the boris. Simmer, covered, until
   limp, 3 to 5 minutes for spinach or 6 to 7 minutes for thicker greens.

Add peas and simmer, covered, 1 more minute. Remove from heat. Sprinkle cashews on top and serve.

3 to 4 servings.

Serving suggestions: This lovely spinach-potato sauté makes a good side dish for beef, lamb, or chicken dinners. For a filling vegetarian meal, try with rice, Fragrant Roasted Mung Bean Stew, and Smoked Eggplant in Ginger-Yogurt Sauce.

Bandhakopir Ghanto
CABBAGE POTATO EXTRAVAGANZA

In this classic dish shredded cabbage is slowly simmered to sweet tenderness. When I was a student I asked a neighbor, who made this dish especially well, how she cooked it. She gave me one secret: to keep the cabbage uncovered during part of the cooking. She also told me to shred the cabbage thinly—the finer the better. The recipe below is one of my favorites. It is lightly spiced but hearty and flavorful.

Although my neighbor used ghee liberally in this dish, I make it an optional item and instead depend on cumin seeds, mustard oil, and the natural juices of the vegetables for flavor.

2½ Tbs. (37 ml) mustard oil
¾ lb. (375 g) peeled potatoes, cut into 1-inch (2.5 cm) cubes
½ tsp. (2 ml) cumin seeds
6 cups (1 liter 500 ml) finely shredded cabbage
1 tsp. (5 ml) seeded, chopped fresh green chili (or to taste)
¼ cup plus 2 Tbs. (90 ml) water
¾ tsp. (3 ml) salt
½ tsp. (2 ml) turmeric
1¼ tsp. (6 ml) sugar
Dash ground red chili or cayenne pepper (or to taste)
½ cup (125 ml) thawed frozen peas
½ tsp. (2 ml) garam masala
A sprinkling of ghee (optional)

1. Heat 2 tablespoons (30 ml) oil in a 12-inch (30 cm) deep-sided pan or Dutch oven over medium heat. Add potatoes and fry until medium brown, 5 to 8 minutes, stirring often. Remove with a slotted spoon and set aside.
2. Add the remaining ½ tablespoon (7 ml) oil to the pan and heat over medium low heat. Add cumin seeds and fry for a few seconds until

lightly browned. Add cabbage, green chili, and ¼ cup (60 ml) water. Lower heat slightly and cook uncovered until cabbage is limp, 6 to 8 minutes, stirring often. Stir in salt, turmeric, sugar, red pepper, 2 tablespoons (30 ml) water, and the potatoes.

3. Simmer, covered, until potatoes are tender, 18 to 20 minutes, adding peas during the last 2 to 3 minutes. Remove from heat and blend in garam masala. Let stand covered for a few minutes to help develop the flavors. Sprinkle with ghee and serve immediately.

4 to 5 servings.

Serving suggestions: I find that prawns, cabbage, and coconut taste excellent together. Keeping that in mind, I serve this hearty cabbage with rice (or Soft Bread), Prawns in a Pot of Gold (or, for vegetarians, Fresh Cheese and Mung Bean Delight), and Green and White Coconut Chutney.

Bandhakopir Korma
CABBAGE AND POTATOES IN BROWNED-ONION SAUCE

Those who think of cabbage as a lowly vegetable are surprised to find that this dish is positively regal. Potatoes swim in an onion-scented yogurt gravy, their smooth texture providing a contrast to the slight crunch of the cabbage. I often serve this dish at parties.

2½ Tbs. (37 ml) vegetable oil (mustard oil preferred)
1 bay leaf
1 whole dried red chili
5 whole cardamom pods
2-inch (5 cm) cinnamon stick
2 whole cloves
¾ cup (175 ml) finely chopped onion
½ lb. (¼ kg) peeled potatoes (about 2 medium), cut into 1-inch (2.5 cm) cubes
1 tsp. (5 ml) seeded, chopped fresh green chili (or to taste)
¼ tsp. (1 ml) turmeric
½ tsp. (2 ml) salt
1 tsp. (5 ml) sugar
½ cup plus 1 Tbs. (140 ml) water
3 cups (750 ml) cabbage cut into 1½-inch (4 cm) diamond-shaped strips (see Note)
2 Tbs. (30 ml) plain yogurt, lightly beaten until smooth
¼ tsp. (1 ml) garam masala
Garnish: hard-cooked egg wedges

1. Heat oil in a large, deep-sided pan over medium low heat. Fry bay leaf and red chili until the chili darkens. Cook cardamom, cinnamon, and cloves for 5 seconds. Add onion and fry until it is richly browned but not burnt, 8 to 10 minutes, stirring constantly. Add potatoes and cook for 2 minutes, stirring often. Add green chili, turmeric, salt, and sugar and stir a few times.
2. Add water and bring to boil. Lower the heat slightly and simmer, covered, until potatoes are almost tender, 10 to 12 minutes. Place cabbage on top of the potatoes and simmer, covered, 10 more minutes. By this time cabbage will be limp and almost tender.
3. Stir, mixing the vegetables together. Simmer, covered, until both cabbage and potatoes are done, 3 to 5 more minutes. Remove from heat. Gently blend in yogurt so as not to break the potatoes. Return to very low heat for 10 or so seconds. Remove from heat and gently stir in garam masala. Let stand covered for a few minutes to help develop the flavors. Garnish with egg wedges and cilantro and serve immediately.

4 servings.

Serving suggestions: Cabbage blends well with chickpeas, so I serve this savory korma with rice, Chic Tart Chickpeas, and Mellow Tomato Chutney.

Note: To slice cabbage in diamond-shaped strips, slice off a rounded side of the cabbage; the slice should be about an inch (2.5 cm) thick at the thickest part. Place the slice cut side downward. Make several parallel cuts about 1½ inches (4 cm) apart across the slice and several parallel cuts diagonal to the first set of cuts to create a diamond pattern. Cut another slice of the same thickness from one of the remaining rounded sides of the cabbage and repeat as needed until you have the desired amount. The remaining cabbage can be used in other dishes.

Phulcopi Bhapa
STEAMED SPICY CAULIFLOWER

A dish to make on a day you're in a hurry. You simply combine the ingredients and steam them, cutting the cauliflower into larger pieces than the potatoes so they cook in the same amount of time. Your guests will thank you for having toiled over the stove for hours.

1 Tbs. (15 ml) ground cumin
1 Tbs. (15 ml) ground coriander
2 Tbs. (30 ml) water

1½ tsp. (7 ml) sugar

¾ tsp. (3 ml) salt

1 Tbs. (15 ml) peeled fresh ginger, grated or made into a paste
(see "A Glossary of Spices and Ingredients")

1 tsp. (5 ml) seeded, chopped fresh green chili (or to taste)

2 Tbs. (30 ml) mustard oil

4 cups (1 liter) cauliflower (see Note), cut into florets 1½ inches (4 cm) in
diameter

½ lb. (¼ kg) peeled potatoes (about 2 medium), cut into 1-inch (2.5 cm)
cubes

1 cup (250 ml) chopped tomatoes (about 4 Roma or 2 regular tomatoes)

¼ cup (60 ml) water

1 bay leaf

1. Combine cumin and coriander with 2 tablespoons (30 ml) water in a
   small bowl. Add sugar, salt, ginger, and green chili. Add oil and mix
   well. Combine cauliflower, potatoes, and tomatoes in a large bowl. Pour
   the spice mixture over the vegetables and mix thoroughly.
2. Heat the water in a nonstick skillet at least 10 inches (25 cm) in diameter. As soon as it comes to boil, add bay leaf and the vegetable mixture.
   (You do not need to stir.) Simmer, tightly covered, until the potatoes are
   tender and cauliflower is still slightly crunchy, 15 to 20 minutes. Garnish
   with cilantro and serve.

4 servings.

Serving suggestions: You can treat this spicy cauliflower as an appetizer and
dip it in a bowl of Splendid Cilantro Chutney. For an easy supper, pair with
Rice and Mung Beans Flavored with Whole Spices. Or serve with rice,
Chickpea Lamb Treasure, and Country-style Chunky Tomato Chutney
when family members get together.

Note: You can substitute broccoli, which does not blend with the spices as
well but still produces a tasty dish. Reduce the cooking time by 2 to 3
minutes.

Phulcopir Chechki
CAULIFLOWER WITH A HINT OF MUSTARD

Cauliflower is so popular in Bengal that it is sometimes described as "the
rose among vegetables." The florets, which soak up flavors well, are often
added to fish or vegetable dishes. In this dish cauliflower plays solo, its
mellowness complemented by a touch of pungent black mustard.

2 Tbs. (30 ml) vegetable oil (mustard oil preferred)
1 bay leaf
1 whole dried red chili
½ tsp. (2 ml) five-spice
1 cup (250 ml) finely chopped onion
½ tsp. (2 ml) turmeric
3 Tbs. (45 ml) peeled fresh ginger, grated or made into a paste
  (see "A Glossary of Spices and Ingredients")
1 tsp. (5 ml) seeded, chopped fresh green chili (or to taste)
¾ tsp. (3 ml) salt
½ cup (125 ml) water
1½ tsp. (7 ml) black mustard seeds, ground to a powder, moistened with
  1 Tbs. (15 ml) water and allowed to stand for 30 minutes
4 cups (1 liter) cauliflower, cut into florets 1½ inches (4 cm) in diameter
Garnish: toasted sesame seeds

1. Heat oil in a skillet over medium low heat. Fry bay leaf and red chili
   until the chili blackens. Add five-spice and fry until it starts to pop. Fry
   onion until it is richly browned but not burnt, 7 to 10 minutes, stirring
   constantly. Stir in turmeric, ginger, green chili, and salt. Combine the
   water and mustard paste; stir into the onion mixture. Add cauliflower.
2. Simmer, covered, until cauliflower is tender but still firm, 10 to 15 minutes, stirring occasionally and adding 1 tablespoon (15 ml) water if the
   vegetables begin to stick to the bottom of the pan. Remove from heat.
   Let stand covered for 15 minutes to help develop the flavors. (The mustard will mellow and impart a faint pungency.) Sprinkle sesame seeds
   and cilantro on top and serve.

4 to 5 servings.

Serving suggestions: The mustardy flavor of this dish makes it an ideal companion for fish and legume dishes. For a meal with many colors and flavors,
accompany with Shrimp Pullao (or rice), Festive Chickpeas with Coconut
and Whole Spices, and Mellow Tomato Chutney.

VARIATION

BROCCOLI WITH A HINT OF MUSTARD

Substitute an equal amount of broccoli and decrease water to ¼ cup
(60 ml). In step 2, simmer until broccoli is tender but still firm, 8 to 10
minutes.

Phulkopir Dalna
CAULIFLOWER AND POTATOES IN ROASTED RED CHILI SAUCE

On Sundays when friends and relatives come over for dinner, my mother serves this classic dish. Bits of red Roma tomatoes, turmeric-yellow potatoes, and green peas make the platter a visual delight. The rich, warm flavor of dried red chili enlivens the sauce.

1½ Tbs. plus 2 tsp. to 3½ Tbs. (32 to 52 ml) vegetable oil (mustard oil preferred)
1 lb. (½ kg) peeled potatoes (about 3 medium), cut into 1-inch (2.5 cm) cubes
1 tsp. (5 ml) sugar
1 bay leaf
¼ tsp. (1 ml) black mustard seeds
½ tsp. (2 ml) cumin seeds
¼ tsp. (1 ml) turmeric
1 Tbs. (15 ml) peeled fresh ginger, grated or made into a paste (see "A Glossary of Spices and Ingredients")
1 Tbs. (15 ml) garlic, forced through a garlic press or made into a paste (see "A Glossary of Spices and Ingredients")
½ cup (125 ml) chopped tomatoes (2 Roma or 1 regular tomato)
½ tsp. (2 ml) salt
¾ cup (175 ml) water
1 to 2 tsp. (5 to 10 ml) red chili paste (see "A Glossary of Spices and Ingredients")
2 tsp. (10 ml) ground cumin
2 tsp. (10 ml) ground coriander
3 cups (750 ml) cauliflower cut into florets 1¾ inches (4.5 cm) in diameter
¼ cup (60 ml) thawed frozen peas
¼ tsp. (1 ml) garam masala
2 Tbs. (30 ml) fresh lemon juice

1. Heat 2 tablespoons (30 ml) oil in a large skillet over medium heat. Fry potatoes until they turn medium brown, about 5 minutes, turning often. Remove with a slotted spoon and set aside. (Or fry potatoes in 2 teaspoons/10 ml oil. See "Brown-frying of potatoes" in "A Glossary of Spices and Ingredients.")
2. Add the remaining 1½ tablespoons (22 ml) oil to the skillet and heat over medium low heat. Add sugar and stir until it turns light brown. Fry bay leaf, black mustard seeds, and cumin seeds until they start to crackle. Add turmeric, ginger, and garlic and stir several times. Add

tomatoes, salt, and water. Add potatoes, red chili paste, ground cumin, and coriander. Simmer, covered, for 10 minutes.

3. Add cauliflower and simmer, covered, until both cauliflower and potatoes are done, another 10 to 15 minutes; the cauliflower should be crisp-tender. Add peas and simmer, covered, 1 more minute. Remove from heat. Blend in garam masala. Let stand covered for a few minutes to help develop the flavors. Sprinkle lemon juice and cilantro on top and serve.

4 to 5 servings.

Serving suggestions: Enjoy this savory and filling *dalna* with chicken or beef dinners. Teamed with rice, Fragrant Roasted Mung Bean Stew, and Splendid Cilantro Chutney, this cauliflower-potato combination is a vegetarian delight.

Labra

VEGETABLES IN A MINGLING MOOD

A banquet of flavors and a confetti of colors, this vegetable dish is often served in Bengal when a family gathers. I once asked a Bengali man, a master at making labra, what his secret was.

One tip he shared was to cook the vegetables uncovered part of the time. When simmered covered for a long time, vegetables become soft and mashed, but cooked uncovered they develop a rich roasted flavor.

Another trick I learned was to crush a few of the vegetables at the end with the back of a spoon. They surrender their essence, blending to form a unique sauce. The sum is indeed greater than its parts.

2 Tbs. (30 ml) vegetable oil (mustard oil preferred)
1½ tsp. (7 ml) sugar
1 bay leaf
¼ tsp. (1 ml) five-spice
3 Tbs. (45 ml) peeled, minced fresh ginger
½ tsp. (2 ml) turmeric
2 tsp. (10 ml) ground cumin
¾ tsp. (3 ml) salt
¾ cup (175 ml) chopped tomatoes (about 3 Roma or 1½ regular tomatoes)
½ cup (125 ml) water
½ lb. (¼ kg) peeled or unpeeled potatoes (about 2 medium), cut into 1-inch (2.5 cm) cubes
1¼ cups (300 ml) peeled sweet potato or yam cut into 1-inch (2.5 cm) cubes
2 cups (500 ml) cauliflower cut into florets 1½ inches (4 cm) in diameter

1 cup (250 ml) green beans, cut crosswise into 1½-inch (4 cm) lengths
2 cups (500 ml) eggplant cut into 1-inch (2.5 cm) cubes
1 to 3 tsp. (5 to 15 ml) red chili paste (see "A Glossary of Spices
   and Ingredients")
¼ cup (60 ml) thawed frozen peas
½ tsp. (2 ml) garam masala
Garnish: Boris prepared for garnish (see "Dals" chapter), or toasted
   cashews

1. Heat oil in a deep 12-inch (30 cm), preferably nonstick skillet or Dutch
   oven over medium heat. (See "When cooking mixed vegetables" under
   "Vegetable Tips" in this chapter.) Add sugar and fry until it darkens, a
   few seconds. Turn heat to medium low. Fry bay leaf and five-spice until
   they start crackling. Add ginger, turmeric, cumin, and salt, then
   tomatoes and water. Add potatoes and sweet potatoes. Simmer, covered,
   for 15 minutes.
2. Add cauliflower, beans, eggplant, and red chili paste. Simmer, covered,
   for another 10 minutes. Turn heat to medium low. Uncover and cook
   until the vegetables are almost tender, about 10 minutes. (Sprinkle 2 to
   4 tablespoons (30 to 60 ml) hot water over the vegetables if they start to
   stick to the bottom, but do not add any more than necessary; the sauce
   should be thick and clingy.
3. Add peas and simmer, covered, until the vegetables are tender, 3 to
   5 more minutes. Remove from heat. Blend in garam masala. Using the
   back of a spoon, mash a few of the potatoes and sweet potatoes and mix
   in with the sauce. Sprinkle cilantro on top and serve.

4 to 5 servings.

Serving suggestions: This homey dish is particularly good for sharing with
the family. In a typical Bengali home it would be served with rice (or Soft
Bread), Tart Red Lentils, and Mellow Tomato Chutney.

Shukto

TENDER BEGINNING WITH MANY FLAVORS

Shukto, a classic Bengali dish, is the traditional beginning to a meal in
Bengal. A wide array of vegetables is cooked, using minimal spices and oil.
"This light starter prepares you for richer fare to come," my Aunt Gouri
once explained.

Of the many variations of shukto, my favorite is this dish in which
roasted mung beans are the main seasoning. A touch of black mustard paste
further enhances the creamy sauce.

The seven rasas or flavors as described in ancient Indian writings were: sweet, sour, bitter, salty, pungent, astringent, and hot.

2 Tbs. (30 ml) roasted split mung beans (see "Dals" chapter), soaked
   4 hours or overnight in ½ cup (125 ml) of water
2 Tbs. (30 ml) vegetable oil (mustard oil preferred)
½ lb. (¼ kg) unpeeled potatoes (about 2 medium), cut into 1-inch (2.5 cm)
   cubes
¼ tsp. (1 ml) five-spice
1 cup (250 ml) carrots cut crosswise into ¼-inch (6 mm) rounds
2½ cups (625 ml) water
¾ tsp. (3 ml) salt
2 tsp. (10 ml) sugar
1 tsp. (5 ml) black mustard seeds, ground to a powder, mixed with 2 tsp.
   (10 ml) water and allowed to stand 30 minutes
2 cups (500 ml) cauliflower cut into florets 1 inch (2.5 cm) in diameter
2 cups (500 ml) eggplant cut into 1-inch (2.5 cm) cubes
½ cup (125 ml) boris (preferably made with urad dal) (See "Dals" chapter)
1 cup (250 ml) firmly packed slivered Swiss chard, collards, or kale leaves

1. Drain mung beans, reserving the soaking liquid. Puree the beans in a blender with 1 to 2 tablespoons (15 to 30 ml) of the soaking liquid until smooth. Set aside.
2. Heat 1½ tablespoons (22 ml) oil in a deep pan, about 12 inches (30 cm) in diameter, over medium heat. Add potatoes and fry until medium brown, 5 to 8 minutes, turning often. Remove with a slotted spoon and set aside.
3. Add the remaining ½ tablespoon (7 ml) oil to the pan and heat over medium low heat. Fry five-spice until the seeds start popping. Add carrots, potatoes, water, salt, and sugar and simmer, covered, 5 minutes.
4. Add the mung bean paste and black mustard paste. Simmer, covered, 10 minutes, stirring often and adding a tablespoon (15 ml) or so of water or bean-soaking liquid if necessary to prevent sticking. Add cauliflower, eggplant, and boris and simmer, covered, until the vegetables are tender but still firm, another 15 to 20 minutes.
5. Add Swiss chard and simmer, covered, another 3 to 5 minutes or until greens are limp but still retain their color. Remove from heat and let

stand covered for a few minutes to help develop the flavors. Scatter cilantro on top and serve.

4 to 6 servings.

Serving suggestions: Since shukto is not overly spicy, you can match it with many types of sauces. Accompanied by rice, Green Split Peas in Zesty Mustard Sauce, and Ginger Yogurt Chutney, shukto makes a hearty meal.

Dimer Dalna
EGG AND CAULIFLOWER IN SAVORY CUMIN SAUCE

When you taste this dish you know why Bengalis consider eggs not as mere breakfast food but as dinner fare. The golden eggs and cauliflower florets stewed in a rich, dark, cumin-flavored sauce make for hearty fare on a cool evening. I often serve this dish when entertaining vegetarian guests.

2 to 3½ Tbs. (30 to 52 ml) vegetable oil
1½ cups (375 ml) cauliflower cut into florets 1 inch (2.5 cm) in diameter
1 bay leaf
1 whole dried red chili
5 whole cardamom pods
2-inch (5 cm) cinnamon stick
2 whole cloves
1½ cups (375 ml) finely chopped onion
2½ Tbs. (37 ml) peeled, minced fresh ginger
¼ tsp. (1 ml) turmeric
½ tsp. (2 ml) salt
2 tsp. (10 ml) ground cumin
½ cup (125 ml) water
2 Tbs. (30 ml) plain yogurt, preferably at room temperature, lightly beaten
   until smooth
Dash ground red chili or cayenne pepper (or to taste)
4 hard-cooked eggs, shelled, or whites of 8 hard-cooked eggs (see Note)
½ tsp. (2 ml) garam masala

1. Heat 1½ tablespoons (22 ml) oil in a skillet over medium low heat. Fry cauliflower until lightly browned, 2 to 5 minutes. Remove with a slotted spoon and set aside. (Omit this step for a lower-fat dish.)
2. Add 2 tablespoons (30 ml) oil to the same pan and heat over medium low heat. Fry bay leaf and red chili until the chili darkens. Fry cardamom, cinnamon, and cloves for a few seconds. Fry onion until it is richly browned but not burnt, 15 to 18 minutes, stirring constantly.

3. Turn heat to low. Add ginger, turmeric, salt, cumin, cauliflower, water, yogurt, and red pepper and mix well. Simmer, covered, until cauliflower is crisp-tender, 10 to 15 minutes; too much heat will curdle the yogurt. Add the eggs and simmer, covered, another 3 to 5 minutes to warm up the mixture. Remove from heat. Mix in garam masala, garnish with cilantro, and serve.

4 servings.

Serving suggestions: These eggs are delicious with Banquet Bread for brunch. For a vegetarian feast, accompany with Vegetable Pullao (or Pan-raised Bread), Glorious Greens, and Tender Tamarind Chutney.

Note: Traditionally the hard-cooked eggs were lightly fried to add more texture to the whites. To reduce the amount of oil, I have omitted this step. Using a toothpick, my mother pierces the hard-boiled eggs lightly in several places. This allows the spices to penetrate the eggs better.

Chhaner Dalna
FRESH CHEESE AND POTATOES IN SAVORY SAUCE

Protein-rich fresh cheese, made by curdling milk, adds new dimensions of flavor and texture to the vegetarian diet, in addition to its nutritional punch. It resembles ricotta cheese but has a fresher, more delicate flavor. In this dish the cheese is pressed into cubes, which are transformed into tender morsels as they absorb the sauce during cooking. They provide a contrast in color and texture to other vegetable dishes in the same meal.

2 Tbs. plus 2 tsp. to 4 Tbs. (40 to 60 ml) vegetable oil
¾ lb. (375 g) potatoes (about 3 medium), peeled or unpeeled, cut into
    1-inch (2.5 cm) cubes
1 bay leaf
5 whole cardamom pods
2-inch (5 cm) cinnamon stick
2 whole cloves
1 cup (250 ml) finely chopped onion
1 Tbs. (15 ml) peeled, minced fresh ginger
1 tsp. (5 ml) seeded, chopped fresh green chili (or to taste)
¼ tsp. (1 ml) turmeric
2 tsp. (10 ml) ground cumin
2 tsp. (10 ml) ground coriander
1½ cups (375 ml) whey (reserved from the fresh cheese), water, or a combination of the two

½ tsp. (2 ml) salt
½ tsp. (2 ml) sugar
Fresh cheese cubes made from 8 cups (2 liters) milk (see "A Glossary of
    Spices and Ingredients")
½ tsp. (2 ml) garam masala

1. Heat 2 tablespoons (30 ml) oil in a skillet over medium heat. Fry
   potatoes until they turn medium brown, about 5 minutes, turning frequently. Remove with a slotted spoon and set aside. (Or fry in 2
   teaspoons/10 ml oil. See "Brown-frying of potatoes" in "A Glossary of
   Spices and Ingredients.")
2. Add 2 tablespoons (30 ml) oil to the skillet and heat over medium low
   heat. Fry bay leaf, cardamom, cinnamon, and cloves for a few seconds.
   Add onion and fry until it is richly browned but not burnt, about 10
   minutes, stirring constantly.
3. Add ginger, green chili, turmeric, cumin, and coriander and stir a few
   times. Add whey or water, salt, and sugar and bring to boil. Add the
   potatoes and simmer, covered, until tender, 15 to 20 minutes, turning
   occasionally.
4. Add the cheese cubes and simmer, covered, 3 to 5 more minutes to heat
   the mixture through. Remove from heat and gently mix in garam masala
   so as not to break the cheese cubes. Let stand covered for 10 minutes to
   help develop the flavors. Scatter cilantro on top and serve.

4 to 5 servings.

Serving suggestions: This hearty, flavorful dish can be the centerpiece for a
vegetarian dinner. Accompany with rice, Mellow Tomato Chutney, and
Spinach in Spiced Yogurt.

Farashi Beaner Chochori
GREEN BEANS IN MUSTARD-POPPYSEED SAUCE

Here tiny white poppyseeds and brown-black specks of mustard seed dot a
thick, pungent sauce. Strips of green beans shine on its surface. I often
entertain with this simple yet elegant dish.

2 Tbs. (30 ml) mustard oil
¼ tsp. (1 ml) five-spice
1 tsp. (5 ml) seeded, chopped fresh green chili (or to taste)
¼ tsp. (1 ml) turmeric
¼ tsp. (1 ml) salt

1 tsp. (5 ml) sugar

2½ cups (625 ml) green beans cut crosswise into 1½-inch (4 cm) pieces

¼ cup plus 1 Tbs. (75 ml) water

1 tsp. (5 ml) black mustard seeds, ground to a powder, mixed with 2 tsp. (10 ml) water and allowed to stand 30 minutes

2 Tbs. (30 ml) white poppyseeds, made into a paste (see "A Glossary of Spices and Ingredients")

Garnish: raw mild onion rings

1. Heat oil in a 10-inch (25 cm) skillet over medium low heat. Add five-spice and green chili and fry until the five-spice starts popping. Add turmeric, salt, and sugar. Stir in green beans, water, and mustard paste. Simmer, covered, 10 minutes.
2. Add poppyseed paste and simmer, covered, until the beans are done, 5 to 10 more minutes. Remove from heat and let stand, covered, for a few minutes to allow the sauce to thicken more and the flavors to develop. Garnish with cilantro and serve.

4 servings.

Serving suggestions: These green beans perk up any chicken, lamb, or beef dinner. When dining vegetarian style, try them as well with rice, Down-home Chickpea Stew, and Tender Tamarind Chutney.

Baati Chochori
SAVORY VEGETABLE MELANGE "BAATI" STYLE

The name comes from the word *baati*, a small bowl, since traditionally this dish was made in a brass bowl. You might wonder how the dish can be cooked in such a tiny utensil.

Diced vegetables, oil, and spices are mixed together in the bowl, then placed directly over a low flame on an open coal hearth. In the West I find that slow baking in an ovenproof casserole yields a similar result. For a special effect, you might prepare and serve this dish in individual ovenproof bowls.

For the vegetables:

1½ cups (375 ml) peeled sweet potatoes or yams cut into ½-inch (1 cm) or smaller cubes

½ lb. (¼ kg) peeled or unpeeled potatoes (about 2 medium), cut into ½-inch (1 cm) or smaller cubes

The dish called baati chochori *has been immortalized,*
in a story of the same name, by the late author Bibhutibhusan
Banerjee. A dying young woman develops a craving for the dish,
which becomes a symbol of life.

1 cup (250 ml) green beans cut crosswise into ½-inch (1 cm) pieces (or half green beans and half cauliflower), cut into ½-inch (1 cm) or smaller cubes
½ cup (125 ml) chopped tomatoes (2 Roma or 1 regular tomato)
½ cup (125 ml) thawed frozen peas

For the spices:
1 tsp. (5 ml) seeded, chopped fresh green chili, made into a paste, or to taste (see "A Glossary of Spices and Ingredients")
2 tsp. (10 ml) red chili paste (see "A Glossary of Spices and Ingredients")
¼ tsp. (1 ml) turmeric
2 tsp. (10 ml) black mustard seeds, ground to a powder
¾ tsp. (3 ml) salt
1 tsp. (5 ml) sugar
¼ cup (60 ml) water
2 Tbs. (30 ml) mustard oil
1 Tbs. (15 ml) white poppyseeds, made into a paste (see "A Glossary of Spices and Ingredients")
1 Tbs. (15 ml) fresh lemon juice

1. Preheat oven to 375°F (190°C; gas mark 5). Place sweet potatoes, potatoes, green beans, cauliflower, tomatoes, and peas in a lightly oiled 8-inch (20 cm) square baking dish.
2. Combine green chili paste, red chili paste, turmeric, ground mustard, salt, sugar, and water in a small bowl. Pour over the vegetables and coat the pieces well. Stir in mustard oil.
3. Cover tightly with aluminum foil and bake 50 minutes. Stir in poppy paste and bake until the vegetables are tender, another 10 minutes. Remove from oven and let stand, covered, for 15 minutes. With the back of a spoon, mash a few potatoes and sweet potatoes to thicken the gravy. Add lemon juice and thoroughly combine with the vegetables. Serve hot.

5 to 6 servings.

Serving suggestions: A good potluck offering. Also delicious with rice on a day you don't have time to prepare too many dishes. For a more elaborate meal, serve with rice, Festive Chickpeas with Coconut and Whole Spices, and Splendid Cilantro Chutney.

Tomato Bhapa
SPICY STUFFED TOMATOES

These plump, bright red, oval-shaped Roma tomatoes, bursting with a fragrant vegetable stuffing, are reminiscent of springtime tulips. The stuffing, which takes only minutes to prepare, enhances the taste of the tomatoes. An easy, elegant dish that is great for entertaining.

10 Roma tomatoes
2 Tbs. (30 ml) vegetable oil (mustard oil preferred)
¼ tsp. (1 ml) asafetida powder
¾ cup (175 ml) finely chopped onion
1 Tbs. (15 ml) peeled, minced fresh ginger
1 tsp. (5 ml) seeded, chopped fresh green chili (or to taste)
¼ tsp. (1 ml) turmeric
2 tsp. (10 ml) besan (chickpea flour)
¼ tsp. (1 ml) salt
1 Tbs. (15 ml) finely chopped fresh cilantro

1. Remove the dark stem end from 8 of the tomatoes. Carefully hollow out each tomato by removing the pulp and seeds; discard the seeds but save the pulp. Chop enough of the remaining 2 tomatoes, discarding the seeds, to make ¼ cup (60 ml) together with the reserved pulp. Set aside.
2. Heat oil in a small skillet over medium low heat. Sprinkle asafetida over the oil. Fry onion until it is richly browned but not burnt, 8 to 10 minutes, stirring constantly. Add ginger, green chili, and turmeric and stir a few times. Stir in besan. Lower the heat slightly. Add the reserved tomato pulp, salt, and cilantro. Cook until the pulp disintegrates into the sauce, about 2 minutes, stirring often. Transfer to a bowl and let cool slightly.
3. Stuff the hollowed tomatoes with this mixture and place upright in a baking pan. If they will not stand because of their pointy ends, place a crumpled piece of aluminum foil on the bottom of the baking pan and make small hollows in the foil (similar to an egg carton) to support the tomatoes upright. Or place the tomatoes in the cups of a muffin or cupcake tin.

4. Just before serving, preheat oven to 400°F (200°C; gas mark 6). Bake the tomatoes until they are tender but retain their color and shape, 7 to 12 minutes (the timing will vary with the firmness and size of the tomatoes). Do not overbake or the tomatoes will darken and their skin will wrinkle. Serve immediately.

4 servings.

Serving suggestions: When served with rice and Onion-fragrant Red Lentils, these savory tomatoes make for a light meal. For entertaining, I serve them with Vegetable Pullao, Egg and Cauliflower in Savory Cumin Sauce, and Splendid Cilantro Chutney.

Dharosher Chochori
OKRA DELIGHT

In India, okra is called "lady's fingers," because it resembles the slender fingers of a woman. Even those who don't think they like okra enjoy this dish, which is richly sauced with browned onion and a hint of mango powder. Try this dish with legume, potato, or fish dishes.

When shopping for okra, look for bright green color and small size—2 to 3 inches (5 to 8 cm), which indicates tender young pods. I add salt at the end, as otherwise okra can turn mushy.

2½ Tbs. (37 ml) vegetable oil (mustard oil preferred)
1 cup (250 ml) thinly sliced onion
¼ tsp. (1 ml) five-spice
¼ tsp. (1 ml) turmeric
1 Tbs. (15 ml) peeled fresh ginger, grated or made into a paste
   (see "A Glossary of Spices and Ingredients")
1 tsp. (5 ml) seeded, chopped fresh green chili (or to taste)
25 to 30 okra pods, stems trimmed, cut crosswise into 2-inch (5 cm) pieces
¼ cup plus 2 Tbs. (90 ml) water
¼ tsp. (1 ml) aamchoor (mango powder)
¼ tsp. (1 ml) salt

1. Heat 2 tablespoons (30 ml) oil in a skillet over medium low heat. Fry onion until richly browned but not burnt, about 10 minutes. Remove with a slotted spoon and set aside.
2. Add the remaining ½ tablespoon (7 ml) oil to the skillet and heat over medium low heat. Add five-spice. As soon as it starts crackling, add turmeric, ginger, and green chili and stir a few times. (Cover the skillet

partially if the spices splatter the cooking area.) Add okra and water. Lower the heat slightly and simmer, covered, until okra is tender but not mushy, about 15 minutes, stirring often and adding a tablespoon (15 ml) of water only if the mixture sticks to the bottom of the pan. The sauce should be thick and clingy.

3. Stir in mango powder, salt, and browned onion. Cook uncovered for a minute or so to heat through, stirring constantly. Remove from heat. Let stand covered for a few minutes to help develop the flavors. Serve hot.

4 servings.

Serving suggestions: Makes a delightful meal when served with rice (and/or Puffed Bread), Fragrant Roasted Mung Bean Stew, and "Happy Heart" Chutney.

RICE

"**P**lease come to my house for some rice," is the way Bengalis invite you home for some food. *Annagata pran*, a common expression, means that "life depends on rice."

Although most Westerners equate rice with long-grain white rice, many different varieties grow in Bengal and other parts of India. A grain of rice can be short and stout or slightly curved and slender. The taste can vary from gently sweet to delicately nutlike.

Bou-bhat, *wife-rice, is an event that takes place after a wedding when the newlyweds arrive at the groom's house and the bride cooks for her in-laws for the first time. Of the new responsibilities she takes on, the most important is the cooking of rice—a symbol of nurturing and of life.*

Each type has its own special use. Festive rice, made with superior-quality grains and rendered golden by saffron, is not the same as everyday rice. The rice for an elderly person may be different from that given to a growing child. A fine variety, *Gobindabhog*, "rice for God," is reserved for *pullao*, a richly seasoned pilaf, and for rice pudding, a delicate creamy dessert. One dainty type is called "the nail of a sparrow"; a second is named "ocean froth" because of its milky-white appearance; and another is so fragrant that it is called "the grain that maddens the cook with joy."

The cultivation of rice in India predates recorded history. Some botanists believe that rice may have originated in India as a wild plant. It was probably used in China as early as 4000 B.C. The Aryan conquerors, who invaded India around 1500 B.C., incorporated the rice they discovered growing there into their diet. They sometimes cooked it in milk, sweetened it, and offered it to their gods. This dish appears in most religious ceremonies today and is believed to be the origin in the West of rice pudding. The Bengali rice pudding dish *payesh,* derived from the original Sanskrit word *payasa,* is different from Western rice pudding in that it has a rich, nutty flavor, is creamier, and is egg-free. (A recipe appears in the "Sweets" chapter.) When I was a child this delicious treat was a must on birthdays, the equivalent of a Western birthday cake.

Rice is so important in Bengali culture that a child's initiation into the eating of it occurs at a joyous ceremony, *mukhe bhat,* "first rice." This event brings together family and friends. After a brief offering of thanks to the gods, the child gets its first taste of rice and everyone else sits down to a grand feast. With this introduction to rice, Bengalis develop a respect for it that lasts a lifetime.

This may be why Bengalis feel hungry unless rice is a part of every meal. As a child, when I came down with a fever, my mother took away the rice and brought me barley broth instead; I always missed my rice and got better in a hurry.

Other dishes may take a role subordinate to rice. Bengali cooks make plenty of sauce with a chicken dish so "you can moisten the rice." They add extra chili to sautéed minced vegetables because "it will make the rice taste better."

At a wedding, a hostess may serve more than one rice dish. Throughout the meal, she offers steamed rice to complement the spicy dishes and help the guests discern the varied and complex flavors of each. She may also serve a pullao, which is a course by itself. The full flavor of this rice dish, made fragrant by hot spices and sprinklings of ghee, can only be savored when no other course clamors for attention.

Although pullao is the food of the affluent and marks a special occasion, rich and poor alike enjoy *khichuri,* a rice and lentil dish. Many temples serve it when feeding thousands of worshipers during a religious observance. Khichuri can be made in many ways, from plain to princely. Emperor Shahjahan, who built the Taj Mahal, is said to have liked the lavish, princely version whose aroma transports you to another time, another era.

Pitha, rice flour dumplings, prepared for the harvest festival, may have originated in the Aryan days. During festivities Bengalis even use ground rice moistened with water to draw designs that beautify floors, doorways, and patios. These improvisational drawings are splendid examples of folk art practiced by women.

Puffed rice is another popular rice derivative. A boxed cereal to Westerners, it is available fresh in Bengal. Walk through the downtown section of Calcutta and you will find street vendors selling it as a snack mix. (See Puffed Rice "Tea" Salad in the "Teatime" chapter.) They stir-fry crunchy puffed rice with chilies, onions, and spices on a tiny stove, then offer it in newspaper cones. Your eyes may shed a tear or two from the sting of the hot chilies, but your heart's cry will be a happy one.

Even though processed rice is portable and easier to prepare, steamed rice remains the most favored. Cooking it is an art. The grains should be plump, unbroken, and distinct, and rice should arrive at the table fragrant and steaming. Few words are harsher to a Bengali cook than "the rice is burned."

While city dwellers breakfast on tea and toast, Bengali villagers start their day with light, sweet balls made with puffed rice. The best moa, it is said, comes from a town called Jaynagar, a city just south of Calcutta, where a special unrefined palm sugar (not readily available in the West) is made.

"Want moa from Jaynagar?" a vendor who walked the streets near our Calcutta home would shout, a trunk balanced on his head. All the children in the neighborhood would rush out of their houses. I had to elbow my way through to buy these treats.

Rice Tips

■ Both long-grain white rice and brown rice go well with Bengali dishes. For everyday eating I prefer the more nutritious brown rice. The best choice for fine dining is Basmati rice (see "A Glossary of Spices and Ingredients"), which I serve when entertaining Bengali style. The more nutritious but equally fragrant brown Basmati rice is another favorite of mine. This rice cooks in 45 to 50 minutes, as opposed to the 20 minutes or less that white Basmati or long-grain rice takes. You can soak brown Basmati 6 to 8 hours; this will reduce the cooking time to 35 to 40 minutes. The timing given in these recipes is based on white rice. Adjust the timing if using brown rice of any kind.

Rice that is firm, plump, and distinct goes better with Bengali food than soft, sticky rice.

■ I always wash rice (except for enriched, long-grain white rice) before cooking. Washing removes the excess starch, makes rice nonsticky, and gives it a cleaner look. *To wash rice:* If you purchase rice from an open barrel at a bulk food store, you may first want to pick it over for stones and other debris. Cover the rice with water, stir with your fingers or a spoon, then drain. I rinse rice this way three times or until the water runs clear, and finally drain it in a strainer.

In recipes that call for first frying of uncooked rice, drain the washed rice through a sieve. Spread it on a tray in a single layer and let stand for three or more hours or until thoroughly dry. Rice will not fry properly if it is coated with moisture.

- Do not open the cover while rice simmers; this causes moisture to escape and the temperature to fall, which can make the rice sticky.

- In rice recipes that call for raisins, the golden variety, available at some Western supermarkets and Indian groceries, is preferable to the more common darker variety. The pale golden color harmonizes better with the white or turmeric-tinted yellow rice.

- I sometimes add a black cardamom pod, an inch-long (2.5 cm) dark-jacketed variety, to the rice as it simmers. This gives an exotic and slightly smoky flavor to the grains.

- I generally use 50% more water than the amount of white rice. That is, for 1 cup (250 ml) rice I use 1½ cups (375 ml) water; for 2 cups (500 ml) rice, I add 3 cups (750 ml) water; for 3 cups (750 ml) rice, 4½ cups (1 liter 125 ml) water, and so on. For brown rice I use double the amount of water—for each cup (250 ml) of brown rice I use 2 cups (500 ml) of water.

- *To garnish rice:* You can apply these garnish ideas to plain rice, or other rice dishes in this chapter. Mound hot, cooked rice on a preheated platter. Score the surface with parallel diagonal lines, a cross or any design of your choice. Using a small spoon, fill the lines lightly with mild paprika or garam masala. Sprinkle toasted cashews or toasted slivered almonds on top. Finally, place a sprig of cilantro or mint at the center or on one side of rice.

- *Serving suggestions for rice dishes:* Plain rice goes well with any meal and is an excellent foil for sauces. The other rice dishes in this chapter can be served with virtually any fish, meat, or vegetable dishes. A meat pullao or a khichuri, which are substantial, need not be served with other seafood, meat, or legume dishes, but can accompany vegetables. You can also offer a pullao as a separate course at the beginning of a meal and serve plain rice for the remainder of the meal to enjoy the various sauces.

- You can serve a small amount of melted ghee as a table condiment. Put it in a small bowl or, better yet, in a jar with a sprinkler top and let the diners help themselves.

Bhat

PLAIN BOILED RICE

A Bengali household will reserve a special pot for cooking rice so that no other color or flavor can taint the grains. Bengali cooks do not measure the amount of water, but use their eyes as a guide. Or they touch the surface of the rice with a downward-pointing index finger and add water to reach up to the first knuckle.

Many Western cooks think it's tricky to cook rice properly. Actually, it is quite easy. The two key elements are the amount of water used and the control of temperature, both of which are specified below. (See also "Rice Tips" in this chapter.) Another important factor is the size of the pot. You need a pot that is large enough so the rice will have room to expand, but if the pot is too large and there is too much empty space above the rice, then steam may not properly moisten it and the grains may remain hard. For example, when cooking 1 cup (250 ml) of rice, use a pot no larger than 2 quarts (2 liters) in capacity.

Since the dishes accompanying rice contain salt, I have omitted it from this recipe. You can add ¼ teaspoon (1 ml) salt to the boiling water if you wish.

Use Basmati (white or brown), long-grain white rice, or long- or short-grain brown rice.

2 cups (500 ml) rice
3 cups (750 ml) water (4 cups/1 liter if using a brown variety of rice)

1. Bring rice and water to boil in covered pot. When you hear a bubbling sound, turn heat to low. Simmer, tightly covered, until all water is absorbed and rice is tender but firm, 20 to 25 minutes (45 to 50 minutes for brown rice). Do not open the cover except at the end of cooking. Let stand covered for 10 minutes to allow the rice to absorb any remaining steam.

   Rice will stay hot, if kept covered, for about 20 minutes. To serve, toss very lightly (to avoid breaking the kernels) with a wet spoon (so that rice will not stick) or fluff with a fork.

4 servings.

VARIATION

WHEY RICE

Replacing the water with whey (see "A Glossary of Spices and Ingredients"), the liquid by-product of making fresh cheese, gives rice a wonderful, sweet aroma. After tasting it, you may decide to make fresh cheese more often simply for the fragrance the whey adds to rice.

Follow directions for Plain Boiled Rice, increasing the amount of the liquid; use 2 cups (500 ml) whey for each cup (250 ml) white rice. Add an extra ¼ cup (60 ml) for brown rice. Extend the cooking time by 15 minutes.

Bhate
SPICY STEAMED VEGETABLES OVER RICE

The name *bhate* means "over rice," a popular way to start a meal. My mother steams squash or potatoes separately or with rice. She spoons fragrant mustard oil on top of the vegetables, then slivers a fresh green chili over them. Sometimes she sprinkles droplets of ghee over the rice for extra fragrance.

On occasion my mother stuffs a few spoonfuls of red lentils into a piece of cloth to keep the kernels together. She steams this bundle with rice, then seasons the softened lentils with mustard oil and green chili. It tastes delicious.

Two other recipes follow.

Saak Bhate
PUREED GREENS WITH CHILI AND COCONUT OVER RICE

Green chili, coconut, and black mustard form a flavor triangle that enlivens the greens. This peasant dish nourishes your heart and soul.

5½ cups (1 liter 375 ml) firmly packed slivered greens (mustard greens,
    collards, kale, fresh spinach), steamed and pureed (see "Greens"
    in "A Glossary of Spices and Ingredients")
1 Tbs. (15 ml) mustard oil
2 tsp. (10 ml) black mustard seeds, ground to a powder, mixed with 2 tsp.
    (10 ml) water and allowed to stand for 30 minutes
1 tsp. (5 ml) seeded, chopped fresh green chili (or to taste)
¼ tsp. (1 ml) salt
2 Tbs. (30 ml) dried flaked or shredded sweetened coconut, or freshly
    grated or shredded coconut mixed with ¼ tsp. (1 ml) sugar
Plain boiled rice

1. Place the pureed greens in a sieve about 5 inches (12.5 cm) in diameter. Rest the sieve over a tall tumbler to catch the drippings. With the back of a large spoon, press down on the greens to squeeze out moisture. About a cup (250 ml) of liquid will be released into the tumbler; you may save this liquid to use for cooking soups or discard it. When no more moisture comes out, set the greens aside.
2. Heat oil in a skillet over medium low heat. Add mustard paste and green chili and stir a few times, keeping the skillet partially covered if the mustard paste starts to splatter. Add the greens and salt and stir a few times. Add coconut and mix well. Remove from heat. Serve about 2 tablespoons (30 ml) per person on top of boiled rice.

4 servings.

Serving suggestion: Serve as a first course to any meal.

Kumror Bhate
LIME-SPLASHED BUTTERNUT SQUASH OVER RICE

You may be surprised to find how good steamed vegetables can taste when paired with proper condiments. Lime offsets the rich sweetness of the squash, and piquant black mustard seeds further enliven the dish.

2 Tbs. (30 ml) mustard oil
½ tsp. (2 ml) black mustard seeds
1 tsp. (5 ml) seeded, chopped fresh green chili (or to taste)
½ tsp. (2 ml) turmeric
2 cups (500 ml) mashed, cooked butternut squash
½ tsp. (2 ml) salt
3 Tbs. (45 ml) fresh lime or lemon juice
Plain boiled rice
Garnish: mild fresh green chili, thinly slivered

1. Heat oil in a skillet over medium low heat and fry the black mustard seeds. As soon as the seeds start popping, add green chili and turmeric and stir a few times. Add squash and salt.
2. Fry for 2 minutes, stirring often. Remove from heat. Blend in lime juice. Serve a small amount over plain boiled rice garnished with green chili.

4 to 5 servings.

Serving suggestion: Serve as a first course to any meal.

Khichuri

MONSOON NIGHT RICE

The word *khichuri* literally means "a mixture of the unexpected." This dish is popular during the monsoon season, when village markets stay closed. In many homes the kitchen is separated from the living quarters; having to carry many dishes to the dining area in drenching rain poses quite a problem. As a child on monsoon evenings, I would eagerly wait for this one wonderful dish to arrive.

Khichuri comes in many styles. This stewlike version is called *gola*, "meltingly soft" khichuri. In the West, I find that brown rice, which gives the dish a smooth and yet chewy texture, is the best choice. Should you prefer not to use brown rice, select the khichuri recipe titled "Rice and Mung Beans Flavored with Whole Spices," which calls for white rice.

This meal, composed mainly of rice and lentils, is protein-balanced and allows you to add whatever vegetables are on hand. "It's so easy to eat," says my sister Sheila, referring to its smooth texture.

2 to 3½ Tbs. (30 to 52 ml) vegetable oil
1 cup (250 ml) thinly slivered onion (see Note 1)
2 bay leaves
¼ tsp. (1 ml) kalonji seeds
1 Tbs. (15 ml) peeled, minced fresh ginger
1 tsp. (5 ml) seeded, chopped fresh green chili (or to taste)
¼ tsp. (1 ml) turmeric
2 tsp. (10 ml) ground cumin
2 tsp. (10 ml) ground coriander
½ cup (125 ml) short- or long-grain brown rice
1 cup (250 ml) red lentils
¾ tsp. (3 ml) salt
1 tsp. (5 ml) sugar
1 cup (250 ml) carrots cut crosswise into ¼-inch (6 mm) rounds, or peeled
    sweet potatoes cut into 1-inch (2.5 cm) cubes (see Note 2)
3¼ cups (800 ml) hot water
½ cup (125 ml) chopped tomatoes (2 Roma or 1 regular tomato)
1 cup (250 ml) cauliflower cut into florets about 1 inch (2.5 cm) in diame-
    ter, or green beans cut into 1-inch (2.5 cm) pieces (see Note 2)
2 Tbs. (30 ml) fresh lemon juice
A sprinkling of ghee (optional)
Garnish: toasted cashews and hard-cooked egg wedges

1. Heat 2 tablespoons (30 ml) oil in a large, deep, and preferably nonstick
   pan over medium low heat. Fry onion, stirring constantly, until richly

browned but not burnt, 6 to 10 minutes. Remove with a slotted spoon and set aside. Omit this step for a low-fat dish.

2. Heat 1½ tablespoons (22 ml) oil over medium low heat. Fry bay leaves and kalonji for a few seconds. Add ginger and green chili and fry until ginger is lightly browned, about a minute. Add turmeric, cumin, and coriander. Stir in rice and lentils. Add salt, sugar, carrots, and water. Add tomatoes, cover, and bring to boil. Lower the heat slightly and simmer, covered, for 40 minutes.

3. Arrange cauliflower on top of the rice-lentil mixture; do not stir. Simmer, covered, until cauliflower is crisp-tender, 6 to 8 more minutes. Remove from heat and let stand covered a few minutes. Stir in lemon juice, the browned onion (if using), and ghee. Garnish with cashews and egg wedges. Serve hot.

6 to 7 servings.

Serving suggestions: Try with papads, Crisp Fried Eggplant (or Rich Roasted Eggplant), and "Happy Heart" Chutney. Because khichuri is protein-balanced, it need not be served with fish or meat dishes (the only exception being Crisp Fried Fish). Chutneys, raitas, papads, and fried vegetables round out a khichuri meal.

Note 1. In Bengal, khichuri for vegetarians is made without onions. This is the way it is usually prepared during autumn's Durga puja, the biggest festival of the year, and Saraswati puja, the worship ceremony for the goddess of learning.

Note 2. When replacing carrots with sweet potatoes or cauliflower with green beans, keep the amount the same. Too many vegetables can make the dish watery.

Bhuni Khichuri
RICE AND MUNG BEANS FLAVORED WITH WHOLE SPICES

The word *bhuni* means "dry," and this version of khichuri has a drier, firmer texture. Here nine spices and mung beans impart a tantalizing aroma to the rice. An elegant dish that is a specialty of Dhaka, Bangladesh.

½ cup (125 ml) split yellow mung beans
2 cups (500 ml) water
2 to 3 Tbs. (30 to 45 ml) vegetable oil (mustard oil preferred)
1¼ cups (300 ml) thinly slivered onion (or ½ cup/125 ml for a lower-fat dish)

2 bay leaves
5 whole cardamom pods
1 black cardamom (optional, if available)
2-inch (5 cm) cinnamon stick
2 whole cloves
1 cup (250 ml) Basmati or fine long-grain white rice
¼ tsp. (1 ml) turmeric
2 tsp. (10 ml) ground cumin
2 tsp. (10 ml) ground coriander
Dash ground red chili or cayenne pepper (or to taste)
½ tsp (2 ml) salt
¾ tsp. (3 ml) sugar
1¼ cups (300 ml) water
½ cup (125 ml) thawed frozen peas
2 Tbs. (30 ml) fresh lemon juice
A sprinkling of ghee (optional)
Garnish: hard-cooked egg wedges and lemon wedges

1. Roast the mung beans (see "A Glossary of Spices and Ingredients"). Bring water and beans to boil. Simmer, covered, until the beans are tender and most of the water is absorbed, 30 to 35 minutes; a tablespoon or two (15 to 30 ml) of the liquid will remain.
2. Heat 2 tablespoons (30 ml) oil in a skillet over medium low heat. Fry onion, stirring constantly, until richly browned but not burnt, 8 to 10 minutes. (Or fry ½ cup/125 ml onion in 1 tablespoon/15 ml oil.) Remove with a slotted spoon and set aside.
3. Heat 1 tablespoon (15 ml) oil in the same skillet over medium low heat. Fry bay leaf, cardamom, black cardamom (if using), cinnamon, and cloves for a few seconds. Add rice. Fry until rice turns opaque, about 3 minutes, stirring constantly. Add turmeric, cumin, coriander, red pepper, salt, and sugar. Add the mung beans, any remaining bean liquid, and water. Cover and bring to boil.
4. Simmer, covered, until rice is tender and all water is absorbed, 20 to 25 minutes. Sprinkle peas on top of the rice-lentil mixture but do not stir. Simmer, covered, 2 more minutes. Remove from heat. Let stand covered for a few minutes to allow the rice to become firmer and plumper. Add the lemon juice, browned onion, and ghee, and stir gently just until mixed. Garnish with egg and lemon wedges and serve.

4 servings.

Serving suggestions: Great for potlucks and for entertaining vegetarian guests. Serve with papads, Spicy Home Fries, and Mint-Yogurt Sauce.

Doi Bhat

GINGER-SCENTED YOGURT RICE

In this memorable dish, accented by ginger, yogurt blends smoothly with rice. Black mustard seeds add pungency, and specks of green cilantro deliver a fresh taste. Try this dish on a day you want a change from plain rice.

1 cup (250 ml) Basmati or other fine long-grain white rice
1½ cups (375 ml) water
¾ tsp. (3 ml) salt
1½ Tbs. (22 ml) vegetable oil (mustard oil preferred)
¼ tsp. (1 ml) asafetida powder
1 tsp. (5 ml) black mustard seeds
2 Tbs. (30 ml) peeled, thinly slivered fresh ginger
1 tsp. (5 ml) seeded, chopped fresh green chili (or to taste)
1 Tbs. (15 ml) finely chopped fresh cilantro
2 cups (500 ml) plain yogurt, lightly beaten until smooth

1. Bring rice, water, and salt to a boil. Lower heat slightly and simmer, covered, 15 to 20 minutes or until all water is absorbed and rice is tender but firm. Remove from heat and set aside.
2. Heat oil in a 6-inch (15 cm) skillet over medium low heat. Sprinkle asafetida on top of oil. Add mustard seeds. As soon as the seeds start popping, add ginger and green chili. Stir in cilantro and remove from heat. Pour spice mixture over rice and mix well. Blend in yogurt. Serve immediately or at room temperature. Store any leftovers in the refrigerator and bring to room temperature before serving; the flavor improves on standing.

5 to 6 servings.

Serving suggestions: At a picnic or for a light lunch serve with Splendid Cilantro Chutney. For a full meal try with Green Split Peas with Zesty Mustard Sauce and "Happy Heart" Chutney.

Lebur Bhat

LEMON-LACED RICE

The aroma of hot spices fills the air while this dish simmers. Lemon juice is one of the ingredients, and a wedge of lemon, added to the rice as it cooks, imparts a delightful tartness.

1½ Tbs. plus 1 tsp. (27 ml) vegetable oil (mustard oil preferred)
1 bay leaf
5 whole cardamom pods
2-inch (5 cm) cinnamon stick
2 whole cloves
1 Tbs. (15 ml) peeled, minced fresh ginger
1½ Tbs. (22 ml) raisins
1 cup (250 ml) Basmati or long-grain white rice
A lemon wedge (¼ of a lemon, seeds removed)
1½ cups (375 ml) water
½ cup (125 ml) fresh or thawed frozen peas
¼ cup (60 ml) fresh lemon juice
2 tsp. (10 ml) sugar
¼ tsp. (1 ml) black mustard seeds

1. Heat 1½ tablespoons (22 ml) oil in a pan over medium low heat. Fry bay leaf, cardamom, cinnamon, and cloves for a few seconds. Add ginger and fry until lightly browned, stirring often. Add raisins and rice and fry until rice is opaque, about 3 minutes. Add lemon wedge and water. If using fresh peas, add at this point. Bring to boil, then lower heat slightly. Simmer, covered, for 18 to 20 minutes or until all water is absorbed and rice is tender and fluffy.
2. Sprinkle with lemon juice and sugar but do not stir. If using frozen peas, add at this point. Simmer, covered, 1 to 2 more minutes. Remove from heat and set aside.
3. Heat 1 teaspoon (5 ml) oil in a 6-inch (15 cm) skillet over medium low heat. Fry mustard seeds a few seconds until they begin to pop, covering the skillet if necessary to prevent the seeds from flying out. Remove from heat. Pour oil and spice mixture over the rice and mix gently. Discard lemon wedge and serve piping hot.

4 to 5 servings.

Serving suggestions: This lemony rice goes well with fish or seafood dishes. For vegetarians, round out the meal with Vegetables in a Mingling Mood. Ginger Yogurt Chutney, when served on the side, accentuates the clean citrus flavor of this rice dish.

Ghee Bhat
AROMATIC RICE WITH PEAS AND WHOLE SPICES

The name *ghee bhat* literally means "butter-flavored pilaf." The word *pullao*, or pilaf in the Middle East and the West, possibly comes from the Sanskrit words *pal* and *anna,* meaning "meat" and "rice." Originally this lavish rice meal probably included meat. This pullao recipe and those that follow offer shrimp, meat, and vegetable variations.

In this vegetarian version of a pullao, peas, raisins, cashews, and whole hot spices adorn the rice. The fragrance of this exquisite dish is intoxicating.

In a simpler version of this recipe a few drops of ghee are sprinkled over hot cooked rice of a fine variety such as Basmati. During a feast following a wedding or a religious ceremony, rice for children is often prepared this way without spices.

Instead of splurging with ½ cup (125 ml) or so of ghee as is traditional, I use only a moderate amount of oil and optionally sprinkle on ghee at the end, or use an oil and ghee combination. The dish is still tasty.

2 Tbs. (30 ml) vegetable oil (or equal parts ghee and oil)
1 bay leaf
6 to 8 whole cardamom pods
2-inch (5 cm) cinnamon stick
2 whole cloves
¼ tsp. (1 ml) turmeric
1 Tbs. (15 ml) raisins
2 Tbs. (30 ml) unsalted raw cashews
1 Tbs. (15 ml) peeled, minced fresh ginger
¼ tsp. (1 ml) salt
1 tsp. (5 ml) sugar
1 cup (250 ml) Basmati or fine long-grain white rice
½ cup (125 ml) fresh or thawed frozen peas
1½ cups (375 ml) water
A sprinkling of ghee (optional)
Garnish: Brown-fried onions (optional) (see "A Glossary of Spices and
  Ingredients")

1. Heat oil in a pan over medium low heat. Fry bay leaf, cardamom, cinnamon, and cloves. Add turmeric, raisins, and cashews and fry for a few seconds, stirring constantly. Watch carefully to avoid burning. Add ginger, salt, and sugar.
2. Add rice and cook until it turns opaque, about 3 minutes, stirring constantly. Add water and bring to boil. Simmer, covered, until all water is absorbed and rice is fluffy, 18 to 20 minutes. Add peas during the last 5 minutes of cooking. Let stand covered for a few minutes. Sprinkle with the brown-fried onions and the ghee and serve piping hot.

4 servings.

Serving suggestions: You can serve this aromatic dish in place of plain rice with any meal. My favorite accompaniments are Tender Beginning with Many Flavors and Yogurt Coconut Dip.

Tarkarir Pullao
VEGETABLE PULLAO

I love to entertain with this fragrant dish, in which each bite contains a surprise—nuts, raisins, vegetables, or rice. This pullao goes well with meat dishes or as part of a meatless dinner.

2½ to 4 Tbs. (37 to 60 ml) vegetable oil
¾ cup (175 ml) carrots cut into ¾-inch (2 cm) cubes
1 cup (250 ml) cauliflower cut into florets 1 inch (2.5 cm) in diameter
¼ cup (60 ml) green beans cut crosswise into ½-inch (1 cm) pieces
1 bay leaf
6 to 8 whole cardamom pods
2-inch (5 cm) cinnamon stick
2 whole cloves
1 cup (250 ml) finely chopped onion
1 Tbs. (15 ml) peeled, minced fresh ginger
1 tsp. (5 ml) seeded, chopped fresh green chili (or to taste)
2 Tbs. (30 ml) unsalted raw cashews
1 Tbs. (15 ml) raisins (preferably golden)
1¼ cups (300 ml) Basmati or long-grain white rice
¾ cup (175 ml) chopped tomatoes (about 3 Roma or 1½ regular tomatoes)
½ tsp. (2 ml) salt
½ tsp. (2 ml) sugar
½ to 1 tsp. (2 to 5 ml) saffron, ground to a powder and soaked in 1 Tbs.
    (15 ml) warm milk or water for 30 minutes
2 cups (500 ml) hot water
¼ cup (60 ml) frozen thawed peas
A sprinkling of ghee (optional)
Optional garnish: Brown-fried onions and fried fresh cheese cubes
    (see "A Glossary of Spices and Ingredients")

1. Heat 1½ tablespoons (22 ml) oil in a pan over medium heat. Fry carrots, cauliflower, and green beans until the vegetables are lightly browned, 3 to 5 minutes. Remove with a slotted spoon and set aside. (Omit this step for a lower-fat dish; the vegetables will be cooked in step 4.)
2. Add 2½ tablespoons (37 ml) oil to the pan and heat over medium low

heat (see Note). Add bay leaf, cardamom, cinnamon, and cloves and fry for a few seconds. Add onion and fry until translucent, about 2 minutes, stirring constantly. Add ginger, green chili, cashews, and raisins and fry for a minute or so, stirring constantly.

3. Add rice and fry until opaque, 3 or so minutes, stirring constantly. Add tomatoes, salt, and sugar. Blend in saffron and the soaking liquid. Add hot water and bring to boil. Lower the heat slightly and simmer, covered, until most of the water is absorbed and rice is almost tender, about 12 minutes.

4. Place vegetables on top of rice; do not stir. Simmer, covered, until rice is done and vegetables are tender but still firm, 5 to 10 more minutes (if they were not fried in step 1, allow an additional 5 to 7 minutes). Place peas on top of rice during the last 2 minutes of cooking. Remove from heat. Let stand covered for 10 minutes to allow rice to become plumper and fluffier. Sprinkle with ghee for additional flavor and stir gently. Garnish with brown-fried onion and cheese cubes and serve.

4 to 6 servings.

Serving suggestions: For a tasty meal with many colors and flavors, I surround this gorgeous rice platter with Butternut Squash in Mustard Sauce, Glorious Greens, and Ginger Yogurt Chutney.

Note: For a special treat, replace 1 tablespoon (15 ml) of the oil with ghee in step 2.

Chingrir Pullao
EXQUISITE SHRIMP PULLAO

Of the many methods for preparing shrimp pullao, this version, enriched by a touch of coconut milk, is in my opinion one of the best. The tiny pink shrimp peek from a nest of pale yellow rice, inviting you to sample a bite.

2 Tbs. (30 ml) vegetable oil (mustard oil preferred)
2 bay leaves
6 to 8 whole cardamom pods
2-inch (5 cm) cinnamon stick
2 whole cloves
1 cup (250 ml) finely chopped onion
1 Tbs. (15 ml) peeled, minced fresh ginger
1 tsp. (5 ml) seeded, chopped fresh green chili (or to taste)
¼ tsp. (1 ml) turmeric
½ tsp. (2 ml) salt

½ tsp. (2 ml) sugar
1 cup (250 ml) Basmati or fine long-grain white rice
1¼ cups (300 ml) water
½ cup (125 ml) fresh or unsweetened canned coconut milk (stirred until evenly mixed)
¼ lb. (115 g) fresh or thawed frozen bay shrimp

1. Heat oil in a large, deep-sided pan over medium low heat. Fry bay leaf, cardamom, cinnamon, and cloves for a few seconds. Add onion and fry until richly browned but not burnt, 5 to 8 minutes.
2. Add ginger, green chili, turmeric, salt, sugar, and rice and cook about 3 minutes, stirring constantly. Add water and bring to boil. Lower the heat slightly and simmer, covered, until all water is absorbed and rice is tender, 15 to 20 minutes. Pour coconut milk on top of rice but do not stir.
3. Simmer, covered, another 5 minutes. Arrange shrimp on top of rice (see Note). Simmer, covered, until shrimp is done, 3 to 5 more minutes (see "Test for doneness" under "Seafood Tips" in the "Fish and Seafood" chapter). Remove from heat. Let stand covered for a few minutes to allow the rice to become plumper and fluffier. Add chopped cilantro and stir gently. Serve piping hot.

4 servings.

Serving suggestions: This pullao complements Sweet and Tart Pumpkin. For a splash of color I follow with Splendid Cilantro Chutney.

Note: For a richer taste, fry the shrimp in 1 tablespoon (15 ml) oil before adding in step 3.

Mangsher Pullao
IMPERIAL RICE

This dish originated in the Moghul courts. As many as 15 spices and aromatics blend to form the flavors. In Bengal, we may wrap edible silver leaves around a few grains of rice to further enhance the beauty of the dish.

I place the rice in the center of a large oval platter, with tomato wedges, sliced cucumber, and onion rings arranged concentrically around the edges and a sprig of mint nested in the center.

For the marinade:

3 Tbs. (45 ml) peeled, coarsely chopped fresh ginger
½ cup (125 ml) plain yogurt
¼ tsp. (1 ml) turmeric

2 lb. (1 kg) leg of lamb or beef round steak, chuck roast, or sirloin tip, cut
   into 2 × 2 × 1-inch (5 × 5 × 2.5 cm) pieces
2 to 3 Tbs. (30 to 45 ml) vegetable oil
6 to 8 whole cardamom pods
1 black cardamom pod (optional, if available)
2-inch (5 cm) cinnamon stick
2 whole cloves
1 Tbs. (15 ml) minced garlic
2 tsp. (10 ml) ground cumin
1 tsp. (5 ml) fennel seeds, roasted and ground
2 tsp. (10 ml) ground coriander
Dash ground red chili or cayenne pepper (or to taste)
½ tsp. (2 ml) sugar
½ cup (125 ml) water
¾ tsp. (3 ml) salt
2 bay leaves
¼ tsp. (1 ml) cumin seeds
1½ cups (375 ml) finely chopped onion (or ¾ cup/175 ml)
1½ cups (375 ml) Basmati or long-grain white rice
2 Tbs. (30 ml) unsalted raw cashews
⅛ tsp. (.5 ml) mace
Garnish: tomato wedges, cucumber slices, raw onion rings

1. *To marinate the meat:* In a blender, puree ginger and 2 tablespoons
(30 ml) of the yogurt until smooth. In a large bowl, combine the ginger
mixture, the remaining yogurt, and turmeric. Beat lightly by hand until
smooth. Add meat, making sure each piece is well coated. Cover and
refrigerate 4 hours or preferably overnight.
2. Heat 1 tablespoon (15 ml) oil in a large pan over medium low heat. Fry
cardamom, black cardamom, cinnamon, cloves, and garlic until garlic is
lightly browned. (Or fry in ½ tablespoon/7 ml oil for a lower-fat dish.)
3. Add cumin, fennel, coriander, red pepper, and sugar and stir a few
times. Lower the heat slightly. Add the meat with marinade and water.
Simmer, covered, until meat is tender, about 1 hour, stirring occasionally and adding a tablespoon (15 ml) or so of water if the mixture sticks
to the bottom.
4. Add salt. Remove meat with a slotted spoon and set aside. Measure the
broth remaining in the pan and add sufficient water to make 2½ cups
(625 ml). Set aside.
5. Wash and wipe out the pan. Heat 2 tablespoons (30 ml) oil over
medium low heat. Fry bay leaves and cumin seeds just until the seeds
start to darken, a few seconds. Fry onion until richly browned but not
burnt, about 10 minutes, stirring constantly and turning heat to medium

low when the onions start to become dark brown around the edges. (Or fry the spices and ¾ cup/175 ml onion in 1½ tablespoons/22 ml oil.)

6. Add rice and fry until opaque, about 3 minutes. Add cashews, mace, and the meat broth. Bring to boil. Lower the heat slightly and simmer, covered, until rice is tender, 25 to 30 minutes. Place meat and accumulated juices, if any, on top of the rice, but do not stir. Simmer, covered, 5 more minutes. Remove from heat. Let stand covered for a few minutes to allow rice to become plumper and firmer. Gently mix rice and meat together. Place on a preheated platter and surround with tomato, cucumber, and onion rings. Serve hot.

7 to 8 servings.

Serving suggestions: This dish takes center stage on my table. It is usually surrounded by Green Beans in Mustard-Poppyseed Sauce and "Happy Heart" Chutney.

FLATBREADS

Unleavened bread, an ancient food, is a marvel. The simplest varieties require only wheat, water, a griddle, and an open flame. The method of preparation has changed little in thousands of years. Unlike raised loaves, these do not need the rising action of yeast—or even an oven.

Bengali flatbreads come in numerous shapes: round, triangular, square, and so on. They may be spiced, stuffed, layered, or plain, and served with the main meal or at teatime as "fun food."

My favorites have always been the stuffed breads. I would first search through the delicate creases to find the filling. One day it would be cumin potatoes, another day creamed legumes. Each would have a taste of its own and add a different dimension to dining.

Even plain breads have charm. They are prepared fresh just before the family sits down at the table. Watching my mother make chapati—so basic a task—is a joy. She rolls pieces of dough into circular shapes, identical in size, then cooks and stacks them. They are shaped so perfectly that looking down from the top of the stack you cannot see the edges of the ones below.

When visiting Bengal's villages I an entranced by the sight of chapatis cooking on open-air charcoal stoves outside the huts. In the faint light of evening, their robust aroma wafting on the warm breeze creates an almost mystical effect on me.

The three most popular breads in Bengal are rooti or chapati, which is thin, flat, and soft; parota, a flaky layered bread; and luchi, puffy and deep-fried.

Soft breads are the simplest and lightest of the three. Since they are griddle-cooked without using any oil, they don't keep very well and should be eaten within an hour or so.

Layered breads, which are pan-fried using a little oil, have a heavier texture. They keep well and can be made several hours ahead and reheated.

141

You can make them plain or stuff them with spicy vegetables. They are popular as a portable snack.

The puffed breads, which are easy to prepare and can be made ahead, are rich and have a light texture. They are most often used when entertaining large numbers of guests. Although they lose their puffiness if not served immediately, they still taste good.

Flatbread Tips

- The amount of water needed for the dough can vary slightly depending on the weather. With experience you'll be able to adjust the amount.

- Kneading the dough is important, as it makes the bread light and gives it a smooth texture.

- The dough must rest before it is cooked. Let it stand, covered, in a cool dry place or in the refrigerator for the amount of time specified in the recipe.

- For visual appeal, the breads should be rolled in round shapes. This requires some practice, and, in the beginning, they may not turn out to be perfect rounds. Don't be disappointed. Try to roll them as evenly as you can, trimming the edges with a knife if necessary.

- You can place any leftover dough in a plastic bag, close the bag tightly, and refrigerate. The dough will last for several days. Bring to room temperature before using.

- After you have rolled a bread, cook it immediately rather than rolling out all the dough at once. Keep the dough covered with a damp cloth to prevent it from drying out.

  If rolled too thin, a luchi will not puff up. For parota, roll the edges thinner than the center.

- Flatbreads are best served hot from the stove, requiring that the cook prepare them while the diners eat. In the West, this may not be convenient. As you make them, keep them covered with a kitchen towel and serve as soon as several are cooked.

- *Reheating a flatbread:* Enclose it in a piece of aluminum foil, seal tightly, and place in a 350°F (180°C; gas mark 4) oven for 5 to 10 minutes. Prolonged heating will dry out the bread.

- *Serving suggestions for flatbreads:* Flatbreads can accompany any meal, although they are best served with a meat, fish, vegetable, or legume dish that has a thick gravy. I generally serve a simpler flatbread like chapati or rooti with a richly sauced dish but offer the heavier parota with a light vegetable dish.

Chapati
SOFT BREAD

"Flatbreads fascinate me," says my husband. "I like touching my food with my fingers while I eat." To eat with chapati you tear off a small portion and use it to scoop out a little curry. It is an edible spoon, so to speak.

Rice can no longer be served several times a day in Bengal, due to rising costs. Many families occasionally substitute chapati.

Since the making of flatbreads may be new to many Westerners, I have given a half-recipe below. The smaller amount of flour makes the dough easier to knead and handle. Double the recipe if you wish. Use either of the following sets of ingredients to prepare the dough.

1) ⅔ cup (150 ml) atta (chapati flour); see "Chapati Tips"
   ⅓ cup (75 ml) stone-ground wholewheat flour
   ½ tsp. (2 ml) baking powder
   3 Tbs. (45 ml) milk or buttermilk
   5 Tbs. (75 ml) warm (not hot) water
2) ½ cup (125 ml) all purpose flour
   ½ cup (125 ml) wholewheat pastry flour (see "Chapati Tips" on substituting wholewheat flour)
   ½ tsp. (2 ml) baking powder
   ½ Tbs. (7 ml) vegetable oil
   3 Tbs. (45 ml) milk or buttermilk
   7 Tbs. (105 ml) warm (not hot) water
   Additional wholewheat or chapati flour for dusting

1. Sift the flours and baking powder together. Make a well in the center and pour in oil and buttermilk. Mix with your fingers until the mixture resembles coarse crumbs. Gradually add water and mix to form a soft, slightly sticky dough that holds together. Depending on the weather, the amount of water needed can vary slightly.
2. Knead the dough until it is soft and pliable and springs back when lightly pressed with a finger, about 5 minutes. Cover with a damp cloth and let rest at room temperature for at least 30 minutes.
3. Knead the dough a few more times. Pinch off a portion and make a ball about 1¾ inches (4 cm) in diameter by rolling between the palms of your hands. Dust a work surface and a rolling pin with flour. Roll the ball evenly into a disc about 6 inches (15 cm) in diameter and between ⅛ inch (3 mm) and 1/16 inch (1½ mm) thick. Shake off any excess flour from the surface of the chapati.

4. Heat an ungreased skillet (preferably cast iron) or a griddle over medium heat until hot, about 3 minutes.

5. Turn a second burner to medium or medium high heat. Place a nonflammable rack (such as a cake cooling rack) over the second burner. Place the chapati on the skillet. When bubbles begin to appear on the top and the bottom turns lighter in color and becomes mottled with small, light brown spots, turn the chapati. (This should take 30 to 35 seconds; if the brown spots are larger than 1/4 inch/4 mm in diameter, the heat is too high.) Press the surface lightly with a spoon, kitchen towel, or oven mitt and it will puff up in several places. Do this only until the bottom turns lighter in color, about 10 seconds; if you cook too long, the chapati will dry out and become brittle.

6. Using tongs, place the chapati (first-cooked side down) on the rack over the burner and adjust the flame (if using a gas stove) so that it does not touch the chapati. Within 30 or so seconds, the bread will puff up either entirely or in several places. Immediately remove from heat. If using a gas stove, turn the second flame off until ready to cook the next chapati.

7. Continue with the remaining dough, cooking each chapati as it is rolled out rather than rolling them all at once. Adjust the heat under the skillet as necessary so that the chapatis cook the requisite length of time.

Serve immediately or keep covered with a kitchen towel until ready to serve.

Makes 8 chapatis.

Serving suggestion: Serve in place of rice with any meat or vegetarian dinner.

Chapati Tips

■ The flour used to make this bread in India is *atta,* or chapati flour, a specially ground soft wholewheat flour. It has much of the bran and husk left in it, which results in a superior texture and makes it easier to knead. Indian stores in the West sell chapati flour, but it has been processed outside of India and is often too finely ground. I find that adding a little stone-ground wholewheat flour gives it more body, making it similar to Indian atta. The combination of all purpose and wholewheat pastry flour suggested in the recipe also works well.

■ Sifting the flour is not for the purpose of removing the bran but to give the bread a lighter texture. I return any bran remaining on the sifter to the bowl and mix it in with the flour.

■ *Substituting wholewheat flour:* Chapatis are slightly less tender when made with wholewheat flour. Wholewheat pastry flour, which is milled more finely and contains the entire wheat berry, is preferable to regular whole-wheat flour.

- Buttermilk gives the chapatis a light texture and a slightly tangy flavor.
- I omit salt, since chapatis are eaten with dishes that contain salt.
- Warm water makes the dough tender and is especially effective in softening the somewhat coarser Western supermarket flours.
- Do not stack warm chapatis on top of one another or they will stick together and become soggy. I place them on a large tray, not overlapping, and cover them with a kitchen towel. The towel absorbs any rising steam.
- You can use a "chapati fluffer," a small raised platform sold in Indian stores, instead of a rack for the final cooking phase.
- The best chapatis are those that puff up entirely and thereby separate into two thin layers in the middle. These chapatis have a tender, light texture.
- Success in making chapatis depends on the freshness of the flour, the texture of the dough, and the heat. Overcooking or too much heat will make them crisp and crackerlike.

Rooti

PAN-RAISED BREAD

Rooti, or roti, is the generic name for flatbreads, but in Bengal the term also applies to this variation of Soft Bread. Rootis puff up during griddle-cooking and acquire a light, fluffy texture. They are a favorite at breakfast time.

⅔ cup (150 ml) atta (chapati flour); see "Chapati Tips"
⅓ cup (75 ml) stone-ground wholewheat flour
½ tsp. (2 ml) baking powder
½ tsp. (2 ml) salt
1½ tsp. (7 ml) brown or granulated sugar
½ tsp. (2 ml) fennel seeds, roasted and ground
¼ cup (60 ml) plain yogurt
¼ cup (60 ml) warm (not hot) water
Additional wholewheat or chapati flour for dusting

1. Sift together flours, baking powder, and salt. Add sugar and fennel. Blend in yogurt. Mix in the water gradually with your fingers to form a

soft dough. Knead for at least 10 minutes. Cover with a damp cloth and let rest at room temperature for at least 30 minutes.

2. Proceed with steps 3 to 7 of Soft Bread.

Makes 8 rootis.

Serving suggestion: same as for Soft Bread

Dimer Parota
FLAKY BREAD WITH ZIPPY EGG FILLING

Originally, stuffed breads were invented to use leftovers and for ease of carrying lunch to a workplace. They are tastier than plain bread, as the filling makes the dough moist and flavorful. You can vary the fillings tremendously to suit the available ingredients, and they are a good way to introduce additional vegetables into your diet.

In the small towns of Bengal you sometimes see vendors preparing egg-stuffed parotas with amazing speed at roadside stands. I once watched one who used no rolling pin but pressed and released the dough between the palms of his hands until it reached the required size. When he drizzled the beaten egg mixture over the partly cooked bread, it never once spilled over the edge.

For the dough:

1 cup (250 ml) all purpose flour
1 cup (250 ml) wholewheat pastry flour
1 tsp. (5 ml) baking powder
¼ tsp. (1 ml) salt
1 Tbs. (15 ml) vegetable oil
½ cup (125 ml) plain yogurt
5 Tbs. (75 ml) warm (not hot) water

For the filling:

2 eggs, lightly beaten
2 Tbs. (30 ml) very finely minced onion
1 tsp. (5 ml) seeded, minced fresh green chili (or to taste)
2 Tbs. (30 ml) finely chopped fresh cilantro

Additional flour for dusting
Vegetable oil for pan-frying

1. Prepare the dough: Sift the flours, baking powder, and salt into a large bowl. Gradually add oil and yogurt and mix well. Add water a little at a time, mixing with your fingers to form a dough that holds together. Knead for at least 10 minutes until dough is smooth and pliable. Cover with a damp cloth and let rest at room temperature for 1 hour.

2. Prepare the filling: Combine all the filling ingredients and set aside. Be sure all the filling ingredients are mashed or very finely minced so that they do not tear the delicate dough.

3. To cook the parotas: Knead the dough a few more times. Divide into 6 equal portions. Oil your palms lightly and roll a portion between your palms to form a smooth ball. Flatten the ball between your palms. On a lightly floured work surface, roll out into a disc about 8½ inches (21 cm) in diameter.

4. Heat 1 teaspoon (5 ml) oil in a nonstick griddle or skillet at least 9 inches (22.5 cm) in diameter. Place a parota on it. When bubbles appear all over the surface, turn the parota. Drizzle ½ teaspoon (2 ml) more oil around the edges of the parota if the griddle is dry.

5. Cook until the bottom becomes mottled with light brown spots. Drizzle 2 tablespoons (30 ml) of the egg mixture over the surface and spread to within ¼ inch (6 mm) of the edge. With the help of a spatula, lift half of the parota and fold it onto the other half to enclose the filling. Cook for a few seconds to set the egg. (You can lift the top edge very slightly to see if the egg is cooked. Do not overcook or the egg will dry out.) The whole process should take about 1½ minutes. Remove from the griddle and serve immediately.

Makes 6 parotas.

Serving suggestions: Serve with tea, as a snack with Ginger-Raisin Chutney, or in place of rice with a vegetarian dinner.

Gajarer Parota
CARROT-FILLED PAN BREAD

As you unfold the delicate layers of this tasty bread, an aroma drifts up from the stuffing, which is dotted with pretty bits of orange, yellow, and green vegetables. The bread goes well with any meat or vegetable dish, but is also excellent as an appetizer when dipped in Splendid Cilantro Chutney or Tender Tamarind Chutney. You can serve the savory filling alone as a snack or side dish; in that case, do not mince the carrots too finely.

For the filling:

2 Tbs. (30 ml) vegetable oil (mustard oil preferred)
¼ tsp. (1 ml) kalonji seeds

¼ tsp. (1 ml) turmeric
1 Tbs. (15 ml) peeled, minced fresh ginger
2 tsp. (10 ml) seeded, chopped fresh green chili (or to taste)
½ tsp. (2 ml) salt
1 cup (250 ml) very finely minced or mashed cooked carrots
1 cup (250 ml) mashed, peeled, cooked baking potatoes
¼ tsp. (1 ml) garam masala
1 Tbs. (15 ml) fresh lime or lemon juice
2 Tbs. (30 ml) finely chopped fresh cilantro

For the dough:
1 dough recipe from Flaky Bread with Zippy Egg Filling
Vegetable oil for pan-frying, as needed

1. To prepare the filling: Heat oil in a nonstick skillet, about 10 inches (25 cm) in diameter, over medium low heat. Fry kalonji seeds for a few seconds. Stir in turmeric, ginger, green chili, and salt and fry for a minute. Add carrots and fry for 2 minutes, stirring often. (The carrots will absorb the oil and the skillet will become dry.) Add potato and continue to cook for several minutes, stirring often. Remove from heat. Blend in garam masala, lime juice, and cilantro. Transfer to a bowl and let cool.
2. To prepare the parota dough: Follow step 1 of the recipe for Flaky Bread with Zippy Egg Filling.
3. Knead the dough a few more times. Divide into 8 equal portions. Roll each into a smooth ball between the palms of your hands. On a floured work surface, roll out one portion into a flat disc about 6 inches (15 cm) in diameter. Place 2 tablespoons (30 ml) of the filling on the center of the disc and spread evenly to about ¼ inch (6 mm) from the edges. Roll another disc of similar size and place on top of the filled disc. Moisten the meeting surfaces and pinch the edges together, making sure they are completely sealed.
4. Heat a lightly oiled griddle until it begins to smoke, then turn heat to low. Place a parota on the griddle and spoon 1 teaspoon (5 ml) oil all around the edges. As soon as brown spots appear all over the bottom, flip the bread and cook the other side, adding a little more oil if necessary. The whole process will take about 1½ to 2 minutes; these parotas need to be cooked slowly so that they will cook inside. Remove from heat.

Makes 8 parotas.

Serving suggestions: Serve immediately, or reheat briefly in the oven just before serving (see "Flatbread Tips" in this section).

Matarsutir Kachuri
PEA-FILLED PUFFED BUNS

When fresh peas arrived at the market, I would pester my mother to make these teatime snacks. This savory tidbit intensified the taste of tea. Instead of deep-frying them as is the tradition, I cook them on a griddle like a parota. They are less puffy this way, but equally tasty.

For the dough:
1 dough recipe from Flaky Bread with Zippy Egg Filling

For the filling:
1 cup (250 ml) thawed frozen peas
1½ Tbs. (22 ml) vegetable oil (mustard oil preferred)
½ tsp. (2 ml) asafetida powder
1 Tbs. (15 ml) peeled, minced fresh ginger
1 tsp. (5 ml) seeded, chopped fresh green chili (or to taste)
¼ tsp. (1 ml) fennel seeds, roasted and ground
¼ tsp. (1 ml) salt
Dash ground red chili or cayenne pepper (or to taste)
½ tsp. (2 ml) garam masala
Vegetable oil for pan-frying, as needed

1. Prepare the dough following step 1 of Flaky Bread with Zippy Egg Filling.
2. While the dough rests, prepare the filling: Crush the peas using a mortar and pestle, a rolling pin, or a flat, heavy utensil such as a skillet. The peas need not be very smooth. Set aside.
3. Heat oil in a skillet over medium low heat. Sprinkle asafetida over the oil. Add ginger and green chili and stir for about a minute. Add the crushed peas, fennel, salt, and red pepper and mix well. Fry for 2 minutes, stirring constantly. Remove from heat. Mix in garam masala. Transfer the pea mixture to a bowl and let cool to room temperature.
4. Proceed with steps 3 and 4 of Carrot-filled Pan Bread.
Makes 8 buns.

Serving suggestions: Same as for Carrot-filled Pan Bread.

Dhakai Parota
BANQUET BREAD

This was popular in the kitchens of Moslem kings, where cooks would spend hours rolling and rerolling the dough. The result was a delicate, flaky bread with many thin layers. They are less elaborate these days, but are still appreciated as a fine bread. This version of parota is a specialty of Dhaka, now the capital of Bangladesh.

For the dough:

1 dough recipe from Flaky Bread with Zippy Egg Filling
Additional vegetable oil for brushing
Additional flour for dusting
Vegetable oil for pan-frying

1. Prepare the dough following step 1 of Flaky Bread with Zippy Egg Filling. Divide into 8 equal parts.
2. On a lightly floured work surface, roll out one portion into a disc 6 inches (15 cm) in diameter. Brush the top lightly with oil. Using a knife, cut a line from the center to the edge. Lift one cut edge and roll it around the circle to form a cone whose point is at the center of the disc. Place the pointed side down and flatten the cone with your palm. (It will resemble a cinnamon roll.) Using a rolling pin, roll out again into a 6-inch (15 cm) disc. Repeat the process three times. The repeated flattening and rerolling create tiny air pockets, which help make the bread puffy.
3. Proceed with step 4 of Carrot-filled Pan Bread to pan-fry the parotas.
Makes 8 parotas.

Serving suggestions: Serve in place of rice with any meat or vegetarian dish.

Luchi
PUFFED BREAD

Luchis are close to the hearts of Bengalis everywhere and are a must at wedding ceremonies. They puff up like little balloons when immersed in hot oil, acquiring a light, flaky texture. "Your cheeks are like luchis" is a fond expression for a child with dimples.

1 cup plus 1 Tbs. (265 ml) all purpose flour
1 tsp. (5 ml) baking powder
1 Tbs. (15 ml) vegetable oil
6 Tbs. (90 ml) warm water
Additional flour for dusting
Vegetable oil for deep-frying

1. Sift flour and baking powder into a bowl. Make a well in the center, add oil, and blend with your fingers until the mixture resembles coarse crumbs. Gradually add water to form a dough that holds together. Knead until dough is soft and pliable, 5 to 10 minutes. Cover with a damp cloth and let rest at room temperature for at least 30 minutes.

2. Pinch off a portion of the dough and make a ball about 1¾ inches (4 cm) in diameter by rolling between the palms of your hands. On a lightly floured work surface, roll out into a disc about 4½ inches (11 cm) in diameter and ¹⁄₁₆ inch (1½ mm) thick; if rolled too thin, it may not puff up. Shake off excess flour.

3. Heat oil in a deep-fat fryer or saucepan to 375°F (190°C). Carefully drop a disc into the hot oil. It will rise to the surface and puff up immediately, either entirely or in several places. Remove with a slotted spatula and drain on paper towels. Since they cook in a few seconds, I fry one luchi at a time.

Makes 7 to 8 luchis.

Serving suggestions: Traditionally, luchis are served at teatime with Potatoes Braised in a Tart Sauce or at a meal with a well-sauced lamb dish. You can also serve a luchi, lightly sprinkled with powdered sugar, as a snack. Or serve as a dessert with the cream sauce from Milk Balls in Rich Saffron Cream Sauce.

Luchi Tips

■ For a wholesome variation, prepare luchis using one of the wholewheat doughs described in the recipe for Soft Bread. These brown puffs are called pooris.

■ Since luchis are deep-fried, I serve only one or two per person on special occasions, supplementing the carbohydrate in the meal with Plain Boiled Rice. Luchis add variety, taste, and texture to a meal.

■ Luchis made with white flour are supposed to have a yellowish-white color. Do not keep them in hot oil any longer than necessary as they will turn brown.

FISH AND SEAFOOD

Among my fondest childhood memories are images of Bengali fishermen landing their catch on the banks of the Ganges. In the silent hours of dawn they carried the fish to eager shoppers swarming through the market.

Fish is a symbol of prosperity and wealth. Ritual pictures drawn during ceremonial occasions on entranceways and walls, pots and pitchers often show a whole fish.

My father and I would arrive to find hundreds of fish, some still alive and jumping, displayed on platforms. Each vendor proclaimed he had the freshest catch and the best prices. "Buy this *rui*," one would shout, "and you'll eat like a king tonight." My father would bargain for a shad, a carp, or jumbo prawns and carry our purchase home in a jute bag. Together we would present it to my mother. "Oh! What a lovely *eelish*," my mother would exclaim, as her face lit up.

To hide a fish with greens
> —Bengali proverb meaning to conceal superficially

She then lovingly prepared several sumptuous fish dishes with sauces varying from one day to the next—sweet and hot, sour, pungent, or mild. We would eat fish for both lunch and dinner and never tire of it.

Ingenious Bengali cooks like my mother waste no part of a fish. Fish eggs are considered to be so tasty that they "wake up a dead man," according to a popular Bengali saying. My mother stuffs shredded or ground fish into vegetables and they become a treat at teatime.

Bengalis transform small fish into many culinary delights. They may pickle them, make a savory chutney, or even ferment them. In the typically sultry weather of West Bengal, when the appetite wanes, such highly seasoned morsels quickly revive it.

Fish to a Bengali is what beef is to a Texan: Bengalis are enamored of it. The early settlers of Bengal depended on fish as one of their mainstays. Age-old cooking techniques, exotic spices, and love of fish combine to make the fish cookery of Bengal one of the most distinguished in the world.

Prawns, the most popular shellfish in Bengal, are dressed in many imaginative styles such as Prawns in Coconut Cream Sauce. This extraordinary dish, made with fresh coconut milk, is reserved for special occasions. Another splendid taste is prawns and potatoes cooked with black mustard paste.

The Bengali expression "a shallow-water fish" refers to an insignificant person, whereas "a deep-water fish" is a noble person.

Other shellfish take equally well to these delicate treatments. I have adapted recipes to use with shellfish that are available in the West but not usually eaten in Bengal. Scallops produce spectacular results when complemented by thick, rich white poppyseed sauce. Mussels or clams are excellent when simmered in a light, flavorful gravy.

The seafood and other fish come from the coastal areas and the innumerable rivers, lakes, and ponds that dominate Bengal's landscape. In the past, Bengalis preferred freshwater fish—*eelish, rui,* and *pooti*—to ocean fish. The rising prices of freshwater fish, however, have forced many households to reconsider the ocean catch. Although markets in the West don't sell the same types of river fish, it isn't hard to find satisfactory substitutes. I have tested Bengali recipes extensively with fish commonly available in North America—salmon, cod, halibut, rock cod, mackerel, fresh tuna, swordfish, and sturgeon, to name a few. The results have been wonderful.

Except for a spice grinder or, if you want to be authentic, a mortar and pestle, you don't need any special gadgets, utensils, or skills—only a taste for fish.

To fry a fish in its own oil
    —Bengali proverb meaning to get something for nothing

Fish and Seafood Tips

■ Bengalis consider a 4 × 1½ × 1-inch (10 × 4 × 2.5 cm—about 3 ounces/ 75 g or less) piece of fish to be the ideal cooking and serving size. Fish cut in such a size is easier to handle during cooking than a larger fillet, and the sauce penetrates better. Many nutritionists in the West believe 3 to 6 ounces (75 to 175 g) or one to two of these pieces to be an adequate serving size. This is the guideline I have adapted in this book. For larger portions, you can double a recipe or serve a dish to a smaller number of people.

■ When selecting fresh fish, look for shiny skin, clear eyes, and fresh gills. The flesh should spring back when pressed with the finger.

■ You can use the fish of your choice in preparing these recipes. The best are those with a firm texture such as salmon, fresh tuna, halibut, mackerel, and swordfish. Salmon works well with all fish recipes in this book.

Do not confuse yellowtail (hamachi), used in making sushi in Japanese restaurants and a choice fish for many of these recipes, with yellowtail snapper from the Caribbean. For dishes that specifically call for hamachi, snapper will not substitute well. You can, however, use snapper in many of the other recipes.

■ Before starting, wash the fish or shellfish and pat the pieces dry. In many recipes, the fish or shellfish is dusted with turmeric and salt before cooking. This eliminates any fishy smell and also helps prevent the seafood from sticking to the pan.

■ Serve seafoods (especially those with thin sauces) in individual bowls to keep the sauce from mixing with other food on the plate.

■ Since the heat of a chili intensifies the flavor of crab, you may add more than the usual amount of chili, use a hotter variety, or incorporate some of the seeds.

■ You need little or no salt when cooking crabs, clams, or mussels, since their juice provides sufficient salinity.

- Use steaming clams, such as Manila, steamer, or butter clams, for these recipes. Do not use horse clams, razor clams, or geoducks. These have tough meat and require pounding or chopping.

- *Initial frying of fish:* Another place to cut down on fat is in the initial frying of fish. Fish (or prawns or shrimp) is fried in 2 tablespoons (30 ml) oil. The idea here is not to brown the fish but merely to sear it and seal in the juices. To lower the fat content, you can fry it in 1 tablespoon (15 ml) oil in a nonstick skillet. Turn heat to medium and fry for a few seconds. Remove the fish as it becomes firm and opaque so that it does not have a chance to absorb much of the oil.

- *Test for doneness:* Remove the lid (or if steaming, open the pouch). Fish and shellfish (except for clams and mussels) are done when a toothpick inserted in the thickest part and moved gently sideways shows an opaque color within. For clams and mussels, check their respective recipes.

    Overcooking seafood makes it either tough and dry or mushy. Follow the time given in each recipe as a guide, adjusting it, whenever necessary, to the thickness of the ingredient.

Shorshe Diyea Eelish Maach
STEAMED FISH IN CHILI-MUSTARD SAUCE

"It's caviar to me." So says my Uncle Sukumar, referring to this elegant dish made with eelish, a shadlike fish. Bengalis debate whether eelish from the Ganges have more flavor than those from the Padma River. One thing everyone agrees on is that the sauce, intensely flavored with green chili and mustard, tastes delicious with rice.

You can use any fish, although salmon and halibut as well as fresh prawns adapt particularly well to this sauce.

Traditionally the fish is wrapped in banana leaves and steamed alone or placed on top of simmering rice. Banana leaves impart a musky, smoky fragrance to the fish. See "Dishes for the Adventurous" chapter.

"THE SILVER SEASON"
The popular eelish is especially tasty and plentiful during monsoon (June–July) or winter months (December–January). Fishermen rejoice at the piles of freshly caught eelish, gleaming with a silvery sheen.

For the marinade:

1½ tsp. (7 ml) black mustard seeds, ground to a fine powder and mixed with
   3 Tbs. (15 ml) water
1 tsp. (5 ml) seeded, chopped fresh green chili (or to taste)
¼ tsp. (1 ml) turmeric
¼ tsp. (1 ml) salt
3 to 4 Tbs. (45 to 60 ml) mustard oil (see Note 1)

1 to 1¼ lb. (½ kg to 675 g) fish, cut into 4 × 1½ × 1-inch (10 × 4 ×
   2.5 cm) pieces, or raw prawns, shelled and deveined

1. Combine black mustard paste, green chili, turmeric, salt, and mustard
   oil in a bowl (the larger amount of oil will yield more sauce). Add fish,
   tossing gently to coat each piece with marinade. Cover and refrigerate
   for 30 minutes.
       Use any of the following three methods to prepare the fish: steam-
   ing, braising, or steaming over rice. (See "Test for doneness" under
   "Fish and Seafood Tips" in this chapter.)
2. To steam the fish: Steam 10 to 12 minutes or until done. (See "To steam
   fish or shellfish" under "Cooking Techniques.")
3. To braise the fish: Place the fish and marinade in an ungreased skillet
   over low heat. Cover tightly and cook until done, 8 to 12 minutes, stirring occasionally to prevent sticking.
4. To steam the fish over rice: Wrap fish and marinade in a pouch made
   from a single layer of a piece of heavy-duty aluminum foil (see Note 2).
   Seal the edges tightly so that no water can seep through. Cook rice
   according to the directions given under "Plain Boiled Rice" in the rice
   chapter. When most of the water has been absorbed (10 to 15 minutes
   for long-grain white rice), place the aluminum pouch on top. Cover the
   pan tightly and simmer until fish is done, 10 to 12 minutes. (Rice should
   also be ready at about the same time. If not, remove fish but continue to
   cook the rice.)
       Garnish with cilantro and serve immediately.

3 to 4 servings.

Serving suggestions: For a quick family meal, serve with rice and Fiery
Potatoes. I often serve this easy and unusual dish to company with Basmati
rice, Smoked Eggplant in Creamy Sauce (or Yellow Crookneck Squash in
Coriander–Red Chili Sauce), and Splendid Cilantro Chutney.

Note 1: Lowfat alternatives: If possible, do not reduce the amount of oil in
the marinade. The unheated oil simply forms a flavorful cooking medium
for the fish, and the combination of succulent fish juices, mustard oil, and

mustard paste makes a superb gravy for rice. If you prefer, serve each diner only a teaspoon (5 ml) of the tasty sauce, or use half mustard oil and half water.

Note 2: If you double this recipe, place fish in two separate foil pouches so as not to crowd them together.

VARIATION

STEAMED FISH IN GINGER-MUSTARD SAUCE

Add 1 tablespoon (15 ml) peeled fresh ginger, grated or made into a paste (see "A Glossary of Spices and Ingredients"), to the above marinade.

Maacher Jhal
STEAMED FISH IN CHILI-CILANTRO SAUCE

Mustard oil is a must, and green chili and cilantro add a fresh, clean taste to this simple dish. Most fish take well to this sauce, but salmon, black cod, fresh tuna, fresh sardines, and prawns are especially good.

For the marinade:

1 Tbs. (15 ml) seeded, chopped fresh green chili, made into a paste
  (see "A Glossary of Spices and Ingredients")
½ cup (125 ml) cilantro leaves, made into a paste (see "A Glossary of
  Spices and Ingredients")
¼ tsp. (1 ml) salt
⅛ tsp. (.5 ml) black pepper (preferably freshly ground)
3 Tbs. (45 ml) mustard oil, or 2 Tbs. (30 ml) mustard oil and 1 Tbs.
  (15 ml) water
1½ lb. (750 g) fish, cut into 4 × 1½ × 1-inch (10 × 4 × 2.5 cm) pieces, or
  raw prawns, shelled and deveined

1. Combine chili paste, cilantro paste, salt, black pepper, and mustard oil in a large bowl. Add fish, tossing gently to coat each piece.
2. You can either steam or braise the fish. If steaming, see "A Glossary of Spices and Ingredients" for instructions. Otherwise, place fish and marinade in an ungreased skillet over low heat. Simmer, covered, until fish is done, 8 to 10 minutes, turning the pieces once. Serve immediately. If

allowed to stand, the sauce darkens, losing its lovely green color. This does not, however, affect its flavor.

4 servings.

Serving suggestions: The clean taste and greenish hue of this sauce are complemented by the orange color and pleasant spiciness of Butternut Squash in Mustard Sauce. To carry through with the simplicity theme, you can also serve it with rice, Potatoes Pronto, and Yogurt Coconut Dip.

Maacher Dom
FANCY FISH IN CASHEW-PISTACHIO SAUCE

When I visited India recently, a Bengali housewife named Gita Sarkar served me this dish. Gita comes from Dhaka, the capital of Bangladesh. The elegance of this sauce is characteristic of that city's venerable cuisine. Use any rich, firm-fleshed fish; sturgeon, salmon, albacore tuna, yellowtail (hamachi), halibut, and swordfish are good choices.

½ tsp. (2 ml) turmeric
½ tsp. (2 ml) salt
2 lb. (1 kg) fish, cut into 4 × 1½ × 1-inch (10 × 4 × 2.5 cm) pieces
2½ to 3½ Tbs. (37 to 52 ml) vegetable oil (mustard oil preferred)
1 cup (250 ml) finely chopped onion
1 Tbs. (15 ml) peeled fresh ginger, grated or made into a paste
   (see "A Glossary of Spices and Ingredients")
1 tsp. (5 ml) seeded, chopped fresh green chili (or to taste)
2 Tbs. (30 ml) raw cashews, ground in a blender to a coarse powder
1 Tbs. (15 ml) raw pistachios, ground in a blender to a coarse powder
¾ cup plus 2 Tbs. (200 ml) water

1. In a bowl, combine turmeric and ¼ teaspoon (1 ml) of the salt. Add fish, tossing gently to coat each piece. Set aside.
2. Heat 2 tablespoons (30 ml) oil in a skillet over medium low heat. Fry fish, 4 or 5 pieces at a time, just until opaque, about 1 minute, turning once. Remove with a slotted spatula and set aside. (Or fry fish in 1 tablespoon/15 ml oil. See "Initial frying of fish" under "Fish and Seafood Tips" in this chapter.)
3. Add 1½ tablespoons (22 ml) oil to the skillet and heat it. Fry onion until richly browned but not burnt, about 10 minutes, stirring constantly. Add ginger and green chili and stir a few times. Add cashews,

pistachios, the remaining ¼ teaspoon (1 ml) salt, and water and bring to boil. Simmer, covered, until the sauce thickens, 8 to 10 minutes.

4. Add the fish and any accumulated liquid. Simmer until fish is done, 3 to 5 minutes. (See "Test for doneness" under "Fish and Seafood Tips" in this chapter.) Remove from heat. Garnish with cilantro and serve immediately.

5 to 6 servings.

Serving suggestions: Excellent for entertaining. The rich sauce is balanced by the fresh flavors of Glorious Greens. Also can be served with rice, Spicy Home Fries, and Pleasing Plum Chutney.

Maacher Jhol
FISH IN AROMATIC SAUCE

In Bengal, *rui,* a large carplike fish prized for its rich flavor, is often called "the king of fish." It forms the basis of many boldly sauced dishes. My mother prepares rui using the *jhol* technique. In the West, any richly flavored fish will do, but halibut and black cod (also called sablefish) are particularly good choices.

2 Tbs. (30 ml) vegetable oil (mustard oil preferred)
1 bay leaf
1 whole dried red chili
¼ tsp. (1 ml) five-spice
½ lb. (¼ kg) potatoes (about 2 medium), peeled, cut into 2½-inch (6 cm) cubes
¼ tsp. (1 ml) turmeric
2 tsp. (10 ml) ground cumin
2 tsp. (10 ml) ground coriander
⅛ tsp. (.5 ml) black pepper (preferably freshly ground)
½ tsp. (2 ml) salt
1 tsp. (5 ml) sugar
1 tsp. (5 ml) seeded, chopped fresh green chili (or to taste)
2¼ cups (550 ml) eggplant cut into 2½-inch (6 cm) cubes
¾ cup (175 ml) water
1½ lb. (750 g) fish, cut into 4 × 1½ × 1-inch (10 × 4 × 2.5 cm) pieces
½ tsp. (2 ml) garam masala

1. Heat oil in a skillet over medium low heat. Fry bay leaf and red chili until the chili darkens. Add five-spice and fry for a few seconds. As soon

as the five-spice starts crackling, add potatoes and fry for a minute or so. Add turmeric, cumin, coriander, black pepper, salt, sugar, and green chili and mix well.

2. Add eggplant and water. Bring to boil, then lower heat slightly. Simmer, covered, until the vegetables are tender, 15 to 18 minutes. Gently stir in fish. (See Note.)

3. Simmer, covered, until fish is done, 3 to 5 minutes. (See "Test for doneness" under "Fish and Seafood Tips" in this chapter.) Remove from heat. Gently mix in garam masala. Garnish with cilantro and serve.

4 servings.

Serving suggestions: This Bengali favorite is complemented by a leafy green dish such as Splendid Spinach. It also goes well with rice, Cauliflower with a Hint of Mustard, and Mellow Tomato Chutney.

Note: For a richer taste, sauté the fish separately before adding it in step 2. Do so in 2 tablespoons (30 ml) oil in a nonstick skillet in 2 batches just until opaque on the surface, about 1 minute per batch. (Or, fry in 1 tablespoon (15 ml) oil. See "Initial frying of fish" under "Fish and Seafood Tips" in this chapter.)

Shorshe Diyea Maacher Jhol
FISH BRAISED IN LIGHT MUSTARD SAUCE

My mother, grandmothers, and aunts were all accomplished cooks. The male members of the family were equally knowledgeable about food. At the dinner table we discussed the flavors and seasonings of each dish. I remember one discussion about this celebrated *jhol*-style dish—how a little extra chili enlivens it and how the boris provide textural contrast and soak up the thin, flavorful sauce to become plump and delicious. "It's easy to digest," my mother noted.

It's also easy to prepare. Select a fish of your choice; black cod, sturgeon, halibut, and salmon work especially well.

½ tsp. (2 ml) turmeric
½ tsp. (2 ml) salt
1½ lb. (750 g) fish, cut into 4 × 1½ × 1-inch (10 × 4 × 2.5 cm) pieces
2 Tbs. to 2 Tbs. plus 2 tsp. (30 to 40 ml) mustard oil
1 bay leaf
2 tsp. (10 ml) ground black mustard, mixed with 1 Tbs. (15 ml) water and allowed to stand 30 minutes
2 whole fresh green hot chilies (see Note)

1 cup (250 ml) Boris (optional; see "A Glossary of Spices and
  Ingredients")
¾ cup (175 ml) water
1 Tbs. (15 ml) finely chopped fresh cilantro

1. Combine turmeric and ¼ teaspoon (1 ml) salt in a large bowl. Add fish,
   tossing gently to coat each piece. Set aside.
2. Heat 2 tablespoons (30 ml) oil in a skillet (preferably 12 inches/30 cm
   in diameter if using boris) over medium low heat. Fry fish 4 or 5 pieces
   at a time just until opaque, about 1 minute, turning once. Remove with
   a slotted spoon and set aside.
3. Reheat oil remaining in the skillet over medium low heat. If skillet is too
   dry, add the optional 2 teaspoons (10 ml) oil. Fry bay leaf for a few
   seconds. Add black mustard paste and the remaining ¼ teaspoon (1 ml)
   salt. Add green chilies, boris, and water and bring to boil.
4. Lower heat and simmer, covered, 10 to 12 minutes. Add the fish and any
   accumulated liquid. Simmer, covered, until fish is done, 3 to 5 more
   minutes. (See "Test for doneness" under "Fish and Seafood Tips" in this
   chapter.) Remove from heat; the sauce will be thin. Add cilantro. Serve
   at once in individual bowls.

4 servings.

Serving suggestions: This light dish complements mixed vegetable preparations such as Vegetables in a Mingling Mood or Tender Beginning with
Many Flavors. You can add rice and "Happy Heart" Chutney for a full meal.

Note: The whole chilies are used to add a refreshing taste and not to make
the dish excessively hot. So select a mild variety such as jalapeños. My
mother adds several pods, then discards them before serving.

Kishmisher Maach
FISH IN GINGER-RAISIN SAUCE

You might wonder: raisins with fish? It's the gentle sweetness of raisins combined with a bare hint of ginger that makes this dish tasty and unique. Use
sturgeon, yellowtail (hamachi), salmon, fresh mackerel, or fresh tuna if
possible, as this sauce is meant to complement richly flavored fish. Other
firm-fleshed fish will do, but the result will not be as authentic.

2 Tbs. (30 ml) raisins (golden preferred)
¼ cup (60 ml) hot water
1 Tbs. (15 ml) vegetable oil (mustard oil preferred)

2 bay leaves
¼ tsp. (1 ml) asafetida powder
3 Tbs. (45 ml) peeled, minced fresh ginger
1 tsp. (5 ml) seeded, chopped fresh green chili (or to taste)
½ tsp. (2 ml) turmeric
½ cup (125 ml) water
½ tsp. (2 ml) salt
1½ lb. (750 g) fish, cut into 4 × 1½ × 1-inch (10 × 4 × 2.5 cm) pieces

1. Soak the raisins in the hot water until soft and plump, about 30 minutes. Puree in a blender until smooth, finishing the process with a mortar and pestle if necessary. Set aside.
2. Heat oil in a skillet over medium low heat. Fry bay leaves for a few seconds. Sprinkle asafetida over the leaves. Add ginger and green chili and fry until ginger is lightly browned, about 2 minutes, stirring constantly. Stir in turmeric, water, raisin puree, and salt.
3. Bring to boil, then simmer, covered, until the sauce starts to thicken, 7 to 10 minutes. Add fish and simmer, covered, until fish is done, 3 to 5 minutes. (See "Test for doneness" under "Fish and Seafood Tips" in this chapter.) Remove from heat and let stand covered for a few minutes to help develop the flavors. Garnish with cilantro and serve immediately.

3 servings.

Serving suggestions: For a light meal serve with rice, Fiery Potatoes, and Splendid Cilantro Chutney. For an elaborate meal, substitute Vegetable Pullao for the rice and add Spinach in Spiced Yogurt.

Maacher Chochori
COUNTRY-STYLE FISH AND VEGETABLE STEW

Our love for both fish and vegetables shows in this dish. In a traditional chochori-style dish the ingredients are minced, but here they are cut into larger pieces for eye appeal.

Many variations of this dish exist, each using a particular fish and the vegetables that work best with it. In the West, try any firm-fleshed fish.

Even the bones of a large fish are tasty.
—Bengali proverb meaning that even the small deeds
of a person of admirable character are valuable

Salmon, halibut, sturgeon, swordfish, and catfish are particularly good choices, as their rich juices enhance the flavor of the vegetables.

2 to 4 Tbs. (30 to 60 ml) vegetable oil (mustard oil preferred)
1 lb. (½ kg) fish, cut into 1-inch (2.5 cm) pieces
½ lb. (¼ kg) peeled potatoes (about 2 medium), cut into 1-inch (2.5 cm) cubes
1 cup (250 ml) finely chopped onion
1 Tbs. (15 ml) peeled, minced fresh ginger
1 tsp. (5 ml) seeded, chopped fresh green chili (or to taste)
¼ tsp. (1 ml) turmeric
½ tsp. (2 ml) salt
1 tsp. (5 ml) sugar
¾ cup (175 ml) water
1 to 2 tsp. (5 to 10 ml) red chili paste (see "A Glossary of Spices and Ingredients")
1 cup (250 ml) cauliflower cut into florets 1 inch (2.5 cm) in diameter

1. Heat 2 tablespoons (30 ml) oil in a large skillet over medium low heat. Fry fish just until opaque, about 1 minute, turning once. Remove with a slotted spatula and set aside on a plate. Omit this step for a lower-fat dish.
2. Heat oil remaining in the skillet over medium heat. Fry potatoes until lightly browned, 3 to 5 minutes, turning often. Remove with a slotted spoon and set aside in a bowl. Omit this step for a lower-fat dish; they will be cooked in step 3.
3. Add 2 tablespoons (30 ml) oil to the skillet. Fry onion until translucent, about 2 minutes, stirring constantly. Add ginger, green chili, turmeric, salt, and sugar and fry for a minute or so. Add water and red chili paste and bring to boil. Add the potatoes. Lower the heat slightly and simmer, covered, 6 to 8 minutes.
4. Add cauliflower and simmer, covered, until both potatoes and cauliflower are almost done, 8 to 10 more minutes. Add fish and simmer, covered, until done, another 3 to 5 minutes (see "Test for doneness" under "Fish and Seafood Tips" in this chapter). Sprinkle with cilantro and serve.

4 servings.

Serving suggestions: A potluck and buffet favorite. Accompanied by rice, Peanut-topped Greens, and Joyous Ginger-Raisin Chutney, this fish stew can be the centerpiece of a family meal.

Maacher Kalia

FISH IN CREAMY SAUCE WITH CARROTS, POTATOES, AND PEAS

On "Son-in-law's day" in Bengal, a man is usually served an elaborate meal by his mother-in-law. The meal may feature a tasty yogurt-sauced fish dish like this one, which is accented by the orange color of carrots, brilliant green peas, and golden-hued potatoes. Firm-fleshed fish such as fresh tuna, halibut, or sturgeon is the best choice, but even a tender fish like black cod works well if handled with care.

½ tsp. (2 ml) turmeric
½ tsp. (2 ml) salt
1½ lb. (750 g) fish, cut into 4 × 1½ × 1-inch (10 × 4 × 2.5 cm)
  pieces
2 to 4 Tbs. (30 to 60 ml) vegetable oil (mustard oil preferred)
½ lb. (¼ kg) potatoes (about 2 medium), peeled and cut into 1-inch
  (2.5 cm) cubes
1 bay leaf
5 whole cardamom pods
2-inch (5 cm) cinnamon stick
2 whole cloves
¼ tsp. (1 ml) asafetida powder
1 Tbs. (15 ml) peeled fresh ginger, grated or made into a paste
  (see "A Glossary of Spices and Ingredients")
1 Tbs. (15 ml) garlic, forced through a garlic press or made into a paste
  (see "A Glossary of Spices and Ingredients")
1 tsp. (5 ml) seeded, chopped fresh green chili (or to taste)
1 tsp. (5 ml) sugar
½ cup (125 ml) carrots cut crosswise into ¼-inch (6 mm) rounds
½ cup (125 ml) water
½ cup (125 ml) thawed frozen peas
1½ Tbs. (22 ml) plain yogurt, lightly beaten until smooth
½ tsp. (2 ml) garam masala

1. In a bowl combine turmeric and ¼ teaspoon (1 ml) of the salt. Add fish, tossing gently to coat each piece. Set aside.
2. Heat 2 tablespoons (30 ml) oil in a 12-inch (30 cm) skillet over medium heat. Fry potatoes until medium brown, 5 to 7 minutes, turning frequently. Remove with a slotted spatula and set aside. Omit this step for a lower-fat dish; the potatoes will be cooked in step 4.

3. Add 1 tablespoon (15 ml) oil to the skillet and heat over medium low heat. Fry fish, 5 or 6 pieces at a time, just until opaque, turning once. Remove with a slotted spatula and set aside on a plate.

4. Add 1 tablespoon (15 ml) more oil to the skillet and heat over medium low heat. Fry bay leaf, cardamom, cinnamon, and cloves for 5 seconds. Sprinkle asafetida over the spices. Stir in ginger, garlic, green chili, sugar, and the remaining ¼ teaspoon (1 ml) salt and fry for several seconds. Add the potatoes, carrots, and water. Simmer, covered, until the vegetables are almost tender, 15 to 18 minutes, stirring occasionally and adding a tablespoon (15 ml) of water if necessary to prevent sticking.

5. Add peas, fish, and any accumulated liquid. Simmer, covered, until fish is done, an additional 3 to 5 minutes. (See "Test for doneness" under "Fish and Seafood Tips" in this chapter.) Gently transfer fish to a plate with a slotted spatula. Add yogurt to the sauce and mix well. Remove from heat and blend in garam masala. Return fish to the pan. Garnish with cilantro and serve piping hot.

4 to 5 servings.

Serving suggestions: This kalia can be served simply with rice and a condiment such as Mellow Tomato Chutney. For an elaborate meal, add Crisp Fried Eggplant or Rich Roasted Eggplant.

Maacher Tel Jhol

FRAGRANT FISH IN SILKY-THIN SAUCE

This light, aromatic sauce tastes extraordinary, especially during the summer heat. In Bengal we prepare the dish with *pabda*, a silvery river fish. Substitute a firm-fleshed and preferably nonoily fish such as cod, red snapper, walleyed pike, or yellow perch.

½ tsp. (2 ml) turmeric
½ tsp. (2 ml) salt
2 lb. (1 kg) fish, cut into 4 × 1½ × 1-inch (10 × 4 × 2.5 cm) pieces
2 to 2½ Tbs. (30 to 37 ml) mustard oil
2 bay leaves
1 whole dried red chili
¼ tsp. (1 ml) five-spice
1 tsp. (5 ml) seeded, chopped fresh green chili (or to taste)
¼ cup (60 ml) water

1. In a bowl, combine turmeric and ¼ teaspoon (1 ml) salt. Add fish, toss-ing gently to coat each piece. Set aside.
2. Heat 2 tablespoons (30 ml) oil in a 12-inch (30 cm) skillet over medium low heat. Fry fish, 5 or 6 pieces at a time, just until opaque, about 1 min-ute, turning once. Remove with a slotted spatula and set aside on a plate.
3. If the skillet is too dry for frying, add the remaining ½ tablespoon (7 ml) oil. Heat over medium low heat. Fry bay leaves and red chili until the chili darkens. Add five-spice and fry until the spices start spluttering. Add green chili, the remaining ¼ teaspoon (1 ml) salt, and water and bring to simmer. Lower the heat to maintain the simmer. Add the fish and any accumulated liquid. Simmer, covered, until fish is done, 3 to 5 minutes. (See "Test for doneness" under "Fish and Seafood Tips" in this chapter.) Remove from heat. Let stand covered for 10 minutes to help develop the flavors. Garnish with cilantro and serve.

5 to 6 servings.

Serving suggestions: For a meal that celebrates many flavors, I serve this five-spice-enriched fish with rice, Tender Garden Peas and Potatoes, and Spinach in Spiced Yogurt.

Tel Koi

FISH BRAISED WITH GINGER AND RED CHILI PUREE

The dominant flavor in this easily prepared but delectable dish is that of fresh ginger. Freshly ground dried red chili paste and mustard oil also add to its appeal. In Bengal we use *koi*, a river fish sold live, which is similar to the freshwater black bass common to North American lakes. "As sprightly as a *koi*" is an expression that refers to any particularly fresh ingredient.

In the West the best choice is a fish with a high oil content, such as salmon, mackerel, albacore tuna, or yellowtail (hamachi). I also tested the recipe with prawns and, while not authentic, they work especially well. You can braise, steam, or bake the fish. If using a whole mackerel, butterfly it; marinate it in double the amount of marinade and bake it. The traditional way is to cover the fish with oil, but I have significantly reduced the amount of oil and find the dish to be tasty just the same.

For the marinade:
3 Tbs. (45 ml) peeled fresh ginger, grated or made into a paste
  (see "A Glossary of Spices and Ingredients")

2 to 3 tsp. (10 to 15 ml) dried red chili paste (see "A Glossary of Spices and Ingredients")
½ tsp. (2 ml) turmeric
½ tsp. (2 ml) salt
¼ cup (60 ml) mustard oil, or half mustard oil and half water

2 lb. (1 kg) fish, cut into 4 × 1½ × 1-inch (10 × 4 × 2.5 cm) pieces, or raw prawns (large shrimp), shelled and deveined

1. Combine the marinade ingredients in a bowl. Add fish, tossing gently to coat each piece. Cover and refrigerate for 30 minutes.
    See "Test for doneness" under "Fish and Seafood Tips" in this chapter when following any of the following cooking methods.
2. To braise: Place fish and the marinade in an ungreased skillet over medium low heat. Cover and cook until fish is done, 8 to 15 minutes.
3. To steam: See "To steam fish and shellfish" under "Cooking Techniques."
4. To bake: Preheat oven to 350°F (180°C; gas mark 4). Bake fish until done, 10 to 15 minutes.
    Garnish with cilantro and serve.

5 to 6 servings.

Serving suggestions: Try rice, Golden Potatoes in Poppyseed Sauce (or Steamed Spicy Cauliflower), and Pleasing Plum Chutney.

Maach Bhaja
CRISP FRIED FISH

A most popular dish. In Bengal a meal often starts with rice, dal, and a small piece of fried fish. Later you may be served another fish or meat dish, prepared in a spicy sauce that is accompanied by more rice. But this small piece of delicious fried fish stirs an air of anticipation among the diners. A wide variety of fish are suitable for frying. Among the more popular types are salmon, halibut, swordfish, or ling cod.

For the marinade:

½ tsp. (2 ml) salt
3 Tbs. (45 ml) fresh lime or lemon juice
1 Tbs. (15 ml) peeled fresh ginger, grated or made into a paste (see "A Glossary of Spices and Ingredients")
½ tsp. (2 ml) turmeric

Vegetable oil for deep-frying
1½ lb. (750 g) fish, cut into 2½ × 1½ × 1-inch (6 cm × 4 cm × 2.5 cm)
   pieces
1 to 2 Tbs. (15 to 30 ml) ground cumin

1. Just before cooking, mix salt, lime, ginger, and turmeric in a large bowl.
   Add fish, tossing gently to coat each piece.
2. Heat oil in a deep-fat fryer or saucepan to 375°F (180°C). Preheat oven
   to 200°F (110°C; gas mark ¼). Pick up a fish piece with a pair of tongs
   and allow excess marinade to drain back into the bowl. Carefully drop
   fish into the oil and fry until golden brown. Drain on paper towels.
   Repeat with remaining fish pieces. Sprinkle lightly with cumin and serve
   at once, or keep warm in the oven until all fish is fried. Serve a piece to
   each diner as an accompaniment to any meal.

5 to 6 servings.

Besan Diyea Maach Bhaja
FRAGRANT FISH FRY

Fish is also excellent when dipped in a fragrant chickpea flour batter and
then deep-fried.

1 cup (250 ml) besan (chickpea flour)
1 cup (250 ml) water
¼ tsp. (1 ml) salt
Dash ground red chili or cayenne pepper (or to taste)
1 recipe for marinade as described in Crisp Fried Fish
1½ lb. (750 g) firm-fleshed fish, cut into 2½ × 1½ × 1-inch
   (6 cm × 4 cm × 2.5 cm) pieces
Vegetable oil for deep-frying
1 to 2 Tbs. (15 to 30 ml) ground cumin
1 to 2 Tbs. (15 to 30 ml) fennel seeds, roasted and ground

1. In a bowl gradually mix besan with water, stirring constantly so that no
   lumps remain. Add salt and red pepper. Let the batter rest while you
   ready the fish.
2. Prepare the marinade and marinate the fish as in step 1 of Crisp Fried
   Fish. Dip a piece of marinated fish in the batter. Deep-fry as for Crisp
   Fried Fish. Before serving, sprinkle lightly with cumin and fennel.

Chingri Maacher Malai Kari
PRAWNS IN COCONUT CREAM SAUCE

Served on special occasions, this opulent dish has a regal appearance. It outshines many of our other extraordinary fish dishes. When my sister serves this dish, prepared with fresh coconut milk, there is silence at the table, except for the smacking of lips and occasional muffled exclamations of "Oh! so good." In Bengal, the milk extracted from a whole coconut would be used. I have reduced the amount of coconut milk but the dish remains a favorite.

½ tsp. (2 ml) turmeric
½ tsp. (2 ml) salt
1½ lb. (750 g) prawns (large shrimp), shelled and deveined; fish (such as salmon or halibut), cut into 4 × 1½ × 1-inch (10 × 4 × 2.5 cm) pieces; or scallops
2½ to 3½ Tbs. (37 to 52 ml) vegetable oil (mustard oil preferred)
1 bay leaf
5 whole cardamom pods
1 cup (250 ml) finely chopped onion
2 Tbs. (30 ml) peeled, minced fresh ginger
1 Tbs. (15 ml) minced garlic
½ tsp. (2 ml) sugar
Dash ground red chili or cayenne pepper (or to taste)
1 cup (250 ml) fresh or unsweetened canned coconut milk, stirred until evenly mixed, or ¾ cup (175 ml) coconut milk and ¼ cup (60 ml) water
1 Tbs. (15 ml) raw cashews, ground in a blender to a coarse powder

1. Combine turmeric and ¼ teaspoon (1 ml) salt in a bowl. Add prawns, tossing gently to coat each piece.
2. Heat 2 tablespoons (30 ml) oil in a 10-inch (25 cm) or larger skillet over medium heat. Fry prawns 5 or 6 at a time, turning once, just until they change color, about 1 minute; fry fish or scallops just until opaque. Remove with a slotted spatula and set aside on a plate. (Or fry in 1 tablespoon/15 ml oil. See "Initial frying of fish" under "Fish and Seafood Tips" in this chapter.)
3. Add the remaining 1½ tablespoons (15 ml) oil to the pan and heat over medium low heat. Fry bay leaf and cardamom for a few seconds. Fry onion until richly browned but not burnt, 8 to 10 minutes, stirring constantly. Add ginger, garlic, sugar, remaining ¼ teaspoon (1 ml) salt, and red pepper and fry for a minute. Turn heat to low. Remove pan from heat. Add coconut milk, stir a few times, then return to heat, keeping

heat low from this point. (Excessive heat will cause the coconut milk to curdle, affecting its appearance and texture, but the sauce will still taste good.) Cook uncovered, stirring constantly, until the sauce thickens, 7 to 10 minutes.

3. Add the prawns and any accumulated liquid. Cook uncovered until done, 5 to 8 minutes. (See "Test for doneness" under "Fish and Seafood Tips" in this chapter.) If using scallops, cook 3 to 5 minutes. Gently stir in cashews. Let stand covered for a few minutes to help develop the flavors. Remove from heat. Sprinkle with cilantro and serve.

4 servings.

Serving suggestions: For entertaining, make room on the table for Basmati rice, Splendid Spinach (or Potatoes Braised in Rich Tart Sauce), and "Happy Heart" Chutney.

Chingri Posto Diyea
PRAWNS IN POPPYSEED SAUCE

The opulent, nutty poppyseed sauce combines well with shellfish such as prawns. This easily prepared dish exudes an aura of luxury. "You take a bite and think of the days when time was forever," said an elderly Bengali man.

2½ to 3½ Tbs. (37 to 52 ml) vegetable oil (mustard oil preferred)
1½ lb. (750 g) prawns (large shrimp), shelled and deveined, or fish such as
   salmon or halibut, cut into 4 × 1½ × 1-inch (10 × 4 × 2.5 cm) pieces
1 cup (250 ml) finely chopped onion
1 tsp. (5 ml) seeded, chopped fresh green chili (or to taste)
¼ tsp. (1 ml) turmeric
½ tsp. (2 ml) salt
2 Tbs. (30 ml) white poppyseeds, made into a paste (see "A Glossary of
   Spices and Ingredients")
1 cup (250 ml) water
Garnish: red bell pepper strips

1. Heat 2 tablespoons (30 ml) oil in a skillet over medium heat. Fry the prawns or fish 5 or 6 at a time just until they turn pink (or turn opaque in the case of fish), about 1 minute, stirring constantly. Remove with a slotted spatula and set aside on a plate. (Or fry prawns or fish in 1 tablespoon/15 ml oil. See "Initial frying of fish" under "Fish and Seafood Tips" in this chapter.)

3. Add 1½ tablespoons (22 ml) oil to the skillet and heat over medium low heat. Fry onion until richly browned but not burnt, 7 to 10 minutes, stirring constantly. Stir in green chili, turmeric, and salt. Add poppy paste and water and stir until the paste is dissolved. Simmer, covered, 10 minutes.
4. Add the reserved seafood and simmer, covered, 3 to 5 minutes or until done. (See "Test for doneness" under "Fish and Seafood Tips" in this chapter.) Remove from heat. Let stand covered for a few minutes to help develop the flavors. Garnish with pepper strips and cilantro and serve immediately.

4 servings.

Serving suggestions: Excellent at a buffet table. For a family meal, serve with Aromatic Rice with Peas and Whole Spices, Wedding-Day Greens, and Splendid Cilantro Chutney.

VARIATION

SCALLOPS IN POPPYSEED SAUCE

Scallops are excellent when cooked in this thick, rich sauce. They need to be cooked gently, as overcooking toughens them. Follow the recipe above, using 1 pound (½ kg) scallops and, in step 1, frying for a few seconds or until they are opaque.

Chingrir Korma
PRAWN PLEASURE

Pink prawns bathe in a pool of red tomato sauce laced with ground hot spices. If you live in the Pacific Northwest, buy Alaskan spot prawns, the best choice for this dish. You can also substitute fish such as salmon, halibut, or black cod.

2 Tbs. (30 ml) vegetable oil (mustard oil preferred)
1 cup (250 ml) finely chopped onion
1 Tbs. (15 ml) minced garlic
1 Tbs. (15 ml) peeled, minced fresh ginger
½ tsp. (2 ml) turmeric
4 Roma or 2 regular tomatoes, peeled and seeded (see "A Glossary of Spices and Ingredients")
½ tsp. (2 ml) salt

Dash ground red chili or cayenne pepper (or to taste)

1½ lb. (750 g) prawns (large shrimp), shelled and deveined, or fish, cut into 4 × 1½ × 1-inch (10 × 4 × 2.5 cm) pieces

1 Tbs. (15 ml) plain yogurt

¼ tsp. (1 ml) garam masala

1. Heat oil in a deep pan or skillet over medium low heat. Fry onion until richly browned but not burnt, 8 to 10 minutes, stirring constantly. Add garlic and ginger and stir several times. Add turmeric and mix well.
2. Add tomatoes, salt, and red pepper. Lower the heat. Cook, covered, 20 minutes, stirring occasionally and adding a tablespoon (15 ml) of water if mixture sticks to the bottom of the pan. Don't add any more water than necessary.
3. Add prawns and simmer until pinkish-red, 5 to 10 minutes. (See "Test for doneness" under "Fish and Seafood Tips" in this chapter.) Turn heat to very low. Remove from heat, add yogurt, and mix well. Return to heat for only a few seconds to warm up the mixture. Remove from heat. Blend in garam masala. Let stand covered for a few minutes to develop the flavors. Sprinkle cilantro on top.

4 servings.

Serving suggestions: For a family meal serve this korma with rice, Butternut Squash in Mustard Sauce, and Splendid Cilantro Chutney.

Lau Chingri

TENDER BABY SHRIMP IN DELICATE TURNIP SAUCE

This is a case where a few well-chosen ingredients fashion a classic dish. The pink bay shrimp float in a lustrous yellow-tinted sauce thickened with pureed vegetables. Black kalonji seeds provide a faint onion taste, and coconut milk adds a rich, subtle fragrance.

In Bengal we prepare this dish with bottle gourd, a pale green vegetable that resembles cucumber. Since it is not readily available in the West, I substitute turnip or kohlrabi. The result is quite similar and utterly delicious.

2 cups (1 liter) peeled turnip or kohlrabi, cut into ½-inch (1 cm) cubes

2 Tbs. (30 ml) vegetable oil

¼ tsp. (1 ml) kalonji seeds

1 tsp. (5 ml) seeded, chopped fresh green chili (or to taste)

½ tsp. (2 ml) turmeric

½ tsp. (2 ml) salt

½ tsp. (2 ml) sugar
¼ cup (60 ml) fresh or unsweetened canned coconut milk, stirred until
  evenly mixed
½ lb. (¼ kg) fresh or thawed frozen bay shrimp
1 Tbs. (15 ml) finely chopped fresh cilantro

1. Steam the turnip cubes (or cook in boiling water to cover) until tender,
   about 15 minutes. Puree 1 cup (250 ml) in a blender until smooth. Set
   the cubes and puree aside separately.
2. Heat 2 tablespoons (30 ml) oil in a large pan over medium low heat.
   Fry kalonji seeds and green chili for 5 seconds. Add turmeric, salt,
   sugar, and reserved turnip puree. Turn heat to low. Remove from heat,
   add coconut milk, and stir a few times. Return to heat and simmer,
   uncovered, 5 to 8 minutes. (Excessive heat will cause the coconut
   milk to curdle, affecting its appearance and texture, but the sauce
   will still taste good.)
3. Add shrimp and reserved turnip cubes. Cook, uncovered, until shrimp is
   done, 3 to 5 minutes. (See "Test for doneness" under "Fish and Seafood
   Tips" in this chapter.) Add cilantro. Remove from heat and serve.

4 servings.

Serving suggestions: Goes well with rice and Tempting Mint Chutney for a
family meal. Accompany with Vegetable Pullao, Green Beans in Mustard-
Poppyseed Sauce, and Splendid Cilantro Chutney for a company dinner.

Kakra Malai Kari
CRAB IN COCONUT CREAM SAUCE

Crab is extraordinary when cooked Bengali style. In this dish, pinkish-red
chunks of crab are bathed in a golden yellow sauce. "A sublime taste sensa-
tion," declared a Western friend while savoring crab cooked in this manner.
I have reduced the amount of coconut milk, depending instead on the
natural crab juices and the aromatic combination of onion, ginger, and chili
to form a tasty sauce.

2½ Tbs. (37 ml) mustard oil
2 bay leaves
1 whole dried red chili
5 whole cardamom pods
2 whole cloves
1 cup (250 ml) finely chopped onion

1 Tbs. (15 ml) peeled, minced fresh ginger
1 tsp. (5 ml) seeded, chopped fresh green chili (or to taste)
¼ tsp. (1 ml) turmeric
⅛ tsp. (.5 ml) salt
½ Tbs. (7 ml) sugar
2 lb. (1 kg) fresh crab, cleaned and cut into pieces
¼ cup (60 ml) water
½ cup (125 ml) fresh or unsweetened canned coconut milk, stirred until
   evenly mixed

1. Heat oil in a large, deep pan over medium low heat. Fry bay leaves and
   red chili until the chili blackens. Add cardamom and cloves. Fry onion
   until richly browned but not burnt, 7 to 10 minutes, stirring constantly.
2. Add ginger and green chili and stir several times. Add turmeric, salt,
   and sugar. Add crab and mix well. Add water and bring to boil. Cover
   and cook, without lowering heat, for 2 to 3 minutes.
3. Turn heat to low. Remove pan from heat and add coconut milk. Return
   pan to heat and cook, uncovered, until crab is done, stirring occasionally, another 3 to 5 minutes. (Excessive heat will cause the coconut milk
   to curdle, affecting its appearance and texture, but the sauce will still
   taste good.) Remove from heat. Serve piping hot.

3 to 4 servings.

Serving suggestions: When served with rice, Broccoli with a Hint of Mustard, and Joyous Ginger-Raisin Chutney, this crab dish makes a memorable
meal.

Pyaz Diyea Maacher Jhol
STEAMED CLAMS BENGALI STYLE

Clams are not usually served in Bengal, but I find that they are well suited
to this simple, lightly flavored sauce. Your tastebuds are so satisfied that you
need few other courses to complete the meal.

2 Tbs. (30 ml) mustard oil
¼ tsp. (1 ml) black mustard seeds
1 cup (250 ml) finely chopped onion
2 Tbs. (30 ml) peeled, minced fresh ginger
1 tsp. (5 ml) seeded, chopped fresh green chili (or to taste)
¼ tsp. (1 ml) turmeric
⅛ tsp. (.5 ml) salt

1 tsp. (5 ml) sugar
¼ cup (60 ml) water
2 lb. (½ kg) Manila, butter, or steamer clams, scrubbed and rinsed
1 Tbs. (15 ml) finely chopped fresh cilantro

1. Heat oil in a large pan over medium heat. Fry mustard seeds until they start popping, a few seconds. Fry onion until richly browned but not burnt, 7 to 10 minutes, stirring constantly. Stir in ginger and green chili. Add turmeric, salt, sugar, and water. Bring to boil and simmer, covered, 5 minutes.
2. Raise heat to medium and add clams. Cover and cook 5 to 8 minutes, shaking the pan occasionally; after 3 to 4 minutes, peek every minute or so and remove those clams that have opened completely. Remove from heat. Discard any clams that remain closed. Arrange clams on a preheated platter and pour sauce over them. Sprinkle cilantro on top. Serve piping hot.

4 servings.

Serving suggestions: This is a favorite first course of mine. Serve also as part of a light meal with rice, Yellow Crookneck Squash in Coriander-Red Chili Sauce, and Splendid Cilantro Chutney.

Masala Diyea Maacher Jhol
SPICY STEAMED MUSSELS

Mussels are plentiful on both coasts of North America. This Bengali-style treatment will make you an instant fan of this delicious mollusk.

2 Tbs. (30 ml) mustard oil
¼ tsp. (1 ml) five-spice
1 cup (250 ml) finely chopped onion
1 Tbs. (15 ml) peeled, minced fresh ginger
1 tsp. (5 ml) seeded, chopped fresh green chili (or to taste)
¼ tsp. (1 ml) turmeric
½ cup (125 ml) water
2 lb. (1 kg) mussels, scrubbed and rinsed
Salt (optional)
½ tsp. (2 ml) garam masala

1. Heat oil in a large, deep pan over medium low heat. Fry five-spice until the spices start crackling. Fry onion, ginger, and green chili until onion

is translucent and soft, 2 to 3 minutes, stirring constantly. Add turmeric and mix well. Add water. Raise heat to medium high and bring to boil.

2. Add mussels, cover, and cook 4 to 5 minutes. If mussels have opened, remove pan from heat immediately. If not, continue to cook, checking every minute or so. As soon as most of them are open, remove from heat. Discard any mussels that are still closed. Transfer mussels with a slotted spatula to a preheated deep platter. Sample the sauce and, if necessary, add salt. Mix in garam masala. Pour over the mussels. Sprinkle cilantro on top and serve immediately.

4 first-course or 2 main-course servings.

Serving suggestions: Great for sharing with friends as an appetizer. Serve as part of a light meal with rice, Tender Garden Peas and Potatoes, and Yogurt Coconut Dip.

POULTRY AND MEAT

"Today is Sunday. We get to eat meat!" said a Bengali child.

Bengalis, many of whom are strict vegetarians, may live sumptuously without meat. But for the sizable number who are not strictly vegetarians, meat is a rare and greatly appreciated treat.

The expression pullao-mangsha, *"Pilaf and a meat curry," is a metaphor for fine dining.*

Since meat is scarce and commands a high price, Bengalis cook it with loving care. My mother prepares an elaborate list of ingredients before cooking meat, almost as if its presentation were a ritual. She dusts the meat lightly with selected seasonings "to make it easily digestible." She tenderizes it in a marinade of yogurt and spices for several hours. The fragrance of onion and garlic, sautéed into a rich brown sauce and laced with bay leaf and whole spices, permeates the house.

Only then does she add the meat. A slow simmer produces a flavorful gravy, cumin-brown on some occasions and tinged with tomato on others.

The presence of so many highly refined meat dishes in Bengali cuisine often comes as a surprise to Westerners. Actually, these items may be older than some of our vegetarian fare. Cave drawings hint that the ancient monarchs were fond of hunting. Even Brahmins, the highest-caste Hindus, were allowed to eat certain types of flesh. Only during certain religious observances was the public barred from meat consumption. In his volume on the history of the Bengalis, Nihar Ranjan Roy describes an ancient wedding feast that included mutton, deer, and poultry.

Meat eating was deemphasized during the Buddhist period. Asoka, the Buddhist king who ruled India from 273 to 232 B.C., barred the killing of animals. Yet as Buddhism waned in India, many people resumed eating animal protein. In the ensuing centuries, vegetarians lived side by side with nonvegetarians.

Starting in the 12th century, lavish meat dishes came into vogue during the period of Moslem rule. Abul Fazl, advisor to the great 16th-century emperor Akbar, compiled a survey of the empire titled *Ain-e-Akbari,* or *Institutes of Akbar.* In it he describes the cooking styles of the period, providing recipes for dishes such as meat-filled triangular pastries and spicy meatballs on a bed of rice.

Although there is a variety of modern recipes, not all types of meat are consumed. Hindus shun beef and neither Hindus nor Moslems eat pork. The most popular meats today are chicken, goat, and mutton.

The custom is to eat meat in small portions. A full-bodied gravy, enriched by the meat juices, highlights the dish. You may also find mellow chunks of vegetables, such as potato or cauliflower, bathed in the gravy with bite-sized pieces of meat. Meat lends flavor as well as nutritive value to the dish.

Bengalis also use ground lamb in many different ways. By cooking it with onion, garlic, and spices, they create dishes that are quick, filling, and inexpensive. They may also combine ground meat with aromatic spices to create elegant croquettes fit for a princely palate.

Food is a full-time delight in Calcutta. Flavors pile up on flavor . . . the cloying Keatsian glory of the roasted mutton to which thick-spiced gravy lovingly clings.

—from P. Lal's Calcutta, by P. Lal

Meat Tips

■ *Serving sizes for poultry and meat:* Bengalis consume meat in small portions, filling the bulk of their diet with vegetables. Many Western nutritionists advise the same, insisting that a 3- to 6-ounce (80 to 175 g) portion of meat is adequate for a meal. Keeping that in mind, I have provided some recipes where the portions of meat may seem smaller than usual. You can double these recipes if you wish to serve a larger amount of meat. To provide bigger portions, you can also prepare those meat dishes that specify six or eight servings and serve to a group of, say, four people.

■ The skin is removed in all chicken recipes in this chapter. By removing the fatty layer, you not only improve the flavor and texture of the dish but also eliminate unnecessary saturated fat—and spices penetrate skin-less meat better. You can make a few tiny surface slits in the flesh to allow spices to penetrate even more thoroughly.

■ Although chicken breast is popular in the West, other parts of the bird, including the thigh meat, can be used satisfactorily. If using boneless breast meat, which tends to be drier, increase the amount of water slightly.

■ When buying lamb, consider buying leg cuts; they generally have a lower fat content than other parts of the lamb.

■ Lean ground lamb is rarely sold packaged in the West. When ground lamb is available packaged, it is generally made from inferior cuts with a high fat content. You can buy a leg of lamb and either grind it yourself or ask the butcher to grind it. If you decide to buy prepackaged ground lamb, consider parboiling it in water, discarding the water and fat, and then using the meat in the recipes. You may, however, lose some flavor this way.

■ For everyday cooking, 30 minutes to an hour of marination is sufficient. But since longer marination makes the meat tastier, for festive occasions I marinate meat and poultry for 24 to 36 hours in the refrigerator.

■ Although for vegetable dishes I often leave potatoes unpeeled, I remove the skin when preparing them for meat dishes. The peeled potatoes soak up the meat gravy more easily and taste delicious, and their smooth texture blends better with that of the meat. Potatoes for meat dishes are generally cut in larger chunks than for vegetable dishes to conform to the size of the meat pieces.

■ Use a nonstick, deep-sided pan or Dutch oven, at least 10 inches (25 cm) in diameter, for cooking meat. This is especially helpful when handling large volumes of ingredients.

■ *Initial frying of chicken:* Chicken is usually lightly browned in the initial stages of a recipe. As is the case with fish, this frying seals in the natural juices. To reduce the amount of oil, usually 2 tablespoons (30 ml), omit this step. The flavor will be slightly less intense, but the dish will still be tasty.

- Meat and poultry are simmered slowly to allow the flavors and the sauce to develop and permeate the meat. So cook for the amount of time specified in the recipe, even though it may seem longer than you're used to.
- *To test for doneness:* Slash across the center of a piece of meat. If it is still pink inside, the meat needs to be cooked longer.

Shorshe Diyea Murgi
MUSTARD-DRENCHED CHICKEN

The first time I ate chicken in a mustard gravy, I was taken by its unusual flavor. It has since become one of my favorite dishes for potlucks and picnics. Since this dish tastes best when slightly chili-hot, either add extra chilis or throw some of the seeds in the pan while you cook.

1 Tbs. (15 ml) black mustard seeds, ground to a powder and mixed with
   2 Tbs. (30 ml) water
½ tsp. (2 ml) turmeric
⅛ tsp. (.5 ml) black pepper (preferably freshly ground)
2½ lb. (1 ¼ kg) chicken pieces, skinned
2 Tbs. (30 ml) vegetable oil
2 Tbs. (30 ml) peeled, minced fresh ginger
2 Tbs. (30 ml) minced garlic
1 tsp. (5 ml) seeded fresh green chili, thinly sliced (or to taste)
¼ cup (60 ml) water
¾ lb. (375 gs) potatoes (about 3 medium), peeled and cut into 2-inch
   (5 cm) cubes
½ tsp. (2 ml) salt

1. Combine mustard paste, turmeric, and black pepper in a bowl. Add chicken pieces and toss to make sure each piece is well coated. Cover and refrigerate 1 hour.
2. Heat oil in a deep pan, at least 10 inches (25 cm) wide, over medium low heat. Add ginger, garlic, and green chili and fry for 1 minute, stirring constantly. Add the chicken and fry just until chicken turns opaque, turning the pieces once. Add water and lower the heat slightly. Simmer, covered, 10 minutes, stirring occasionally and adding a tablespoon (15 ml) water if necessary to prevent sticking.
3. Add potatoes. Simmer, covered, until both chicken and potatoes are tender, an additional 20 to 30 minutes, stirring occasionally and adding

a tablespoon (15 ml) or so of water if the mixture sticks to the bottom. Add salt and mix well. Remove from heat. Let stand covered for a few minutes. Serve piping hot.

6 servings.

Serving suggestions: At a picnic serve with Banquet Bread. For a light meal, try with Plain Boiled Rice and Splendid Cilantro Chutney. If you need a more substantial meal, serve with Vegetable Pullao (or Soft Bread), Glorious Greens (or Yellow Crookneck Squash in Coriander–Red Chili Sauce), and Ginger-Yogurt Chutney.

Murgi Jhalsano
CHICKEN ROASTED WITH FRAGRANT SPICES

The familiar roast chicken takes on a new dimension when emboldened by spices such as cumin and turmeric. Although easy to make, this dish is quite simply extraordinary.

For the marinade:

2 Tbs. (30 ml) peeled fresh ginger, grated or made into a paste
    (see "A Glossary of Spices and Ingredients")
2 Tbs. (30 ml) garlic, forced through a garlic press or made into a paste
    (see "A Glossary of Spices and Ingredients")
½ tsp. (2 ml) turmeric
2 tsp. (10 ml) ground cumin
½ tsp. (2 ml) sugar
3 Tbs. (45 ml) plain yogurt
¼ tsp. (1 ml) salt

2 lb. (1 kg) chicken pieces, skinned
1 to 2 lime or lemon wedges, seeded
Garnish: raw mild onion rings, tomato wedges, and radish slices

1. Combine all the marinade ingredients in a large bowl. With a sharp knife, make a few slits ⅛ inch (3 mm) deep in the surface of the chicken pieces. Add chicken to the marinade and toss to coat well. Cover and refrigerate at least 8 hours, preferably 24 to 36 hours, turning every few hours.
2. Preheat oven to 350°F (180°C; gas mark 4). Roast chicken until tender, 45 to 50 minutes, turning once. Place the pieces under the broiler for 2 to 3 minutes to brown lightly, turning once.

Arrange chicken pieces on a preheated platter and squeeze lime on top. Place onion rings, tomato wedges, and radish slices around the edges. Serve immediately.

5 servings.

Serving suggestions: Good as a buffet item. As part of a meal, serve this Indian roasted chicken with Aromatic Rice with Peas and Whole Spices, Tender Garden Peas and Potatoes, and Splendid Cilantro Chutney or Country-style Chunky Tomato Chutney.

Murgi Posto
CHICKEN IN RICH GINGER-POPPYSEED SAUCE

This dish particularly delights Westerners. The roasted white poppyseeds, which may be new to them, both thicken the gravy and impart a delightful nutty flavor. It's easy to eat with both rice and flatbread.

¼ tsp. (1 ml) turmeric
¼ cup (60 ml) peeled fresh ginger, grated or made into a paste
   (see "A Glossary of Spices and Ingredients")
2 Tbs. (30 ml) garlic, forced through a garlic press or made into a paste
   (see "A Glossary of Spices and Ingredients")
1 tsp. (5 ml) seeded fresh green chili, made into a paste (see "A Glossary
   of Spices and Ingredients")
2½ to 3 lb. (1¼ to 1½ kg) chicken pieces (legs, thighs, breasts), skinned
2 Tbs. (30 ml) vegetable oil
2 bay leaves
5 whole cardamom pods
2 whole cloves
1 cup (250 ml) finely chopped onion
⅛ tsp. (.5 ml) turmeric
1 tsp. (5 ml) sugar
Dash ground red chili or cayenne pepper (or to taste)
1 cup (250 ml) water
2 Tbs. (30 ml) white poppyseeds, made into a paste
   (see "A Glossary of Spices and Ingredients")
½ tsp. (1 ml) salt

1. Combine ¼ teaspoon (1 ml) turmeric, ginger, garlic, and green chili in a bowl. With a sharp knife, make a few slits ⅛ inch (3 mm) deep in the surface of the chicken pieces. Toss chicken gently in the ginger mixture,

making sure each piece is well coated. Cover and refrigerate for 30 minutes.

2. Heat oil in a pan over medium low heat. Fry bay leaves, cardamom, and cloves for a few seconds. Add onion and fry until richly browned but not burnt, 6 to 10 minutes, stirring constantly. Stir in ⅛ teaspoon (½ ml) turmeric, sugar, and red pepper. Add the chicken with marinade and cook for about 1 minute, turning the pieces once. Add water and lower heat. Simmer, covered, until chicken is tender, about 30 minutes, turning occasionally and adding a tablespoon (15 ml) or so of water if the mixture sticks to the bottom.

3. Stir in poppyseed paste and salt. Simmer, covered, until the sauce thickens, 10 to 15 minutes, stirring occasionally and adding a tablespoon (15 ml) or so of water if the mixture sticks. Remove from heat. Let stand covered for 10 minutes to help thicken the sauce and develop the flavors. Scatter cilantro on top and serve.

6 to 8 servings.

Serving suggestions: Lemon-laced Rice or Vegetable Pullao complements the fine white poppyseed sauce. Rich Roasted Eggplant (or Peanut-topped Greens) and Tempting Mint Chutney will complete the meal.

VARIATION

BEEF IN RICH GINGER-POPPYSEED SAUCE

Beef is excellent when cooked in this sauce. Instead of chicken, use 2 pounds boneless beef (such as round steak, sirloin steak, or chuck roast), cut into 2 × 2 × 1-inch (5 × 5 × 2.5 cm) pieces. Increase water to ¾ cup (175 ml). In step 2, cook beef until tender, about 70 minutes.

Murgir Dom

CHICKEN IN CORIANDER-YOGURT SAUCE

The dom style of cooking is said to have been developed to feed construction workers in northern India in the 18th century. The ingredients were simple, because people could not afford rich oil or spices. Food cooked in its own juices in a covered pan, its edges tightly sealed with a doughy flour-and-water mixture. A ruling monarch smelled the food one day while on excursion and was so intrigued that he ordered it to be included in the royal menu.

In this dish the chicken is braised in an aromatic puree of onion and ginger, which is further enhanced by cumin and coriander.

1 cup (250 ml) coarsely chopped onion
1 Tbs. (15 ml) peeled, chopped fresh ginger
2 to 3 Tbs. (30 to 45 ml) vegetable oil
2½ lb. (1 ¼ kg) chicken pieces, skinned
½ tsp. (2 ml) turmeric
2 tsp. (10 ml) ground cumin
2 tsp. (10 ml) ground coriander
Dash ground red chili or cayenne pepper (or to taste)
½ tsp. (2 ml) sugar
¼ cup (60 ml) hot water
¼ tsp. (1 ml) salt
¼ cup (60 ml) plain yogurt, lightly beaten until smooth

1. Puree onion and ginger in a blender or food processor until smooth. If the mixture does not blend well, add a tablespoon (15 ml) or so of water; do not add any more water than necessary. Set aside.
2. Heat 2 tablespoons (30 ml) oil in a large skillet over medium to medium high heat. Fry chicken in 2 batches until it turns opaque and is lightly browned, 2 to 3 minutes, turning often. Remove with a slotted spoon and set aside. (Or fry in 1 tablespoon/15 ml oil. See "Initial frying of chicken" in this chapter.)
3. Add 1 tablespoon (15 ml) oil to the skillet and heat over medium low heat. Fry the onion-ginger puree for 1 minute, stirring and covering partially to prevent the mixture from splattering the cooking area. Add turmeric, cumin, coriander, red pepper, and sugar and stir several times. Add hot water.
4. Add chicken and mix well with the spices. Lower the heat. Simmer, covered, until chicken is tender, about 30 minutes, turning the pieces occasionally and adding a tablespoon (15 ml) or so of hot water if the mixture sticks to the bottom of the skillet. (You can get by without using any water, but you'll need to turn the chicken pieces more frequently to ensure that they do not burn.) Turn heat very low. Remove half the chicken with a slotted spoon. Add salt and yogurt and stir for a few seconds. Return chicken to the skillet and remove from heat. Garnish with cilantro and serve.

6 to 8 servings.

Serving suggestions: Serve this flavorful dom with Aromatic Rice with Peas and Whole Spices (or Banquet Bread), Cauliflower with a Hint of Mustard, and Pleasing Plum Chutney.

Robibarer Murgi
SAVORY SUNDAY CHICKEN

On Sundays three generations of our family would dine together at my grandfather's house in Calcutta. This flavorful dish, which was often the highlight of the meal, would come with plenty of robust tomato-onion sauce. With the skin removed, the meat was juicy and literally fell off the bones.

2½ to 5½ Tbs. (37 to 82 ml) vegetable oil
3½ lb. (1 ¾ kg) chicken pieces, skinned
1 lb. (½ kg) potatoes (about 4 medium), peeled and cut into 1½-inch
   (4 cm) cubes
2 cups (500 ml) finely chopped onion
½ tsp. (2 ml) turmeric
1 tsp. (5 ml) sugar
1½ Tbs. (22 ml) peeled fresh ginger, grated or made into a paste
   (see "A Glossary of Spices and Ingredients")
1 Tbs. (15 ml) garlic, forced through a garlic press or made into a paste
   (see "A Glossary of Spices and Ingredients")
1 tsp. (5 ml) seeded, chopped fresh green chili (or to taste)
2 tsp. (10 ml) ground cumin
2 tsp. (10 ml) ground coriander
1 ¼ cups (310 ml) water
1½ Tbs. (22 ml) tomato paste
¾ tsp. (3 ml) salt
3 Tbs. (45 ml) plain yogurt
1 tsp. (5 ml) garam masala
Garnish: raw mild onion rings, cucumber slices

1. Heat 2 tablespoons (30 ml) oil in a 12-inch (30 cm) skillet over medium heat. Fry chicken pieces in 2 batches, turning frequently, until opaque and lightly browned, 3 to 5 minutes per batch. Remove with a slotted spoon and set aside. (Omit this step for a lower-fat dish.)
2. Add 1 tablespoon (15 ml) oil to the skillet and reheat over medium heat. Fry potatoes until they turn medium brown, 6 to 8 minutes, turning frequently. Remove with a slotted spoon and set aside. (Omit this step for a lower-fat dish.)
3. Add 2½ tablespoons (37 ml) oil to the skillet and heat over medium low heat. Add onion and fry until richly browned but not burnt, 10 to 20 minutes, stirring constantly. Stir in turmeric and sugar. Add ginger, garlic, green chili, cumin, and coriander and fry for a few seconds. Add water. Blend in tomato paste. Add the chicken and any accumulated

juices. Simmer, covered, 10 minutes. Add the potatoes and simmer, covered, until both chicken and potatoes are tender, another 20 to 25 minutes.

4. Remove from heat. Remove half the chicken and potatoes with a slotted spoon. Add salt, yogurt, and garam masala to the skillet and mix gently. Return chicken and potatoes to the skillet and mix well with the sauce. Let stand covered for a few minutes to allow the flavors to develop. Garnish with onion rings, cucumber, and cilantro and serve.

8 to 9 servings.

Serving suggestions: For a full meal serve with rice (or Puffed Bread), Glorious Greens, and Ginger Yogurt Chutney. You can mop up any leftover sauce the next day with Pan-raised Bread.

Murgi Malai Kari
CHICKEN IN COCONUT CREAM SAUCE

Bengalis rarely use flour to thicken gravy, insisting that the ingredients, properly chosen, should melt into a sauce of proper consistency. In this dish, coconut milk enriches the sauce and joins hands with a few carefully chosen spices to produce an elegant dish fit for a banquet.

2½ to 4½ Tbs. (37 to 67 ml) vegetable oil
3 lb. (1½ kg) chicken pieces, skinned
1½ cups (375 ml) finely chopped onion
1 Tbs. (15 ml) peeled, minced fresh ginger
1 Tbs. (15 ml) minced garlic
1 tsp. (5 ml) seeded, chopped fresh green chili (or to taste)
¼ tsp. (1 ml) turmeric
1 tsp. (5 ml) sugar
¼ cup (60 ml) water
¾ tsp. (3 ml) salt
½ cup plus 1 Tbs. (140 ml) fresh or unsweetened canned coconut milk, (stirred until evenly mixed)

1. Heat 2 tablespoons (30 ml) oil in a skillet over medium heat. Fry chicken pieces in 2 or 3 batches until opaque and lightly browned, about 1 minute per side, turning once. Remove with a slotted spoon and set aside. (Omit this step for a lower-fat dish.)

2. Add 2½ tablespoons (37 ml) oil to the skillet and heat over medium low heat. Add onion and fry until richly browned but not burnt, 15 to 20

minutes, stirring constantly. Add ginger, garlic, green chili, turmeric, and sugar and fry for a few seconds. Add water and the chicken. Lower the heat.

3. Simmer, covered, until chicken is tender, about 40 minutes, stirring as often as necessary to ensure that the meat doesn't stick to the bottom of the skillet.

4. Remove from heat and remove chicken with a slotted spoon, leaving the sauce in the skillet. Add salt and coconut milk. Place over low heat and cook uncovered until the sauce thickens slightly, 8 to 15 minutes, stirring occasionally. (Excessive heat will cause the coconut milk to separate, affecting its appearance and texture. The sauce will, however, still taste good.)

5. Return the chicken to the pan and mix well with the sauce. Remove from heat. Let stand covered for a few minutes to further thicken the sauce and develop the flavors. Garnish with cilantro and serve.

8 servings.

Serving suggestions: I frequently serve this dish for company accompanied by rice (or Banquet Bread), Green Beans in Mustard-Poppyseed Sauce, and "Happy Heart" Chutney or Tempting Mint Chutney.

Murgi Do-pyaza
CHICKEN IN SAVORY ONION SAUCE

The word *do-pyaza,* which means "double onion," is a style of cooking in which onion is used in two different ways: as a paste and brown-fried. Another characteristic of a "double onion" dish is that the weight of onion should nearly equal the weight of chicken. The result is a delicious dish with a rich, spicy gravy, well-suited for entertaining.

2½ cups (625 ml) chopped onion
1 Tbs. (15 ml) peeled, chopped fresh ginger
1 Tbs. (15 ml) finely chopped garlic
1 tsp. (5 ml) seeded, chopped fresh green chili (or to taste)
2½ to 4 Tbs. (37 to 60 ml) vegetable oil
2½ cups (625 ml) thinly slivered onion
1 bay leaf
5 whole cardamom pods
2-inch (5 cm) cinnamon stick
2 whole cloves
½ tsp. (2 ml) turmeric

2 tsp. (10 ml) ground cumin
2 tsp. (10 ml) ground coriander
½ tsp. (2 ml) sugar
⅛ tsp. (.5 ml) black pepper (preferably freshly ground)
Dash ground red chili or cayenne pepper (or to taste)
2 lb. (1 kg) chicken pieces, skinned
3 Tbs. (45 ml) plain yogurt, lightly beaten until smooth
½ tsp. (2 ml) salt
Garnish: tomato wedges and cucumber slices

1. Puree chopped onion, ginger, garlic, and green chili in a blender in batches until smooth. Add a tablespoon (15 ml) or so of water if needed, but don't add any more water than necessary. Set aside.
2. Heat 2 tablespoons (30 ml) oil in a large, deep 10-inch (15 cm) pan over medium heat. Add the slivered onion and fry until richly browned but not burnt, 12 to 15 minutes, stirring constantly and adjusting the heat as necessary. Remove with a slotted spoon and set aside.
3. Add 1 to 2 tablespoons (15 to 30 ml) of the remaining oil to the skillet and heat over medium low heat. (The larger amount of oil will help prevent the onion from sticking and will add more flavor.) Fry bay leaf, cardamom, cinnamon, and cloves for a few seconds. Add the pureed onion mixture and fry, stirring, for 2 minutes. Add turmeric, cumin, coriander, sugar, black pepper, and red pepper and fry for 2 minutes, stirring constantly. Add chicken and mix well with the spices. Lower the heat. Simmer, covered, for 30 to 40 minutes, stirring occasionally and adding a tablespoon (15 ml) or so of water to prevent sticking.
4. Add yogurt and salt and stir for a few seconds; do not overcook or yogurt may separate. Add the slivered onions and mix well. Remove from heat and let stand covered for a few minutes to help develop the flavors. Garnish with tomato wedges, cucumber slices, and cilantro and serve.

5 servings.

Serving suggestions: This savory chicken goes well with rice (or Carrot-filled Pan Bread), Potatoes Braised in Rich Tart Sauce, and Joyous Ginger-Raisin Chutney. For a festive occasion, I substitute Vegetable Pullao for rice.

Saak Diyea Mangsha
LAMB SWIMMING IN CREAMY GREEN SAUCE

Shahjahan was a 17th-century Indian ruler who loved art passionately. It is also believed that he had definite opinions about food and demanded spicy dishes without fresh green chili. A few meat dishes in this chapter, like this dish made without green chili, commemorate the "shajahani" style that was born during his reign.

Even those who turn up their noses at spinach enjoy this dish, in which a puree of the leaves of hearty greens is enriched by lamb broth. The rich, green gravy coats chunks of tender lamb. "A totally sensuous eating experience," says my husband.

For the marinade:

½ cup plus 1 Tbs. (140 ml) plain yogurt, lightly beaten until smooth
½ tsp. (2 ml) turmeric
1½ Tbs. (22 ml) peeled fresh ginger, grated or made into a paste
  (see "A Glossary of Spices and Ingredients")
1 Tbs. (15 ml) garlic, forced through a garlic press or made into a paste
  (see "A Glossary of Spices and Ingredients")

2 lb. (1 kg) lamb (leg of lamb) or beef (round steak, chuck roast, or sirloin
  tip), cut into 2 × 2 × 1 inch (5 × 5 × 2.5 cm) pieces
2 Tbs. (30 ml) vegetable oil
1½ cups (375 ml) finely chopped onion
½ tsp. (2 ml) salt
1 tsp. (5 ml) sugar
½ cup (125 ml) water
3 cups (750 ml) firmly packed slivered leaves of collards, kale, or Swiss
  chard, steamed but not pureed (see "A Glossary of Spices and
  Ingredients")
3 Tbs. (45 ml) dried flaked or shredded sweetened coconut, or freshly
  grated or shredded coconut mixed with ¼ tsp. (1 ml) sugar
3 Tbs. (45 ml) finely chopped fresh cilantro
About ¼ cup (60 ml) water
Garnish: raw mild onion rings

1. Combine the marinade ingredients. Toss meat gently in the mixture, making sure each piece is well coated. Refrigerate for 1 hour.
2. Heat oil in a large pan over medium low heat. Add onion and fry until richly browned but not burnt, 15 to 18 minutes, stirring constantly. Lower the heat. Add salt, sugar, and meat. Immediately add ½ cup (125 ml) water. Simmer, covered, until meat is tender, about 1 hour.
3. Meanwhile, combine the greens, coconut, and cilantro in a bowl. Pour about 2 tablespoons (30 ml) water (or liquid left from steaming the greens) into a blender container. Add half the greens mixture and puree until smooth. Repeat for the remaining greens mixture, using no more water than necessary. Set puree aside.

4. When meat is ready, add the greens puree. Cook uncovered just until the mixture starts to bubble, stirring constantly. Serve immediately. If cooked for too long or allowed to stand, the greens will darken; this will not, however, affect their flavor. Garnish with onion rings.

5 servings.

Serving suggestions: Serve with Puffed Bread (or Soft Bread) for lunch. For a main meal, serve with Lime-splashed Butternut Squash over Rice (or plain rice), Sour Spicy Fries, and Ginger Yogurt Chutney.

Haaree Kabab
LAMB IN CHILI-MUSTARD SAUCE

A mustard-enriched sauce, so typically Bengali, characterizes this unusual dish. Thinly sliced green chili imparts a pleasant afterglow.

For the marinade:

¼ cup (60 ml) plain yogurt, lightly beaten until smooth
2½ Tbs. (37 ml) peeled fresh ginger, grated or made into a paste (see "A Glossary of Spices and Ingredients")
1 Tbs. (15 ml) garlic, forced through a garlic press or made into a paste (see "A Glossary of Spices and Ingredients")
¼ tsp. (1 ml) salt

2 lb. (1 kg) leg of lamb or beef such as round steak, sirloin tip, or chuck roast, cut into 2 × 2 × 1-inch (5 × 5 × 2.5 cm) pieces
1½ tsp. (7 ml) black mustard seeds, ground to a powder
1 tsp. (5 ml) seeded fresh green chili, thinly sliced (or to taste)
1½ Tbs. (22 ml) mustard oil
½ tsp. (1 ml) salt
Garnish: green bell pepper strips

1. Combine the marinade ingredients in a bowl. Add meat and toss to well coat each piece. Covered and refrigerate for 1 hour.
2. Place the meat and marinade in a large skillet over low heat. Simmer, covered, for 1 hour. Combine ground black mustard, green chili, mustard oil, and salt in a small bowl and pour over the meat. Simmer, covered, for 15 more minutes or until meat is done, stirring occasionally, adding a tablespoon (15 ml) or so of water to prevent sticking. Remove from heat. Transfer meat and gravy to a preheated platter. Sprinkle with green pepper strips and cilantro and serve.

5 servings.

Serving suggestions: When I'm looking for an easy-to-do meal, I serve mustard-flavored lamb with rice and Steamed Spicy Cauliflower. For a special-occasion dinner, try it with rice (and/or Puffed Bread), Rich Roasted Eggplant (or Cauliflower and Potatoes in Roasted Red Chili Sauce), and Tempting Mint Chutney.

Kabiraji Cutlet
HERBAL DOCTOR'S BURGER

Just why this dish is so named is not known, but a guess might be that a certain herbal doctor in a village prescribed it to a patient. The question remains: Did the spices or the meat cure the patient?

For the spices:

½ cup (125 ml) minced onion
2 Tbs. (30 ml) peeled, minced fresh ginger
2 tsp. (10 ml) minced garlic
1 tsp. (5 ml) seeded, chopped fresh green chili (or to taste)
2 Tbs. (30 ml) finely chopped fresh cilantro
½ tsp. (2 ml) asafetida powder
2 tsp. (10 ml) ground cumin
2 tsp. (10 ml) ground coriander
¾ tsp. (3 ml) salt
1 tsp. (5 ml) sugar
⅛ tsp. (.5 ml) black pepper (preferably freshly ground)
Dash ground red chili or cayenne pepper (or to taste)

1 lb. (½ kg) extra lean ground beef or lamb (see "Meat and Poultry Tips" in this chapter)
3 eggs, lightly beaten
½ cup (125 ml) breadcrumbs (see "A Glossary of Spices and Ingredients")
Vegetable oil for pan-frying

1. Combine all spices in a large bowl. Gently mix in ground meat without squeezing out the moisture. Pinch off a portion of this mixture, shaping it into a circular patty about 1½ inches (4 cm) in diameter and ½ inch (1 cm) thick. Repeat with the remainder.
2. Dip patties in the egg, then coat lightly on both sides with the breadcrumbs.
3. Heat 1½ tablespoons (22 ml) oil in a skillet over medium low heat. Fry 3 or 4 patties at a time until cooked through, 5 to 6 minutes on each side; a toothpick inserted in the thickest part and moved gently to one

side should not show a pink color. Do not press down on the patties
during frying as this can cause the burgers to lose their natural juices.
Makes 18 patties.

Serving suggestions: For lunch serve 2 of these burgers per person in pita
pockets with shredded lettuce and alfalfa sprouts. As part of a main meal,
serve 3 to 4 per person with rice (or Soft Bread), Smoked Eggplant in
Creamy Sauce, and Green and White Coconut Chutney.

Badam Diyea Mangsha
BEEF IN RICH CASHEW SAUCE

This extravagant cashew sauce melds with fine cuts of meat to create a
sumptous dish. "I used to think all curries were hot," said a Western friend.
"In this dish I find the flavors to be subtle, yet complex." I often serve this
aromatic dish when I entertain.

2 to 4 Tbs. (30 to 60 ml) vegetable oil
¾ lb. (375 g) potatoes (about 3 medium), peeled and cut into 2-inch
    (5 cm) cubes
1 bay leaf
1 whole dried red chili
5 whole cardamom pods
2-inch (5 cm) cinnamon stick
2 whole cloves
2 cups (500 ml) finely chopped onion
2 Tbs. (30 ml) peeled, minced fresh ginger
1 Tbs. (15 ml) minced garlic
1 tsp. (5 ml) seeded, chopped fresh green chili (or to taste)
½ tsp. (2 ml) turmeric
2 tsp. (10 ml) ground cumin
¼ tsp. (1 ml) sugar
2 lb. (½ kg) beef filet mignon, boneless sirloin, boned T-bone steak,
    New York strip, or round steak, or lamb leg or shoulder steak,
    cut into 2 × 2 × 1-inch (5 × 5 × 2.5 cm) cubes
½ cup (125 ml) water
2 Tbs. (30 ml) plain yogurt
1 Tbs. (15 ml) raw cashews or almonds, ground in a blender to a coarse
    powder
½ tsp. (2 ml) salt
½ tsp. (2 ml) garam masala
Garnish: raw mild onion rings

1. Heat 2 tablespoons (30 ml) oil in a pan over medium heat. Fry the potatoes until they turn medium brown, 6 to 7 minutes. Remove with a slotted spoon and set aside. (Omit this step for a lower-fat dish.)
2. Add 2 tablespoons (30 ml) oil to the pan and heat over medium low heat. Fry bay leaf, red chili, cardamom, cinnamon, and cloves for a few seconds. Add onion and fry until richly browned but not burnt, 18 to 20 minutes, stirring constantly.
3. Stir in ginger, garlic, green chili, turmeric, cumin, and sugar. Add meat and water. Lower the heat and simmer, covered, 30 minutes. Add the potatoes and simmer, covered, until both meat and potatoes are tender, about 30 more minutes. Turn heat very low. Blend in yogurt, nuts, and salt and remove from heat. (Prolonged heating will curdle the sauce, detracting from its appearance and texture.) Stir in garam masala. Decorate with onion rings and cilantro.

5 servings.

Serving suggestions: For a family meal, accompany with rice, Splendid Spinach, and Ginger Yogurt Chutney. When entertaining, team with Pureed Greens with Chili and Coconut over Rice (or plain rice), Sweet and Tart Pumpkin, and Smoked Eggplant in Ginger-Yogurt Sauce.

CHUTNEYS
AND RAITAS

The word chutney, or *chatney* in Bengali, likely derives its origin from the word *chat,* meaning to pass lightly over as with the tongue. (Some say the word comes from the Persian word *chasney,* meaning "relish.") The true meaning is to stimulate the appetite without filling the belly. The traditional way to enjoy chutney is to take a dab with your fingers and just savor it.

> Lotus stalks were peeled and cut into small pieces, then cooked
> with salt, sugar and tamarind paste to make a chutney.
> —on chutney in ancient India; from *Saga*
> *of Indian Food* by Indira Chakravarty

A chutney is both a condiment and a sauce, served in small amounts and eaten by itself. Its sour, fiery, sweet-sour or hot-sweet taste provides a transition between courses—a "palate refresher," as they say in Bengal. Chutneys vary not only in flavor but in texture as well; some are smooth, others have an uneven texture.

Chutney is believed to have originated in the peasant kitchen. Perhaps this is why a villager once impressed me with his ardor for this meal-enhancing condiment. His simple midday sustenance consisted of a mound of rice, a small serving of vegetables, and a dollop of chutney. He was wearing a *dhuti,* a long strip of cloth, and sitting cross-legged on a straw mat on the floor. He looked like a king enthroned in the presence of his royal repast. Chutney transformed a simple act of survival into a delightful experience.

And chutney is for lavish feasts as well. At a family wedding that featured a 12-course dinner, our guests indulged in several rich dishes such as *kormas* and *kalias,* rice of course, and two kinds of chutney.

A chutney gives zest to a meal. It catches us by surprise and lifts our mood. Since desserts are generally eaten only on special occasions, it's the taste of a chutney that lingers after dinner.

These chutneys are not jamlike concoctions that come in bottles; my mother prepared them fresh daily to suit her whim or to complement other dishes. Whatever chutney my mother made each day sparked my childhood curiosity. If mangoes were in season, she would choose a young fruit whose bold pink or yellow skin was splashed with lingering green. At another time, she would pick some purple plums for their pleasantly sharp taste.

My mother put together chutneys from herbs, vegetables, or even fish. Sometimes she simply pounded the ingredients together, as in the case of mint chutney. At other times, as for the much-loved tomato chutney, she simmered red, ripe tomatoes with ginger and five-spice, producing a delicate sauce. She also made a more robust chutney with fish or shrimp and tamarind, which always became the high point of the meal.

Chutneys aren't the only subtle delights; *raitas,* various fruits and vegetables dressed with spiced yogurt, are other cherished meal mates. They are different from Western salads in that the dressing constitutes a larger proportion of the dish.

He has yogurt on his plate and rice in his mouth and yet he wants more.

—Bengali proverb describing an unreasonable person

The cooling raitas are sometimes served in place of chutneys to offset rich dishes. They also provide a counterpoint to lamb dishes and rice preparations, and as a dip for flatbreads. An added benefit is that they are a rich source of protein and other nutrients, which are especially important in a vegetarian diet. Like chutneys, they enhance any meal, simple or elaborate.

Chutney Tips

- For blender-made chutneys: For best results, blend just until smooth. Overblending can cause the chutney to separate and lose its texture.

■ You can store freshly made chutneys in the refrigerator for a few days.

■ *Selecting white vinegar:* In recipes that call for white vinegar, I prefer using mild and flavorful rice vinegar, available at Asian markets and some Western supermarkets. If using stronger white wine vinegar, dilute slightly with water.

■ *Serving suggestions for chutneys:* When serving chutney with a meal, I strive, as usual, for variety in color, texture, and flavor. A tomato-based chutney will, for example, go well with a green vegetable dish. A light, soothing raita might balance a heavier meat dish. I usually don't serve a mustard-flavored chutney with an entree made with mustard.

■ Chutney also goes well with Western food—hot and cold meats, stews, and sausages. You can spread chutney on sandwich breads or use it as a dip for chips and crackers. A party theme can be built around varieties of chutneys. (See Menus chapter.)

■ With a main meal, serve chutney in small amounts—usually about ¼ cup (60 ml), or only 1 to 2 teaspoons (5 to 10 ml) for strongly flavored chutneys—in individual bowls or at one side of the dinner plate. Often-times Bengalis will mix some rice with a chutney before eating it.

Aamer Dil Khush Chatney
"HAPPY HEART" CHUTNEY

"A mango is the choicest fruit of India," said 14th-century Indian poet Amir Khusrau. I always loved mangoes; a mango was one of the first things I learned how to draw.

Made with ripe mangoes, this peach-colored condiment has a wonderful aroma and a soft, smooth texture. True to its name, it pleases your heart. It is a lovely companion to both vegetable and meat dishes.

3 cups (750 ml) fresh ripe mango pulp, slivered (see "A Glossary of Spices and Ingredients"), or canned mango pulp (see Note)
¼ cup (60 ml) water or liquid from canned mango
2 tsp. (10 ml) peeled, minced fresh ginger
¼ tsp. (1 ml) salt
2 Tbs. (30 ml) sugar, or 1 tsp. (5 ml) if using canned mango
2 tsp. (10 ml) vegetable oil (mustard oil preferred)
⅛ tsp. (.5 ml) asafetida powder
½ tsp. (2 ml) five-spice, roasted and ground
Dash ground red chili or cayenne pepper (or to taste)

1. Place mango, water, ginger, and salt in a pan over low heat. Simmer, covered, until mango is soft, about 30 minutes (15 minutes if using canned mango). Add sugar and cook, covered, for 1 minute. Remove from heat and set aside.
2. Heat oil in a 6-inch (15 cm) pan over medium low heat. Sprinkle asafetida over the oil. Fry five-spice powder and red pepper for a few seconds. Pour mixture over the cooked mango and stir gently. Let stand covered for 15 minutes to help develop flavor. Serve warm, at room temperature, or chilled.

4 servings.

Serving suggestions: This versatile chutney goes well with any meal. It is also a good accompaniment to papads, especially the hot and spicy varieties.

Note: If using the canned mango sold in Asian and Indian markets, select 3 cans of mango slices in syrup, each 15 ounces (425 g); the drained weight is 9 ounces (250 g). Drain, reserving the liquid from one of the cans. I use the leftover liquid to make blended fruit drinks.

Tomator Misti Chatney
COUNTRY-STYLE CHUNKY TOMATO CHUTNEY

Red is the color associated with festivities in Bengal, so this chutney, made with ripe Roma tomatoes, has a merrymaking quality. The velvety-smooth sauce, with chunks of tomatoes breaking the surface, goes well with both vegetarian and meat dishes.

1 Tbs. (15 ml) vegetable oil (mustard oil preferred)
1 whole dried red chili
¼ tsp. (1 ml) five-spice
1 Tbs. (15 ml) peeled, minced fresh ginger
½ tsp. (2 ml) salt
Dash ground red chili or cayenne pepper (or to taste)
3 cups (750 ml) loosely packed seeded, thinly sliced tomatoes (about
    8 Roma or 4 regular tomatoes)
1½ Tbs. (22 ml) sugar
¼ tsp. (1 ml) five-spice, roasted and ground
1 Tbs. (15 ml) fresh lime or lemon juice
1 Tbs. (15 ml) finely chopped fresh cilantro

1. Heat oil over medium low heat in a skillet. Sauté red chili until it darkens. Fry five-spice for a few seconds or until the spices start crack-

ling. Add ginger and fry until it is lightly browned. Add salt, red pepper, and tomatoes. Cover and cook until the tomatoes are very soft and disintegrate into a sauce, 8 to 10 minutes, mashing pieces with the back of a spoon. Add sugar and mix well. Remove from heat.

2. Add five-spice powder, lime juice, and cilantro. Let stand covered for 10 minutes. Serve immediately or at room temperature.

6 to 8 servings.

Serving suggestions: Serve with rice or Pan-raised Bread at any meal. Particularly good with Onion-fragrant Red Lentils. I also enjoy this chutney over rice as a simple lunch.

Tomator Chatney
MELLOW TOMATO CHUTNEY

This refined tomato chutney is made in city kitchens and is suited for a buffet table. My sister Sheila laboriously removes the skin and seeds from the tomatoes, retaining only their juicy flesh. The dish is mildly sweet and tender, yet has the assertiveness of the black mustard seeds.

1 lb. (½ kg) Roma tomatoes (about 9 to 10)
1½ Tbs. (22 ml) mustard oil
¼ tsp. (1 ml) black mustard seeds
3 Tbs. (45 ml) peeled fresh ginger, grated or made into a paste
   (see "A Glossary of Spices and Ingredients")
¼ tsp. (1 ml) turmeric
½ tsp. (2 ml) salt
1½ Tbs. (22 ml) sugar
1 to 2 tsp. (5 to 10 ml) dried red chili paste (see "A Glossary of Spices and Ingredients")

1. Peel and seed the tomatoes (see "A Glossary of Spices and Ingredients"). Set aside.
2. Heat oil in a skillet over medium low heat. Fry black mustard seeds until they start popping. Fry ginger until it is lightly browned. Stir in turmeric. Add the tomatoes, salt, sugar, and red chili paste. Lower the heat slightly. Cover and cook until the sauce is thick, about 30 minutes. (This slow cooking will help develop a rich, mellow flavor.) Remove from heat and let stand covered for a few minutes. Serve warm or at room temperature.

4 servings.

Serving suggestions: I place this colorful, vitamin A- and C-rich chutney on the table whenever I need an extra nutritional boost. Rice or Soft Bread provides the bulk; Steamed Fish in Chili-Cilantro Sauce and Smoked Eggplant in Creamy Sauce will complete the meal.

Tomato Kasundi
SWEET AND SOUR TOMATO-MUSTARD CHUTNEY

While traveling in Bengal you might notice bottled yellow sauces called *kasundi* being sold at the markets. A small amount of this pungent sauce, usually mustard-based, is eaten with rice in a meal. This warm and mellow chutney is made in the popular *kasundi* style, with finely ground black mustard as a main ingredient.

This chutney is also pleasantly tart. In Bengali cuisine, we achieve tartness by using lime, tamarind, dry mango powder, or white vinegar, each of which has its unique brand of sour taste. Here mild white vinegar creates a sauce that my husband describes as "richly sour."

1½ Tbs. (22 ml) vegetable oil
1 Tbs. (15 ml) peeled fresh ginger, grated or made into a paste
   (see "A Glossary of Spices and Ingredients")
1 Tbs. (15 ml) garlic, forced through a garlic press or made into a paste
   (see "A Glossary of Spices and Ingredients")
1 tsp. (5 ml) seeded, chopped fresh green chili (or to taste)
¼ tsp. (1 ml) turmeric
2 tsp. (10 ml) ground cumin
2 tsp. (10 ml) black mustard seeds, ground to a powder, mixed with 1 Tbs.
   (15 ml) water, and allowed to stand 30 minutes
3 cups (750 ml) chopped tomatoes (about 8 Roma or 4 regular tomatoes)
½ tsp. (2 ml) salt
2½ tsp. (12 ml) sugar
¼ cup (60 ml) mild white vinegar

1. Heat oil in a skillet over medium low heat. Fry ginger, garlic, and green chili until ginger and garlic turn lightly brown. Add turmeric and cumin and stir a few times. Add black mustard paste. Add tomatoes, salt, and sugar.
2. Simmer, covered, 30 minutes, stirring often and mashing the tomatoes with the back of a spoon. Add vinegar and simmer, covered, 5 more minutes. Remove from heat. Let stand covered for 15 minutes. Serve at room temperature.

4 servings.

Serving suggestions: Serve this salsalike chutney with papad or a platter of raw or steamed vegetables such as radishes, carrot sticks, broccoli, bell pepper strips, and boiled new potatoes.

Tetuler Chatney
TENDER TAMARIND CHUTNEY

This silky-textured chutney hints of roasted cumin and has a balance of sweet and tart tastes. It is excellent either as a dip for raw or steamed vegetables or as a topping.

A 2 × 4 × ¾-inch piece (5 × 10 × 2 cm or 70 g) tamarind, broken off from
    a block of dried tamarind, chopped in pieces, and soaked in ½ cup
    (125 ml) warm water in a nonmetallic bowl for 15 to 30 minutes (do not
    substitute tamarind concentrate)
1 Tbs. (15 ml) peeled, coarsely chopped fresh ginger
Additional water for blending, as needed
1 Tbs. (15 ml) mustard oil
¼ tsp. (1 ml) black mustard seeds
½ tsp. (2 ml) five-spice, roasted and ground
2 tsp. (10 ml) ground cumin (see Note)
⅛ tsp. (.5 ml) salt
Dash black salt
3½ Tbs. (52 ml) sugar

1. Using your fingers, remove the dark, flat-oval tamarind seeds from the pulp. Also remove any fibers or hard membranes. Place the remaining contents of the bowl in a blender with ginger and blend to a thick puree, adding water a tablespoon (15 ml) at a time, if necessary, until the desired consistency results. Do not add any more water than needed. Depending on the brand, the consistency of the tamarind puree will vary slightly. (See "A Glossary of Spices and Ingredients.") Strain the puree through a fine sieve.
2. Heat oil in a 6-inch (15 cm) pan over medium low heat. Add black mustard seeds. When the seeds start popping, add the ground five-spice and cumin and stir a few times. Add the tamarind puree, then stir in salt, black salt, and sugar. Remove from heat and let cool.

3 to 4 servings.

Serving suggestions: Serve with a platter of sliced boiled potatoes, raw celery sticks, and lightly steamed cauliflower or broccoli. Street vendors in Calcutta make a sought-after dish by drizzling tamarind chutney over boiled potatoes; see Savory Potatoes with Three Sauces.

Note: Rather than use store-bought ground cumin, I roast and grind 1 teaspoon (5 ml) cumin seeds just before preparing this chutney. By doing so just prior to cooking, you allow the spice to release its flavor more fully in a dish where the ingredients are cooked very briefly.

A ripe coconut in a monkey's paw!
—Bengali proverb, said when one is unable to take advantage of opportunities at hand

Narkeler Chatney
GREEN AND WHITE COCONUT CHUTNEY

In this chutney, specks of shimmering green cilantro leaves dot a glistening coconut puree. It is easily prepared in the blender. For best results use freshly grated coconut, but even packaged coconut tastes good.

½ cup (125 ml) water
2 Tbs. (30 ml) fresh lemon juice
1 cup (250 ml) dried flaked or shredded sweetened coconut, or freshly
    grated or shredded coconut mixed with ½ tsp. (2 ml) sugar
⅓ cup (75 ml) firmly packed coarsely chopped fresh cilantro leaves
1 Tbs. (15 ml) peeled, coarsely chopped fresh ginger
½ tsp. (2 ml) seeded, chopped fresh green chili (or to taste)
1 tsp. (5 ml) ground cumin
¼ tsp. (1 ml) salt
1 tsp. (5 ml) vegetable oil (mustard oil preferred)
½ tsp. (2 ml) black mustard seeds

1. Place water, lemon juice, coconut, cilantro, ginger, green chili, icumin, and salt in the order given in the container of a blender. Blend until reduced to a thick puree, adding a little more water if necessary. Pour into a small bowl.
2. Heat oil in a 6-inch (15 cm) skillet over medium low heat. Add black mustard seeds. When the seeds start crackling, remove from heat. Add to the contents of the bowl.

4 servings.

Serving suggestions: This chutney is a nice counterpoint for Pan-raised Bread and is also good with rice or papad at any meal. Fish dishes, especially Crisp Fried Fish and Steamed Fish in Chili-Cilantro Sauce, respond well to this coconut concoction.

Kuler Chatney
PLEASING PLUM CHUTNEY

When in season, luscious, juicy plums make one of the best chutneys. My mother chooses small, intensely flavored Indian plums. In the West, you can try any type of plum—the darker varieties give a rich reddish-brown color to the mixture.

Does one eat the pit because the plum is sweet?
—Bengali proverb meaning that you should
show discretion in your pleasure

I serve this chutney during the summer heat, when its delicate sweet-sour taste tempts the palate.

1 Tbs. (15 ml) vegetable oil
1 bay leaf
1 whole dried red chili
¼ tsp. (1 ml) black mustard seeds
¼ tsp. (1 ml) turmeric
1 lb. (½ kg) pitted, slivered ripe plums (7 to 8 medium)
½ cup (125 ml) water
¼ tsp. (1 ml) salt
2½ Tbs. (37 ml) sugar

1. Heat oil in a pan over medium low heat. Fry bay leaf and red chili until the chili darkens. Add black mustard seeds and fry until they start popping, partially covering the pan to prevent the seeds from flying out. Stir in turmeric.
2. Immediately add plums, water, salt, and sugar. Bring to boil. Simmer, covered, until the plums are tender but still hold their shape, 2 to 5 minutes.
3. You can serve as is, but I prefer to thicken the sauce. Remove plums with a slotted spoon. Bring the mixture in the pan to a simmer over medium low heat. Cook, uncovered, until thickened, about 5 minutes. Return the plums to the pan. Let stand covered for a few minutes to help develop the flavors. Allow to cool.

4 servings.

Serving suggestions: I enjoy this chutney over rice at any meal, especially one that features seafood. For a festive menu, serve with Fragrant Roasted Mung Bean Stew, Monsoon Night Rice, and Fancy Fish in Cashew-Pistachio Sauce, or Lamb Swimming in Creamy Green Sauce.

Aadar Chatney
JOYOUS GINGER-RAISIN CHUTNEY

Ginger not only perfumes this dish but also provides spiciness. Raisins and dates infuse the chutney with sweetness and blend surprisingly well with the ginger.

1 cup (250 ml) raisins, soaked in 1 cup (250 ml) warm water for 15 minutes
8 pitted dates, chopped
¼ cup plus 2 Tbs. (90 ml) peeled, coarsely chopped fresh ginger
½ tsp. (2 ml) sugar
½ tsp. (2 ml) salt
¼ cup plus 1 Tbs. (75 ml) fresh lime or lemon juice

Drain the raisins, reserving the soaking liquid. Place ½ cup (125 ml) of the soaking liquid and the remaining ingredients in a blender and puree, scraping the sides often, just until thoroughly blended.
4 servings.

Serving suggestions: Savor this gently sweet chutney with rice, Pan-raised Bread, or papad at any meal, or dip "Queen Pleasing" Meat Croquettes into it. Also try with any one of the following entrees—Vegetables in a Mingling Mood, Herbal Doctor's Burger, or Beef in Rich Cashew Sauce.

VARIATION

For a slightly different taste and a sweeter chutney, omit dates but increase raisins to 1½ cups (375 ml). Soak the raisins in 1½ cups (375 ml) water.

Ada Doi Chatney
GINGER-YOGURT CHUTNEY

This cooling condiment complements rich pullao, lamb, and chicken dishes. It's simple to make and yet has a luxurious texture. I don't know its origin but guess that it was a welcoming sight in royal dining rooms after an excessively indulgent meal.

1½ cups (375 ml) plain yogurt
3 Tbs. (45 ml) fresh lemon juice
1 Tbs. (15 ml) sugar
¼ tsp. (1 ml) salt
½ tsp. (2 ml) ground cumin
1 Tbs. (15 ml) peeled fresh ginger, grated or made into a paste
  (see "A Glossary of Spices and Ingredients")
Dash ground red chili or cayenne pepper (or to taste)
1 Tbs. (15 ml) finely chopped fresh cilantro

In a bowl combine all the ingredients. This can be served immediately, but for best flavor refrigerate for an hour or so.
4 servings.

Serving suggestions: Serve as a dip for "Queen Pleasing" Meat Croquettes. Either rice or Soft Bread is a perfect accompaniment at a meal that could feature entrees such as Broccoli with a Hint of Mustard, Cabbage and Potatoes in Browned Onion Sauce, and Lamb in Chili-Mustard Sauce.

Maacher Chatney
TART TANTALIZING FISH

This tangy chutney awakens the tastebuds in a hurry. Made with fish fillet, small fish, or shrimp, it is a piquant touch with any meal.

To teach a fish how to swim
   —Bengali proverb describing a redundant activity

Use any firm-fleshed fish that you like, but halibut, marlin, salmon, sturgeon, swordfish, and shark are good choices. Avoid fish with a tender texture, such as cod, sole, or flounder. Double the recipe if you decide to serve it as an entree.

2 Tbs. (30 ml) vegetable oil (mustard oil preferred)
1 whole dried red chili
½ tsp. (2 ml) kalonji seeds

1 Tbs. (15 ml) peeled, minced fresh ginger
1 tsp. (5 ml) seeded, chopped fresh green chili (or to taste)
½ tsp. (2 ml) turmeric
½ tsp. (2 ml) salt
1½ tsp. (7 ml) black mustard seeds, ground to a powder, mixed with 1 Tbs.
   (15 ml) water and allowed to stand for 30 minutes
½ cup (125 ml) water
½ tsp. (2 ml) sugar
1 tsp. (5 ml) tamarind concentrate
1 lb. (½ kg) fish, cut into 2 × 1 × 1-inch (5 × 2.5 × 2.5 cm)
   pieces, or fresh or thawed frozen raw shrimp

1. Heat oil in a skillet over medium low heat. Fry red chili until it darkens.
   Add kalonji seeds and fry for 5 seconds. Add ginger and green chili and
   fry until ginger is lightly browned. Add turmeric, salt, and mustard paste
   and stir several times. Add water and sugar and bring to boil.
2. Simmer, covered, until the sauce thickens slightly, 5 to 10 minutes. Add
   tamarind and stir to dissolve in the sauce. Add fish and simmer, covered,
   until fish is done, 3 to 5 minutes. (See "Test for doneness" under "Fish
   and Seafood Tips.") Cook uncovered for a minute or so to allow the
   sauce to thicken more. Remove from heat. Let stand covered for a few
   minutes to help develop the flavors. Place cilantro sprigs at the center.
   Serve immediately or at room temperature.

4 small servings.

Serving suggestions: This provocative chutney draws interest as a buffet
item. For a light meal, serve with rice and Tender Garden Peas and
Potatoes. For a full meal, serve with Glorious Greens, and Rice and Mung
Beans Flavored with Whole Spices.

Chingrir Achar
SWEET AND TART SHRIMP CHUTNEY

Here pink shrimp are veiled in a velvety soft sauce. This dish is good as a
condiment on a buffet table, but after tasting it, you may decide to serve it
as a main course. In that case, double the recipe and serve with Basmati
rice.

2 Tbs. (30 ml) vegetable oil
¾ lb. (375 g) fresh or thawed frozen bay shrimp
1 Tbs. (15 ml) minced garlic

2 tsp. (10 ml) ground cumin
¼ tsp. (1 ml) salt
1½ tsp. (7 ml) sugar
Dash ground red chili or cayenne pepper (or to taste)
¼ cup (60 ml) mild white vinegar

1. Heat oil in a skillet over medium low heat. Fry shrimp just until they turn pink. Transfer with a slotted spoon to a bowl and set aside.
2. Fry garlic in the juice that has accumulated in the skillet for a few seconds. Add cumin, salt, sugar, and red pepper and stir for about 1 minute.
3. Add vinegar and simmer, covered, 3 or so minutes. Add the shrimp and any accumulated juice. Simmer, covered, until heated through, about 1 more minute. Remove from heat. Serve hot or at room temperature.

4 servings.

Serving suggestions: Serve with rice or papad at any meal. Complements entrees such as Steamed Spicy Cauliflower, Splendid Spinach, and Festive Chickpeas with Coconut and Whole Spices.

Tarkarir Chatney
SWEET AND TART VEGETABLE CHUTNEY

The hearty texture, the contrast of flavors, and the accent of spices may induce you to serve this dish as part of a meal and not just as a dip. It's excellent with plain brown rice. Chop the vegetables slightly smaller than a sugar cube.

2 Tbs. (30 ml) vegetable oil (mustard oil preferred)
¼ tsp. (1 ml) asafetida powder
½ tsp. (2 ml) black mustard seeds
1 Tbs. (15 ml) minced, peeled fresh ginger
1 tsp. (5 ml) seeded, chopped fresh green chili (or to taste)
¼ tsp. (1 ml) turmeric
1 cup (250 ml) peeled or unpeeled chopped potatoes
1¼ cups (300 ml) peeled, chopped sweet potatoes or yams
1½ cups (375 ml) chopped eggplant
¼ tsp. (1 ml) salt
2 Tbs. (30 ml) sugar
¾ cup (175 ml) water
2 tsp. (10 ml) tamarind concentrate

1. Heat oil in a large skillet over medium low heat. Sprinkle asafetida over the oil. Fry black mustard seeds for a few seconds. As soon as the seeds start popping, add ginger and green chili. Fry until ginger is lightly browned. Stir in turmeric.
2. Add potatoes and mix well. Add sweet potatoes, eggplant, salt, sugar, and water. Bring to boil and simmer, covered, until vegetables are tender, 20 to 30 minutes. Stir in tamarind. With the back of a spoon, mash some of the potatoes and sweet potatoes to thicken the gravy. Remove from heat.

4 servings.

Serving suggestions: Serve hot as a side dish at a main meal, or at room temperature as an accompaniment for papad. This is also good potluck fare.

Pudinar Chatney
TEMPTING MINT CHUTNEY

This chutney bursts with the bouquet of fresh mint. It is excellent as a dip with chips or papad and goes well with any meal, particularly lamb and beef dishes.

3 Tbs. (45 ml) water
1 Tbs. (15 ml) finely chopped onion
1 Tbs. (15 ml) finely chopped garlic
1 tsp. (5 ml) seeded, chopped fresh green chili (or to taste)
½ tsp. (2 ml) salt
1¾ tsp. (8 ml) sugar
2½ Tbs. (37 ml) tamarind puree, or more according to taste (see Note)
2 cups (500 ml) firmly packed fresh mint leaves

Place the ingredients in a blender container in the order given. Blend until a smooth puree forms. Refrigerate for 30 minutes. Serve chilled.
Makes about ¾ cup (175 ml).

Note: This chutney tastes better made with tamarind puree than with tamarind concentrate. Should you use the concentrate, start with 1¼ teaspoon (6 ml), then adjust according to your taste.

Dhane Patar Chatney
SPLENDID CILANTRO CHUTNEY

A speedy chutney that goes well with papad as well as with most meals. Even those who are not fans of cilantro are often surprised by the perky, pleasant taste of this sauce, made mellow by lemon, ginger, and coconut.

6 Tbs. (90 ml) fresh lemon juice
4 tsp. (20 ml) sugar
2 Tbs. (30 ml) peeled, chopped fresh ginger
2 tsp. (10 ml) coarsely chopped garlic
1 tsp. (5 ml) seeded, chopped fresh green chili (or to taste)
2 Tbs. (30 ml) dried flaked or shredded sweetened coconut
¼ tsp. (1 ml) salt
2 cups (500 ml) firmly packed coarsely chopped fresh
   cilantro leaves

Place the first 7 ingredients and half the cilantro in the container of a
blender in the order given. Blend just until the ingredients are ground;
do not liquefy. Add the remaining cilantro and blend again.
4 servings.

Serving suggestions: This brilliant, all-purpose chutney is a good accompaniment to most meals, particularly seafood and vegetarian dishes.

Alur Raita

POTATO SALAD IN YOGURT-MUSTARD SAUCE

That potato and yogurt have an affinity becomes evident in this dish. The
warm, powerful taste of cumin accents the cool, smooth sauce.

1 Tbs. (15 ml) mustard oil
¼ tsp. (1 ml) asafetida powder
½ tsp. (2 ml) black mustard seeds
½ tsp. (2 ml) ground cumin
¼ tsp. (1 ml) black mustard seeds, ground to a powder
½ lb. (¼ kg) peeled, cooked potatoes (about 2 medium), cut into 1-inch
   (2.5 cm) cubes
1½ cups (375 ml) plain yogurt, lightly beaten until smooth
½ tsp. (2 ml) salt
⅛ tsp. (.5 ml) black pepper, preferably freshly ground

1. Heat oil over medium low heat in a skillet. Sprinkle asafetida over the
   oil. Add mustard seeds and fry until they start popping. Stir in cumin
   and black mustard powder. Add potatoes and mix well. Cook for a minute or so. Remove from heat.
2. Combine yogurt with salt and pepper in a bowl. Add the potato mixture. Refrigerate for at least 30 minutes to develop flavors. Serve chilled.
4 to 5 servings.

Serving suggestions: A favorite snack of mine is this raita served with Soft Bread. The raita is also a good foil for seafood dishes and any vegetarian leafy green or eggplant dish.

Pudinar Raita
MINT YOGURT SAUCE

Although composed only of yogurt and spices, this sauce with a mint fragrance has a feel of luxury.

2 Tbs. (30 ml) coarsely chopped fresh mint leaves
1 cup (250 ml) plain yogurt
½ tsp. (2 ml) ground cumin
¼ tsp. (1 ml) salt
2 tsp. (10 ml) vegetable oil (mustard oil preferred)
¼ tsp. (1 ml) asafetida powder
¼ tsp. (1 ml) cumin seeds

1. Puree mint and ½ cup (125 ml) of the yogurt in a blender. Pour into a bowl. Add the remaining ½ cup (125 ml) yogurt and beat lightly with a fork until smooth. Add ground cumin and salt. Set aside.
2. Heat oil in a 6-inch (15 cm) pan over medium low heat. Sprinkle asafetida over the oil. Fry cumin seeds for a few seconds until they darken slightly. Pour this mixture over yogurt and stir to mix. Allow to cool, then refrigerate for at least 30 minutes.

4 small servings.

Serving suggestions: This versatile chutney can add spark to any meal, particularly chicken, lamb, or beef dinners.

Beguner Raita
SMOKED EGGPLANT IN GINGER-YOGURT SAUCE

The rich, smoky flavor of eggplant makes this a memorable salad. It is splendid at a brunch or buffet, or as a snack. Team with rice, Soft Bread, or papad at any meal and follow with a legume dish.

1 medium eggplant, about 1 lb. (½ kg)
2 Tbs. (30 ml) vegetable oil (mustard oil preferred)
½ tsp. (2 ml) black mustard seeds

2 Tbs. (30 ml) peeled, minced fresh ginger
1 tsp. (5 ml) seeded, chopped fresh green chili (or to taste)
½ tsp. (2 ml) salt
1 tsp. (5 ml) sugar
½ cup (125 ml) plain yogurt
1 Tbs. (15 ml) finely chopped fresh cilantro

1. Smoke and roast the eggplant under a broiler, over a gas flame, or on a barbecue grill. (See "A Glossary of Spices and Ingredients.") Set aside.
2. Heat oil in a skillet over medium low heat. Fry the black mustard seeds for a few seconds until they start popping. Add ginger and green chili and stir until ginger is lightly browned. Add eggplant and fry for a minute or so, stirring often. Remove from heat.
2. Combine salt, sugar, yogurt, and cilantro in a bowl. Add the eggplant mixture. Allow to cool to room temperature. Refrigerate for at least 30 minutes to help develop the flavors.

4 servings.

Palong Saaker Raita
SPINACH IN SPICED YOGURT

Although rarely seen in Indian restaurants, this yogurt salad is one of the best. I choose the healthiest leaves out of a bunch of spinach and let them steep in the savory yogurt sauce.

1½ Tbs. (22 ml) vegetable oil (mustard oil preferred)
¼ tsp. (1 ml) asafetida powder
½ tsp. (2 ml) black mustard seeds
1 tsp. (5 ml) seeded, chopped fresh green chili (or to taste)
1 cup (250 ml) firmly packed slivered fresh spinach leaves
½ tsp. (2 ml) salt
⅛ tsp. (.5 ml) ground black pepper (preferably freshly ground)
2 tsp. (10 ml) ground cumin
1½ cups (375 ml) plain yogurt, lightly beaten until smooth
2 Tbs. (30 ml) finely chopped fresh cilantro

1. Heat oil in a skillet over medium low heat. Sprinkle asafetida over the oil. Add black mustard seeds and fry for a few seconds. As soon as the seeds start popping, stir in green chili. Add spinach and mix well. Cook for a minute or so, just until spinach is wilted. Remove from heat.

2. Combine salt, pepper, cumin, yogurt, and cilantro in a bowl. Add the spinach mixture. Allow to cool to room temperature. Refrigerate for at least 30 minutes to help develop the flavors.

4 small servings.

Serving suggestions: This savory raita adds to the appeal of lamb, beef, and chicken dishes. Vegetarians can pair it with a potato dish such as Spicy Home Fries.

Narkeler Raita
YOGURT COCONUT DIP

When I need to prepare a dip in a hurry, I use this recipe. The cool, smooth sauce with a bare hint of sweetness is always popular with guests.

1½ Tbs. (22 ml) vegetable oil (mustard oil preferred)
½ tsp. (2 ml) black mustard seeds
1 Tbs. (15 ml) peeled fresh ginger, grated or made into a paste
   (see "A Glossary of Spices and Ingredients")
1 tsp. (5 ml) seeded, chopped fresh green chili (or to taste)
1 cup (250 ml) dried flaked or shredded sweetened coconut, ground in a
   blender to a coarse powder, or freshly grated or shredded coconut mixed
   with ½ tsp. (2 ml) sugar (see Note)
¼ tsp. (1 ml) salt
1 cup (250 ml) plain yogurt, lightly beaten until smooth

1. Heat oil in a skillet over medium low heat. Fry the mustard seeds until they start to pop. Add ginger and green chili, keeping the skillet partially covered to avoid splattering the cooking area. As soon as ginger is lightly browned, turn heat to low. Add coconut and stir several times. Remove from heat.
2. Combine salt and yogurt in a bowl. Add the coconut mixture. Refrigerate for at least 30 minutes to help develop the flavors.

4 to 5 small servings.

Serving suggestions: This raita is perfect for dunking boiled potatoes, lightly steamed vegetables, and vegetable fritters. Try also with any vegetarian or fish dish, some excellent choices being Vegetables in a Mingling Mood and Steamed Fish in Chili-Cilantro Sauce.

Note: If available, use freshly grated or thawed, frozen shredded coconut, sold in Asian markets, to give this raita a fresh flavor.

TEATIME

Let's have tea." You hear this phrase often in Bengal. At four o'clock every day we gather with family and friends to sip a cup of golden tea and discuss politics, poetry, and one of our most avid pastimes—cinema. We munch on teatime snacks and solve the world's problems.

Tea is an intensely social drink, and many Bengalis prefer to entertain at teatime rather than at dinner. Dinner requires longer preparation in the kitchen, food being the main reason for such a gathering. With tea your attention is directed more to the company and less to the food. The snacks that accompany tea, mostly finger foods, are fun, easy to prepare, and inexpensive; you can invite a crowd. I remember, for instance, when one of my aunts came to visit, my mother invited 50 people for tea. Between cups of tea, plates of delicious tidbits, and lively, witty discourse, the afternoon event lasted until 9 P.M.

Teatime also marks the transition from the workday to leisure hours. If Bengalis happen to be away from home at that hour, they head for a tea stall or sweet shop or walk up to a street vendor, usually with friends. There they can indulge in Lentil Wafers or a portion of Hot and Savory Party Mix, always with a comforting cup of tea. These mini-meals tide people over until the dinner hour, which in our hot climate occurs late in the evening after the temperature falls.

This is why Bengali cuisine abounds in a wide variety of savory snacks. Although delights such as Gold Bars or Divine Dumplings go well with tea, sweets play a smaller role than savories at teatime, as they are associated more with festive occasions. In many Western countries where teatime is not a tradition, however, these appetizers would still be a welcome treat during the cocktail hour, at brunch, or as between-meal snacks.

Another pleasant custom is "bed tea," which most hotels in Bengal still practice. I first experienced it as a child when traveling with my family. At seven in the morning, I was awakened by a knock at the door of our hotel room. A turbaned, white-gloved waiter stood there with a dainty tea tray in his hands. On it were a pot of Fragrant Milk Tea and a small plate of sweets. That early tea is all I remember of the day.

Even the selection of tea is an art. At better tea establishments you can usually taste tea before buying it. During a recent visit to Calcutta, I shopped for tea at the College Street Market. The tea seller brewed me fresh cups from different varieties; each was irresistible. It was hard to choose only one, so I ended up buying several types.

Besides tea, other popular beverages include fruit juices and blended fruits. Coconut water, the cool, refreshing fluid (different from coconut milk) that is inside a young coconut, is a perennial favorite. On the streets of Calcutta, merchants squatting on street corners beside heaps of pineapple-sized green coconuts sell this refreshing beverage. They lop the top off a coconut with a machete-like knife and insert a straw before handing it to a customer. On a warm day, you can see office workers, schoolchildren, shoppers, and workers standing on the sidewalk sipping this faintly sweet, cooling drink.

Sugarcane juice, when freshly squeezed, is another treat. Street vendors in Bengal feed stalks of sugarcane through a hand-operated press and extract the juice into glasses for passersby. The sweet, aromatic beverage always reminds me of Bengal's villages—lush green fields, fish-filled streams, and trees bowing down with fruit.

Mangoes, watermelons, and limes are typical ingredients for a variety of blended fruit drinks, known as *sharbats.* They were popular in the palaces of Moslem kings centuries ago. It is said that a chilled glass of Delicate Lime Drink appeased many a royal temper made short by the crushing heat of Bengali summers. Even now a dash of nutmeg, a pinch of white pepper, or a sprinkling of rose petals often decorates these coolers, reminiscent of days of leisure, laughter, and luxury.

Tea, the most popular beverage in our country, is to be taken morning, noon and night and on every occasion and with meals, formal or informal.

—from a package of Kohinoor brand
tea, purchased in Calcutta

Cha

FRAGRANT MILK TEA

This hearty, aromatic beverage rivals coffee in its richness. Unlike most teas that are brewed solely with water, this tea is brewed with water, milk, and cardamom. For an even spicier flavor, I add a thin slice of peeled fresh ginger, several whole cloves, and a cinnamon stick to the pot while the tea is brewing. Serve at any time or following a meal.

The Bengali custom is to serve tea always hot, never iced.

2 cups (500 ml) water
4 tsp. (20 ml) loose black tea leaves, preferably a fine-quality Darjeeling, or in a pinch 3 teabags (see Note)
5 whole cardamom pods, tops slightly opened
2 cups (500 ml) whole or 2% lowfat milk
Sugar to taste (optional)

1. Combine water, tea, and cardamom in a large pan. Bring to boil over medium heat. Simmer, covered, until the color turns deep amber, 5 to 10 minutes. (Allow sufficient time to brew. Otherwise, when milk is added in the next step, the tea will be weak.)
2. Add milk and raise heat to medium. Cook uncovered and watch carefully to make sure that the mixture does not boil over. When the mixture starts to bubble and acquires a pinkish color, remove from heat. Strain into a teapot rinsed with hot water or individual cups. Sweeten to taste and serve. (This tea tastes best when slightly sweetened.)

4 servings.

Note: You can use decaffeinated teas, but not Chinese black teas with a smoky flavor.

Lebur Lassi

LIME YOGURT COOLER

Lassi, a yogurt drink popular throughout India, lifts many weary spirits. Calcutta vendors pour lassi back and forth between tall glasses to make it frothy, the bubbly top being a part of its appeal. "Indian milkshake" is how one Westerner has described it.

Lassi can be served alone or with a meal and is a counterpoint to fiery hot food. It is especially good during summer. Enjoy it immediately after it's made; if made to wait it will probably separate. Should this occur, blend again before serving.

¾ cup (175 ml) plain yogurt
½ cup (125 ml) water
3 ice cubes
2 tsp. (10 ml) sugar
2 Tbs. (30 ml) fresh lime juice
¼ tsp. (1 ml) salt
Dash nutmeg (optional)

Puree yogurt, water, ice cubes, sugar, lime juice, and salt in a blender until smooth and bubbly. (The ice cubes will be crushed.) Pour into a chilled glass. Sprinkle nutmeg on top and serve.
1 serving.

*A wise man will accustom himself to the pure and fine water,
or to the excellent lemonade.*

—François Bernier, French traveler, on visiting Bengal
between 1659 and 1667. From the book *Travellers to
India*, by A. Yusuf Ali.

Lebur Sharbat
DELICATE LIME DRINK

Many types of limes and lemons are available in Bengal. One variety has a chiffon-light skin; another is called *gandharaj,* "the king of fragrance."

This beverage, made with either lime or lemon, has a clean, tart taste and a cooling effect. It is particularly good with Hot and Savory Party Mix.

7 Tbs. (105 ml) fresh lime or lemon juice
¼ cup (60 ml) sugar
5 cups (1 liter 250 ml) water
¼ tsp. (1 ml) salt
Ice cubes

Blend all ingredients except ice cubes in a blender. Add ice cubes and pour into chilled glasses.
4 servings.

Gholer Sharbat
FROTHY WHEY DRINK

In days when butter was made at home, the liquid that was left after churn-
ing milk was appreciated as a beverage. Whey, a nearly identical by-product
of making fresh cheese, can also be enjoyed in a similar manner when
blended with lime and spices.

2 cups (500 ml) whey, left from making channa (fresh cheese), chilled
   (see "A Glossary of Spices and Ingredients")
¼ cup (60 ml) fresh lime or lemon juice
4 tsp. (20 ml) sugar
⅛ tsp. (.5 ml) salt
Dash kalonji seeds, ground

Blend whey, lime juice, sugar, and salt in a blender. Sprinkle kalonji powder
on top. Pour into 2 chilled glasses and serve immediately. If allowed to sit,
the frothy part will separate from the liquid at the bottom; if this occurs,
blend again before serving.
2 servings.

> She entered with a tray—
> puffed rice, coconut cake,
> milk in a black marble cup,
> and juice from a green coconut.
>
>   —from *Later Poems of Rabindranath Tagore,*
>   translated by Aurobindo Bose

Jhal Muri
PUFFED RICE SALAD

Puffed rice, a popular Bengali cereal similar to Rice Krispies, adds crunch
to this appetizing salad. Some call this tasty potato and puffed rice combination a *pullao,* the term used for a much more elaborate rice main dish.
Serve with tea, as a snack, or for breakfast.

1 cup (250 ml) puffed rice (see Note)
2 Tbs. (30 ml) vegetable oil

¾ cup (175 ml) thinly slivered onion
1 Tbs. (15 ml) minced garlic
1 Tbs. (15 ml) peeled, minced fresh ginger
1 tsp. (5 ml) seeded, chopped fresh green chili (or to taste)
2 cups (500 ml) peeled, cooked potatoes cut into 1-inch (2.5 cm) cubes
2 tsp. (10 ml) ground cumin
1 Tbs. (15 ml) raisins
¼ cup (60 ml) unsalted dry roasted peanuts
½ tsp. (2 ml) salt
1 tsp. (5 ml) sugar
Dash ground red chili or cayenne pepper (or to taste)
2 tsp. (10 ml) fresh lime or lemon juice

1. Preheat oven to 350°F (180°C; gas mark 4). Spread puffed rice in a single layer on an ungreased baking sheet. Bake until crisp, about 15 minutes; do this just before serving or the puffed rice will lose its crispness.
2. Meanwhile, heat oil in a skillet over medium low heat. Fry onion, garlic, ginger, and green chili until onion is translucent, about 2 minutes. Lower the heat slightly. Add potatoes and cumin and mix well. Add raisins, peanuts, salt, sugar, and red pepper. If the mixture is too dry and sticks to the bottom of the pan, sprinkle with a few drops of water. Remove from heat. Arrange the potato mixture on a platter, sprinkle lime juice on top, and cover with the warmed puffed rice. Serve at once.

3 to 4 servings.

Note: The puffed rice sold in Indian stores is slender and crunchy, whereas that sold in health food stores is softer and puffier. Either kind is delicious as a topping for this salad when baked until crisp as described above.

Alu Kabli
"STREET-STYLE" TANGY POTATOES

Street hawkers in Calcutta are famous for this. After I finish one helping, I immediately want another. This easy, oil-free dish can be made ahead of time. For best flavor, bring it to room temperature before serving. Serve as a snack or side dish.

1 lb. (½ kg) potatoes (about 4 medium), peeled and cut into ½-inch
   (1.2 cm) cubes
½ tsp. (2 ml) salt

3 Tbs. (45 ml) fresh lime or lemon juice
1 cup (250 ml) cooked chickpeas (see "A Glossary of Legumes" in the Dals
  chapter) or canned chickpeas, drained
⅛ tsp. (.5 ml) black pepper (preferably freshly ground)
2 tsp. (10 ml) ground cumin
¼ tsp. (1 ml) black salt (see Note)
Dash ground red chili or cayenne pepper (or to taste)
½ tsp. (2 ml) garam masala
Garnish: raw mild onion rings

1. Boil the potatoes with water to cover and salt until tender but not
   mushy, 15 to 20 minutes. Drain. Drizzle lime juice over the still-hot
   potatoes. They will absorb the juice immediately.
2. Combine potatoes and chickpeas in a large bowl. In a small bowl mix
   black pepper, cumin, black salt, red pepper, and garam masala. Toss vegetables gently with spice mixture. Garnish with cilantro and onion
   rings. Serve at room temperature or slightly chilled.

4 servings.

Note: Black salt, sold in Indian stores, gives many of these snack dishes a
zing. Do not omit it or substitute another seasoning.

Papri Chat
SAVORY POTATOES WITH THREE SAUCES

Another street favorite. On a tiny plate you'll find boldly spiced potato
cubes drizzled with a yogurt sauce, which is layered with a cilantro chutney
and a tart tamarind chutney. With each mouthful you savor a panorama of
tastes, truly a joyful experience. I have omitted the dollar-sized, deep-fried
wheat wafers that form a bed for the potatoes in order to reduce the fat
content of the dish and ease its preparation.

For the potato filling:

1 lb. (½ kg) potatoes (about 4 medium), peeled and cut into ¾-inch (2 cm)
  cubes
2 Tbs. (30 ml) fresh lime or lemon juice
½ tsp. (2 ml) ground cumin
Dash ground red chili or cayenne (or to taste)
¼ tsp. (1 ml) aamchoor (dry mango powder)
¼ tsp. (1 ml) salt
Dash black salt

For the yogurt sauce:

½ cup plus 2 Tbs. (150 ml) plain yogurt
¼ cup (60 ml) cultured buttermilk
⅛ tsp. (.5 ml) salt
1 tsp. (5 ml) sugar

1 recipe Splendid Cilantro Chutney
1 recipe Tender Tamarind Chutney
Garnish: garam masala

1. Boil the potatoes in salted water to cover until tender but not mushy, 15 to 20 minutes. Drain. Drizzle lime juice over the still-hot potatoes; they will absorb it immediately. Add cumin, red pepper, aamchoor, salt, and black salt. Set aside.
2. *To make the yogurt sauce:* Combine all the sauce ingredients in a bowl. Set aside.
3. For each individual serving, place 2 to 3 tablespoons (30 to 45 ml) of the potato mixture on a small plate. Drizzle first with yogurt sauce, then with cilantro chutney, and finally with tamarind chutney. Sprinkle lightly with garam masala.

4 or more servings.

Serving suggestions: Serve as a snack or as the first course of a meal.

Alu Chotpot
PRONTO POTATOES

The word *chotpot* refers to someone who is smart and quick. Prolong the enjoyment of tea with this "smart" and savory potato-onion combination. If you use leftover cooked potatoes, you can prepare the dish in minutes. Serve as a snack or side dish, particularly with seafood.

1½ Tbs. (22 ml) vegetable oil (mustard oil preferred)
¼ tsp. (1 ml) black mustard seeds
2 cups (500 ml) thinly slivered onion
1 tsp. (5 ml) seeded, chopped fresh green chili (see Note)
¼ tsp. (1 ml) turmeric
½ tsp. (2 ml) salt
Dash ground red chili or cayenne pepper (or to taste)
1 lb. (½ kg) peeled or unpeeled potatoes (about 4 medium), cut into 1-inch (2.5 cm) cubes, or leftover cooked potatoes
¼ cup plus 2 Tbs. (90 ml) water (omit if using cooked potatoes)

2 Tbs. (30 ml) fresh lime or lemon juice
Garnish: fresh green mild chili slivers

1. Heat oil in a skillet over medium low heat. Fry black mustard seeds until they start popping. Fry onion until translucent, about 2 minutes. Stir in green chili, turmeric, salt, and red pepper. Add potatoes and mix well. If using cooked potatoes, simmer covered until warm, and omit step 2.
2. Add water and bring to boil. Simmer, covered, 15 to 20 minutes or until potatoes are tender. If the sauce is still thin, mash a few potatoes with the back of a spoon and mix in with the gravy.
3. Remove from heat. Sprinkle lime juice on top. Garnish with chili slivers and cilantro and serve immediately.

4 servings.

Note: Green chili is used here to add a refreshing taste, not heat. Also, the slight crunch of the chili contrasts with the smooth, mellow texture of the potatoes. So choose a mild variety of chili but use plenty of it. A good choice is the mild variety of jalapeño pepper sold in Western supermarkets. Adjust the hotness of the dish with cayenne pepper.

Alur Bora
PIQUANT POTATO CROQUETTES

These savory nibbles are a real success at parties. I prepare the ingredients ahead of time, but fry or bake the croquettes after the guests arrive. An impatient teenager once ate an uncooked croquette and claimed to have enjoyed it just the same.

They are best when deep-fried, as is the tradition, but are also tasty when baked. I usually deep-fry half of the croquettes and bake the other half, then serve them together with a variety of chutneys.

2 Tbs. (30 ml) vegetable oil
¼ tsp. (1 ml) asafetida powder
½ cup (125 ml) finely chopped onion
1 Tbs. (15 ml) peeled, minced fresh ginger
1 tsp. (5 ml) seeded, chopped fresh green chili (or to taste)
⅛ tsp. (.5 ml) turmeric
1 lb. (½ kg) potatoes (about 4 medium), peeled, cooked, and mashed
1 tsp. (5 ml) ground cumin
Dash ground red chili or cayenne pepper (or to taste)
½ tsp. (2 ml) salt

1 Tbs. (15 ml) minced fresh cilantro
2 Tbs. (30 ml) besan (chickpea flour)
½ tsp. (2 ml) baking powder
1 egg, lightly beaten
2 Tbs. (30 ml) fresh lemon juice
Vegetable oil for deep-frying (optional)

1. Heat oil in a skillet over medium low heat. Sprinkle asafetida over the oil. Fry onion until translucent and soft, about 2 minutes. Add ginger and green chili and stir a few times. Lower the heat slightly and stir in turmeric. Add potatoes, cumin, red pepper, and salt and mix well. Transfer the potato mixture to a large bowl and let cool, then add cilantro.

2. Combine besan and baking powder in a separate bowl. Gradually add to the potatoes. Add egg and lemon juice and mix until all ingredients are evenly distributed. Let rest for a few minutes; the mixture will firm up as it stands. Pinch off pieces of dough and roll into balls about 1½ inches (4 cm) in diameter. Set aside. (You can refrigerate them up to a day, but bring them to room temperature before baking or frying.)

3. *To bake:* Preheat oven to 350°F (180°C; gas mark 4). Arrange the balls on a lightly oiled cookie sheet. Bake 20 to 25 minutes, raising the heat to 450°F (230°C; gas mark 8) during the last 3 to 4 minutes of baking to brown the balls lightly and give them a slightly crunchy texture.

4. *To deep-fry:* Just before serving, heat oil in a deep-fat fryer or pan to 375°F (190°C). Heat oven to no more than 200°F (100°C; gas mark ¼). Carefully drop 3 or 4 croquettes into the oil using a slotted spatula. Fry for several seconds until medium brown all over, turning once. Remove and drain on paper towels. Serve immediately or keep warm in the oven until all are fried. Makes 25 or more croquettes.

Serving suggestions: Serve at teatime or as part of a meal with Tender Tamarind Chutney, Tempting Mint Chutney, and/or Green and White Coconut Chutney.

Variation: You can surprise your guests by stuffing these balls with a variety of fillings before frying or baking. Use a dab of any of the above chutneys or a meat filling as below.

VARIATION

MEAT-FILLED POTATO CROQUETTES

Prepare the meat filling. Proceed with the ground meat as described in step 1 of "Queen Pleasing" Meat Croquettes. Do not shape the meat into balls.

Instead, pan-fry the meat using 1 to 1½ tablespoons (15 to 22 ml) oil for several minutes or until done. Drain thoroughly and let cool. See "To stuff the croquettes" below.

VARIATION
FISH-FILLED POTATO CROQUETTES

You can also use this tasty fish filling in pita halves for making sandwiches.

¼ cup (60 ml) water
½ lb. (¼ kg) fish, such as halibut, salmon, or tuna, cut into 4-inch (10 cm)
    square pieces
1 Tbs. (15 ml) mustard oil
¼ tsp. (1 ml) asafetida powder
⅛ tsp. (.5 ml) turmeric
¼ tsp. (1 ml) salt
1 tsp. (5 ml) seeded, chopped fresh green chili (or to taste)
1 Tbs. (15 ml) fresh lemon juice

1. Bring the water to boil in a skillet. Lower the heat and add fish. Simmer, covered, until fish is done, 3 to 5 minutes. (See "Test for doneness" under "Fish and Seafood Tips" in the "Fish and Seafood" chapter.) Remove fish with a slotted spoon. Use the poaching water in cooking other fish dishes or discard it. Rinse and wipe out the skillet.
2. Remove and discard fish skins. Shred the flesh using your fingers or the back of a fork. Set aside.
3. Heat oil in the same skillet over medium low heat. Sprinkle asafetida over the oil. Add turmeric, salt, and green chili. Add the fish and fry for about 2 minutes, stirring constantly. Let cool to room temperature. Blend in lemon juice.

To stuff the croquettes:

Gently insert your little finger halfway into the ball. Place a little chutney or pickle, ground meat or fish filling in the indentation, and reshape into a smooth ball that doesn't show any cracks on the outside. Fry or bake as above.

Begum Bahar Kabab
"QUEEN PLEASING" MEAT CROQUETTES

The name comes from an old story. This dish pleased a finicky *begum*, the wife of a Moslem king. The beautiful queen is said to have lounged on her throne, fanned by her attendants. She would sip lemon *sharbat* and munch on these exotic, spicy croquettes.

Traditionally these croquettes are deep-fried, but they can also be baked oil-free. When entertaining, I deep-fry a few and bake the rest, serving them together on a platter with an assortment of chutneys.

For the croquettes:

2 Tbs. (30 ml) very finely minced onion
1 Tbs. (15 ml) seeded, chopped fresh green chili (or to taste)
2 Tbs. (30 ml) unsalted raw cashews, ground in a blender to a coarse
    powder (see Note)
1 Tbs. (15 ml) unsalted raw pistachios, ground in a blender to a coarse
    powder (see Note)
2 tsp. (10 ml) ground cumin
2 tsp. (10 ml) ground coriander
1 tsp. (5 ml) peeled fresh ginger, grated or made into a paste
    (see "A Glossary of Spices and Ingredients")
1 tsp. (5 ml) garlic, forced through a garlic press or made into a paste
    (see "A Glossary of Spices and Ingredients")
1 tsp. (5 ml) garam masala
¼ tsp. (1 ml) salt
1 Tbs. (15 ml) finely chopped fresh cilantro
¾ lb. (350 g) extra lean ground beef or lamb (see "Meat Tips" in the
    "Poultry and Meat" chapter for suggestions on buying)
2 Tbs. (30 ml) fresh lemon juice

Vegetable oil for deep-frying (optional)

1. Combine all ingredients for the croquettes except meat and lemon juice in a bowl. Add meat and lemon juice and mix gently to keep from squeezing out the moisture. Pinch off portions of this mixture and roll into balls, about 1½ inches (4 cm) in diameter.
2. *If baking:* Preheat oven to 350°F (180°C; gas mark 4). Place a rack on a cookie sheet. Arrange the balls on the rack to allow the fat to drain out. Bake until a toothpick inserted in the middle of one croquette and pulled gently to one side does not show a raw red color, 12 to 15 minutes. Raise heat to 450°F (230°C; gas mark 8) and bake until the balls are lightly browned, 3 to 5 minutes; do not let them burn.
3. *If deep-frying:* Heat oil in a deep-fat fryer or pan to 375°F (190°C). Heat oven to no more than 200°F (110°C; gas mark ¼). Carefully drop 3 or 4 balls into the oil using a spatula. Remove each as soon as it turns medium brown on all sides, less than a minute. Drain on paper towels.

Serve immediately or keep warm in the oven until all have been fried. Makes 25 croquettes.

Serving suggestions: Serve with tea or as an appetizer with Tempting Mint Chutney, Joyous Ginger-Raisin Chutney, and/or Green and White Coconut Chutney.

Note: For lighter croquettes, replace part of the cashew-pistachio powder with an equal amount of wholewheat breadcrumbs. (See "A Glossary of Spices and Ingredients" for instructions on how to make crumbs at home.)

The nightingales have eaten all the rice; how can we pay the rent?
—Bengali nursery rhyme

Chirer Misti Pullao
SWEET RICE FLAKES WITH NUTS AND RAISINS

Rice flakes (*chiura* or *poha*), also called flat rice or beaten rice, are available in Indian stores. They are made commercially by first flattening and then drying cooked rice. These light flakes are easy to digest and make a delightful snack or breakfast item.

When friends and relatives drop in unannounced at teatime, as is customary in Bengal, my mother prepares this dish in minutes. Here the ingredients are simple, but the end result is heavenly. The rice flakes are light as air; the nuts are chewy and full of flavor. Serve as a snack or for breakfast.

2½ Tbs. (37 ml) vegetable oil
1 cup (250 ml) chiura (rice flakes)
1 Tbs. (15 ml) unsalted raw cashews
1 Tbs. (15 ml) unsalted raw pistachios
2 Tbs. (30 ml) raisins (preferably golden)
1 Tbs. (15 ml) peeled, minced fresh ginger
⅛ tsp. (.5 ml) salt
1 Tbs. (15 ml) sugar

1. Heat 1½ tablespoons (22 ml) oil in a skillet over medium heat. When the oil is very hot and almost smoking, add the rice flakes; they will absorb the oil and start puffing up within a few seconds. (Make sure the

oil is very hot, or else they will not puff.) As soon as all the flakes have puffed, remove gently with a slotted spatula and set aside. (Handle them gently once they have been fried, as they will be quite fragile.)

2. Heat the remaining 1 tablespoon (15 ml) oil in the same skillet over medium low heat. Add cashews, pistachios, raisins, ginger, and salt. Cook until ginger turns light brown, about 1 minute, stirring constantly. Remove from heat. Toss nut mixture gently with the rice flakes. Sprinkle sugar on top and serve piping hot.

2 to 3 servings.

Both yogurt and rice flakes are auspicious symbols in Bengal. Following an ancient wedding-day custom, the mothers of both the bride and the groom will eat sweetened yogurt and rice flakes (softened first by rinsing) for breakfast in their respective homes.

Mohonbhog
ENCHANTMENT BARS

Every Bengali child knows the story of Apu, a young village boy depicted in the novel *Pather Panchali,* or *Song of the Road,* by Bibhutibhusan Bandyapadhyaya. It is the story on which the world-renowned "Apu Trilogy" films were based.

In one of the more touching scenes of the novel, Apu is taken in by a wealthy family and served *mohonbhog.* The delicious dish contains raisins. Apu's mother did not use raisins in mohonbhog; Apu realizes for the first time in his life the poverty into which he was born.

I always loved the days when I'd return home from school in the afternoon and find my mother making mohonbhog. She never forgot the raisins.

These bars are good in lunch boxes, for picnics, at potlucks, and as dessert.

2 Tbs. (30 ml) vegetable oil
1 cup (250 ml) regular Cream of Wheat®
½ cup (125 ml) unsalted raw cashews or blanched almonds, ground in a
   blender to a coarse powder
½ cup (125 ml) sugar

2 Tbs. (30 ml) raisins (preferably golden)
2 cups (500 ml) whole or 2% lowfat milk
2 Tbs. (30 ml) chopped unsalted cashews or almonds, lightly toasted
2 Tbs. (30 ml) chopped unsalted raw pistachios
A sprinkling of ghee (optional)

1. Heat oil in a 10-inch (25 cm) skillet over medium low heat. Fry Cream
   of Wheat®, stirring constantly, until light brown, 8 to 15 minutes; do
   not burn.
2. Stir in ground cashews, sugar, and raisins. Lower the heat slightly. Stir in
   milk a little at a time so that no lumps form. When all the milk has
   been absorbed, continue to cook, stirring often, until the mixture solidifies and pulls away from the sides of the pan, about 5 minutes. Stir in
   the ghee.
3. Remove from heat and spread the mixture evenly in an 8-inch (20 cm)
   square baking dish. Sprinkle toasted cashews and pistachios on top and
   press lightly with the back of a spoon. When cool, cut into 1-inch
   (2.5 cm) squares or diamonds.

Makes 20 or more bars.

Nonta Halwa

SAVORY WHEAT PULLAO

A fluffy, chili-hot grain dish with a multitude of flavors, almost a pullao.
"What is this made of?" your family and friends will ask, hardly believing it
is the familiar Cream of Wheat®.

2½ to 3 Tbs. (37 to 45 ml) vegetable oil (mustard oil preferred)
¾ cup (175 ml) regular Cream of Wheat®
1 whole dried red chili
½ tsp. (2 ml) black mustard seeds
1½ cups (375 ml) finely chopped onion
2 Tbs. (30 ml) peeled, minced fresh ginger
1 tsp. (5 ml) seeded, chopped fresh green chili
¼ cup (60 ml) raw cashews
¼ tsp. (1 ml) salt
1 cup (250 ml) hot water
2 Tbs. (30 ml) fresh lime or lemon juice
1 Tbs. (15 ml) finely chopped fresh cilantro
Garnish: fresh mild green chili slivers

1. Heat 1 tablespoon (15 ml) oil in a skillet over medium low heat. Fry Cream of Wheat®, stirring constantly, until light brown, 7 to 10 minutes; do not burn. Remove from the skillet immediately and set aside. Rinse and wipe out the skillet.
2. Heat 2 tablespoons (30 ml) oil in the same skillet over medium low heat. Fry red chili until it darkens. Add mustard seeds and fry until they start crackling. Add onion and fry until richly browned but not burnt, 12 to 15 minutes, stirring constantly. Stir in ginger, green chili, cashews, and salt. Add the Cream of Wheat®.
3. Pour hot water into the skillet and simmer, covered, until all water has been absorbed and the mixture is light and fluffy, 7 to 10 minutes. Add lime juice and cilantro and mix well. Garnish with chili slivers and serve piping hot.

4 to 5 servings.

Serving suggestions: This grain dish is an excellent counterpoint to Fragrant Milk Tea and makes for a satisfying and nutritious snack or breakfast. I also enjoy it in place of rice at a main meal when accompanied by Peanut Cucumber Salad with Chili-Lime Dressing.

Chine Badam O Sosha
PEANUT CUCUMBER SALAD WITH CHILI-LIME DRESSING

Peanuts, which are popular as a snack in Bengal, also provide protein in a vegetarian diet. On warm Calcutta afternoons you will see roadside vendors selling roasted, unshelled peanuts in newspaper cones. People stroll in Maidan, a grassy park in the city center, while sharing peanuts with friends. They say many a romance has started over a cone of peanuts.

Here the crunch of peanuts contrasts with the juiciness of cucumber. Chilies accent this cool salad, so inviting on warm days. You can serve it as a snack, at teatime, or as a salad with a main meal.

2 Tbs. (30 ml) fresh lime (or lemon) juice
1 tsp. (5 ml) sugar
½ tsp. (2 ml) salt
2 cups (500 ml) peeled, seeded cucumber cut into ½-inch (1.2 cm) cubes
¾ cup (175 ml) skinless, unsalted, dry roasted peanuts, coarsely chopped
2 tsp. (10 ml) seeded, chopped fresh green chili (or to taste)
4 romaine leaves
¼ cup (60 ml) skinless, unsalted, dry roasted peanuts, finely chopped

1. In a large bowl, combine lime juice, sugar, and salt. Mix in cucumber, ¾ cup (175 ml) coarsely chopped peanuts, and green chili. Refrigerate 1 hour. (This salad develops flavor as it stands.)
2. Just before serving, stir to mix the ingredients with the accumulated juices. Place a romaine leaf on an individual serving plate and top with a portion of the cucumber mixture. Sprinkle each serving with an equal portion of the remaining ¼ cup (60 ml) chopped peanuts.

4 servings.

Dalmut

HOT AND SAVORY PARTY MIX

This spicy mixture of split chickpeas, peanuts, cashews, raisins, and other savory items is the most favored snack of my childhood. Since it is also nutritious, my mother never stopped me from munching it, although in school I once ate too much and suffered a happy "tummy ache."

Adults are equally fond of this tasty snack. In Calcutta's New Market, a large covered bazaar, you will find numerous vendors selling endless varieties of the colorful mixture in enormous glass jars. Shoppers line up, saying, "I want to buy just a little for my family." They sample everything, then end up with several packages. The range of flavors—hot, sweet, salty—in each bite of dalmut become a high point of the tea hour.

Serve as a snack or at a buffet table. An elegant way to enjoy this savory is to serve it warm on a dainty dessert plate. Eat with a tiny teaspoon while sipping Fragrant Milk Tea.

¾ cup (175 ml) chana dal (split chickpeas), soaked 6 hours or overnight in 2½ cups (625 ml) water
2 Tbs. (30 ml) vegetable oil
¼ tsp. (1 ml) asafetida powder
⅛ tsp. (.5 ml) turmeric
¼ cup (60 ml) raw unsalted cashew halves
¼ cup (60 ml) raisins (preferably golden)
½ cup (125 ml) unsalted roasted peanuts (preferably red-skinned)
1 tsp. (5 ml) ground cumin
¼ tsp. (1 ml) black salt (do not omit)
½ tsp. (2 ml) salt
1½ tsp. (7 ml) sugar
Dash ground red chili or cayenne pepper (or to taste; best if slightly hot)
1 cup (250 ml) *sev* (ready-to-eat chickpea noodles; see Note)

1. Drain chana dal thoroughly. (Use the drained water for cooking rice, soups, or vegetables.) Heat 1 tablespoon (15 ml) oil in a skillet over medium low heat. Add the chana dal and fry until it looks slightly dull and is very lightly browned, 7 to 10 minutes, stirring constantly. The dal will lose its raw taste and will be chewy to taste; do not overcook or it will become soft. Remove and set aside.
2. Heat the remaining tablespoon (15 ml) oil in the same skillet over medium low heat. Sprinkle asafetida over the oil. Lower the heat slightly. Add turmeric, cashews, and raisins and stir until cashews are lightly browned, about 1 minute. Add peanuts and stir several times. Add the dal, cumin, black salt, salt, sugar, and red pepper and mix well. Remove from heat. Add sev. Serve warm (preferably) or at room temperature.

7 to 8 servings.

Note: Sev, ready-made chickpea noodles cut into 1-inch (2.5 cm) lengths, are sold in Indian stores. You can eat them straight from the package, just as you would potato chips. But they are more enjoyable when mixed with other savory items as in the recipe above. The widths of these noodles vary. Some are about ¼ inch (6 mm) wide, others narrower. You can use a mixture of noodles of different widths in the above recipe for variety in appearance and texture.

Papad
LENTIL WAFERS

I attended a feast given by the headmistress of my high school in Bengal when I graduated. The starter for the 10-course meal was crunchy, home-made papads that resembled a fine cracker and were a sheer delight.

Very few families make papad from scratch these days, as the process is laborious. They are usually made with ground lentils, although some varia-tions include ground rice. The dough is rolled paper-thin and traditionally dried in the sun.

In the West you can buy them at Indian grocers. They may be flavored with garlic or asafetida or made fiery with green chili flakes or black pepper. My Western friends enjoy dipping them in chutneys. In fact, you can captivate your guests with nothing other than a heap of papads and bowls of chutneys.

How to cook papads:

The traditional way is to deep-fry them, but I prefer baking, which makes them crisp but keeps them free of oil.

1. *To bake:* Preheat oven to 350°F (180°C; gas mark 4). Place several papads on a large, ungreased baking sheet in a single layer. Bake until they are crisp and lightly and evenly browned all over and bubbles have appeared on the surface, 10 to 20 minutes. If baking more than 7 or 8 in a batch, allow a little more time.

2. *To deep-fry:* You can deep-fry whole, halved, or quartered papads. Cut the papads, if desired, using a pair of kitchen shears. Heat oil in a deep-fat fryer or pan to 375°F (190°C). Heat oven to no more than 200°F (110°C; gas mark ¼). Carefully drop papads or pieces in the oil. In a few seconds they will rise to the surface, turn opaque, and puff up in places. Allow them to become crisp and light brown. Remove with a slotted spatula and drain between layers of paper towel. Serve immediately or keep warm in the oven until all have been fried.

SWEETS

The sights and smells of sweets bring back memories of childhood celebrations when even the simplest treats tasted heavenly. The sweets of my childhood were divided into seasons. In spring and summer, the essence of mango or jackfruit flavored the favorite milk sweets. A dazzling array of confections such as moon cakes and coconut balls would brighten the autumnal festivities. With the coming of winter, it was time for fragrant puddings and plump dumplings with a variety of tantalizing stuffings.

For my sister's wedding, my father hired a local sweetmaker of distinction. Early on the morning of the wedding day, the sweetmaker set up a makeshift shop in our backyard. Sitting cross-legged, he slowly stirred a big pan of milk over a charcoal stove until the milk thickened. Soon thereafter he began to fill large platters with an array of exotic delicacies. The aroma of cardamom and roasted nuts wafted among the guests. My father was a hero. "Wonderful, simply wonderful," murmured the guests, partaking of second helpings.

I spent much time talking to this kindly candy man. His tips are scattered throughout these pages. Above all, he emphasized the need for patience, since many sweets require slow cooking. "Take the time," he said. "After all, it is a gift you make of yourself."

Sweetmaking is considered an art, and Bengalis honor distinctive sweetmakers of yesteryear such as K. C. Das, Girish, and Moira. If traveling to Calcutta, you should not miss the opportunity to visit the sweetshops named after them.

Bengalis follow the ancient custom of incorporating one or more of the "five nectars," which are milk, honey, ghee, sugar, and water, in their sweets. Eggs, however common a dessert ingredient in the West, are absent from these recipes since many Indian vegetarians follow an egg-free diet.

235

Puddings, dumplings, and bar cookies are made without eggs but with no loss of taste.

The basis of most sweets is *khoa,* thickened milk. It's made by slowly simmering milk until it is reduced to a semisolid mass with a nutlike fragrance. Another common base is channa, fresh sweet cheese, made in minutes by curdling milk. Bengalis also incorporate numerous fruits and vegetables, such as mangoes, bananas, and sweet potatoes, to produce an astonishing variety of tastes and enhance the nutritional value of desserts. Nuts, raisins, and spices often add to their appeal as well. For a stunning presentation, sweetmakers may garnish their confections with edible silver or gold leaf, now available in the West. This tissue-thin material, in the past reserved to ornament royal dishes, has a barely perceptible taste and dazzles the eye with its brilliance.

To satisfy the taste of milk with whey
—Bengali proverb referring to a situation in which one must be satisfied with less than an ideal condition

The two most familiar sweets are *rosgolla,* Milk Balls in Rose Syrup, and *Sandesh,* Silk and Satin Bars, often called "the king of sweets." These two varieties, among others, have made Bengali sweets famous throughout India.

"Then tell me what are the things that are required for the worship of God?"
"Flowers, Ganges water, incense, and sandesh."
—from *The Bengali Peasant from Time to Time,*
by Tara Krishna Basu

You will find Bengali sweet vendors in every major Indian city, but the largest number is in Calcutta, the capital of West Bengal. "A sweet shop in every block!" was how my American husband first reacted to this metropolis. In each shop, a profusion of jewellike miniature confections overflowed the display cases, tempting passersby.

Their alluring colors—rose-red, yellow, orange—and fascinating shapes—diamond, pretzellike, spherical—drew us in. Pearl-white puffs floated in clear syrup. Pistachio-green pudding was nestled in reddish-brown earthenware pots. Tom sampled everything, but finally declared *ros malai*, Milk Balls in Rich Saffron Cream Sauce, to be his favorite. He dubbed Bengalis "sweetmakers to the nation."

Later, as I took Tom to visit friends and relatives, we had to *misti-mukh*, "sweeten the palate." Each hostess would offer us a plate filled with delicacies. "You must eat this *sandesh*. I made it especially for you," she would insist. Knowing the time she had spent in front of a stove, I would savor each to its last bite. By day's end my stomach was full, my heart fuller.

The exchange of sweets is an ancient Hindu tradition based on the belief that sweets represent the innate goodness of our being. Even gods are said to delight in these delicacies. The goddess Luxmi prefers puddings, and Lord Krishna is said to like milk-based desserts. During religious events, temple food offerings include large varieties of confections, often called the "food of the gods."

Since a Bengali meal provides many flavors, your tastebuds will be thoroughly aroused even without a dessert. Desserts are generally served on festive occasions and when entertaining. Since most of them are made of milk (which provides protein, calcium, phosphorus, and other nutrients) or legumes (rich in complex carbohydrates, B vitamins, and iron), Bengalis consider them to be nutritious food, not frivolities.

In deference to Western tastes, I have reduced the amount of sugar in these recipes, use only lowfat milk, and eliminate ghee. I serve small portions of these delectable sweets, all within the limits of a lowfat diet, with a large platter of sliced fresh fruits. Following Bengali custom, I may sprinkle lime juice and thin slivers of young ginger over fresh papayas and mangoes. On other occasions, I may end the meal with peaches, strawberries, or persimmons in a creamy saffron sauce.

Bengali sweets, despite their wide range of tastes and textures, are little known outside India. This is probably due to the Western perception that they are overly sweet and high in fat. But once introduced to the lowfat, reduced-sugar versions presented in this book, many of my Western friends develop a great fondness for them. "Bengali sweets are heavenly," one recently told me, "and so enticingly dainty."

Sweet Tips

- If the recipe calls for boiling or reducing milk, choose a deep, heavy-bottomed, preferably nonstick pan at least 10 inches (25 cm) in diameter. A pan with a large surface area helps evaporate the moisture from the milk faster.

  Lightly oil the bottom and sides of the pan before pouring in milk.

(Use a small piece of paper towel saturated with vegetable oil for this purpose.) This will help prevent the milk from sticking.

■ Bay leaves are sometimes added to impart flavor during the preparation of sugar syrup or when reducing milk. If available, use the fresh leaves of bay laurel trees, common in California.

■ Rosewater, kewra water, cardamom, or nutmeg commonly flavors the sweets. Use them according to your taste.

■ How to tell when simmering rosgollas, or milk balls, are ready? Lift a ball out of the simmering syrup with a slotted spoon and gently place in a glass of cold water. If the ball sinks, it is done. Return the ball to the cooking syrup.

■ Reducing milk can take 30 minutes to an hour, depending on the quantity. I usually cook other dishes while watching over the milk. Just make sure that you keep the spoon used to stir the milk separate.

■ Except where noted, most sweets can be made a day or two ahead and refrigerated.

Rosgolla
MILK BALLS IN ROSE SYRUP

These spongy milk balls, soaked in a light sugar syrup, are dear to the heart of all Bengalis. Bagh Bazaar, a neighborhood in Northern Calcutta, is famous for its rosgolla; the dessert was created there in the 19th century by a sweetmaker named Moira. When expatriate Bengalis get together, a question frequently asked is, "Have you tried making rosgolla?"

The first key to preparing them successfully lies in kneading the fresh cheese to make it smooth and pliable. The second is the consistency of the sugar syrup in which the balls are cooked. The syrup should be very thin so that it penetrates the balls and makes them puff up.

For the milk balls:

Fresh cheese (see "A Glossary of Spices and Ingredients")
1 tsp. (5 ml) regular Cream of Wheat®
18 to 20 sugar cubes

For the cooking syrup:

1 cup (250 ml) sugar
6 cups water

For the soaking syrup:

1 cup (250 ml) sugar
4 cups (1 liter) water

1 bay leaf
4 whole cardamom pods
Flavoring: rosewater (optional)
Garnish: chopped raw pistachios (optional)

1. For use in this recipe, make sure that the fresh cheese is well drained; too much moisture may cause the milk balls to crack as they cook. Place the well-drained and well-kneaded cheese on a board. Sprinkle Cream of Wheat® evenly over the cheese and knead again to uniformly incorporate it. Let rest a few minutes.
2. Prepare the cooking syrup: Bring sugar and water to boil in a deep, heavy-bottomed pan at least 10 inches (25 cm) in diameter. Boil for 2 to 3 minutes, then reduce heat and keep warm.
3. Pinch off portions of the cheese and roll into balls, about 1 inch (2.5 cm) in diameter. Gently insert your little finger halfway into each ball, place a sugar cube in the indentation, and reshape into a smooth ball that doesn't show any cracks on the outside.
4. Raise heat under the cooking syrup and bring to a gently bubbling simmer. Reduce heat slightly but make sure that the syrup remains at a simmer. Place each ball on a spoon and gently lower it into the syrup. Cover and simmer for 25 to 30 minutes. The balls will expand slightly during this time.
5. Meanwhile, prepare the soaking syrup. Bring sugar, water, bay leaf, and cardamom to boil. Boil for 3 to 4 more minutes; keep warm.
6. When the balls are cooked, remove carefully with a slotted spoon and place in the soaking syrup. Let cool, then refrigerate overnight or up to 3 days. By this time the balls will have absorbed some of the syrup and will be plump and juicy. Sprinkle with rosewater.

Makes 18 to 20.

Serving suggestions: Place 1 or 2 balls on an individual serving plate. Drizzle a little syrup over them. Scatter pistachios on top. You can't go wrong if you serve rosgolla at the end of any Bengali meal.

Ros Malai

MILK BALLS IN RICH SAFFRON CREAM SAUCE

This elegant dish is worth the time it takes to prepare; you can proudly serve it to your most honored guests. One might mistakenly assume the rich sauce to be inappropriate for healthful dining—yet it can be prepared with lowfat milk, which is slowly simmered until reduced to a thick, creamy consistency. Its flavor is further enhanced by the addition of finely ground saffron. As with other sweets, I serve this in small portions, but even the taste of a few spoonfuls will elevate your dining pleasure to the maximum.

I make the rosgolla a day or two ahead of time, but prepare the cream sauce early on the same day I intend to serve it and store it in the refrigerator. The sauce tastes best when chilled.

1 recipe for Milk Balls in Rose Syrup (see earlier in this chapter)

For the cream sauce:

4 cups (1 liter) whole or 2% lowfat milk (see Note 1)
5 whole cardamom pods
1 Tbs. (15 ml) sugar
1 Tbs. (15 ml) unsalted raw cashews or almonds, ground in a blender to a coarse powder (see Note 2)
1 Tbs. (15 ml) shelled unsalted raw pistachios, ground in a blender to a coarse powder (see Note 2)
½ tsp. (2 ml) saffron, ground to a powder, mixed with 2 tsp. (10 ml) warm (not hot) water, and allowed to stand for 10 minutes
A few saffron threads soaked in 1 tsp. (5 ml) warm milk or water (optional)
Garnish: slivered unsalted raw pistachios

1. Soak rosgollas in syrup but do not add rosewater. Keep refrigerated until ready to use.
2. Prepare the cream sauce: Lightly oil the bottom and sides of a wide pan. (See "Sweets Tips.") Add milk and cardamom pods and bring to boil over medium to medium high heat. Stir constantly until foaming subsides, then lower heat to medium. Cook until reduced to the consistency of whipping cream, 20 to 30 minutes, stirring the milk down each time it rises and foams. Stir frequently and scrape the bottom and sides to incorporate any accumulated milk solids into the liquid milk mixture; if any skin forms on the surface, gently stir it into the liquid as well.
3. Add sugar, cashews, and pistachios. Remove from heat and transfer the sauce to a bowl. It will thicken more as it cools. When cool, add saffron and refrigerate. Just before serving, lift the optional saffron threads from the warm milk in which it has been soaking with a fork and gently swirl them through the cream sauce, making a color pattern. Garnish with slivered pistachios.

Serving suggestions: Pour 2 tablespoons (30 ml) of sauce on a dessert plate. With a slotted spoon, lift 1 or 2 rosgollas from the syrup and place them atop the sauce. Serve at the end of any Bengali meal. You can also prepare this delectable sauce alone to serve with fresh fruits.

Note 1: If reducing dietary fat is not a concern, replace the milk with half and half, which makes a richer, creamier sauce; cook for only about 15 minutes in step 2. Although restaurants in the West sometimes use canned condensed milk for the sauce, preparing it in the traditional slow-cooking way gives far better results.

Note 2: For a very lowfat diet, you can reduce the amount of nuts or omit them altogether.

Cham-Cham
PLEASURE BOATS

These milky-white ovals, floating in a clear sweet sauce, are irresistible. They are a close cousin to Milk Balls in Rose Syrup, but merit a place of their own. The areas of Faridpur and Tangail in Bangladesh are known for this delicious treat.

For the dumplings:
Fresh cheese (see "A Glossary of Spices and Ingredients")
1 tsp. (5 ml) regular Cream of Wheat®
10 to 12 unsalted raw pistachios, chopped

For the syrup:
1 cup (250 ml) sugar
4 cups (1 liter) water
Flavoring: dash of rosewater (optional)

1. Follow step 1 of Milk Balls in Rose Syrup to prepare the dough with fresh cheese and Cream of Wheat®.
2. Prepare the dumplings: Pinch off portions of the dough and roll into balls about 1 inch (2.5 cm) in diameter. Gently insert your little finger halfway into each ball, place 1 or 2 pistachio bits in the indentation, and reshape into a smooth ball that doesn't show any cracks on the outside. Flatten into an oval about 2 inches (5 cm) long and ¾ inch (2 cm) thick. (Use any remaining pistachios for garnish.)
3. Make the syrup: Bring sugar and water to boil in a deep pan about 10 inches (25 cm) in diameter. Boil for 10 minutes, then lower the heat. Place each ball on a spoon and gently lower into the syrup. Simmer, covered, 1 hour.
4. Transfer cham-chams and any remaining syrup to a large bowl. Let cool, then refrigerate for several hours or, for best results, up to 2 days. Sprinkle with rosewater and decorate with any remaining pistachios.

Makes about 20 cham-chams.

Serving suggestions: Serve as you would Milk Balls in Rose Syrup. Cham-chams are also excellent when smothered with the cream sauce as described in Milk Balls in Rich Saffron Cream Sauce.

Golap Jaam
MILK PUFFS IN CARDAMOM SYRUP

These tender, spongy puffs delight the eye with their rich brown color. A cardamom seed hidden inside bursts on the palate with its exotic flavor. This classic dessert can be made ahead and is perfect for a buffet. Even though they are deep-fried (and have no lowfat alternative), I prepare them once a year as a special treat. I serve only one per person, making sure the rest of the meal is nutritious and well balanced. I don't believe an occa-sional deviation from an otherwise lowfat diet will adversely affect my health.

Literally "the rose fruit," these puffs are aptly named after *jaam*, a small, juicy, purplish-red fruit, which they closely resemble. While traveling in Bengal, you may come across variations. *Kaalo jaam*, the "dark fruit," is a larger and darker version. The city of Baharampur, located in the northern part of West Bengal, is famous for *channa bora*, a variation made with *channa*, fresh cheese.

Lady Kenny, another variation, was designed in the early part of this century when Calcutta was the capital of British India and Lord Canning was the Viceroy. Once Lady Canning came to visit a small town in Bengal. The town's best sweetmaker labored for days to prepare a delicacy that would be fit for a queen. He stuffed the milk puffs with thickened milk and raisins, soaked them in syrup, then rolled them in sugar. Lady Canning was said to have been delighted. "Lady Kenny," the variation named after her and available throughout Bengal, has since become popular.

For the cooking syrup:

1 cup (250 ml) sugar
3 cups (750 ml) water

For the balls:

1 cup (250 ml) instant dry milk
3 Tbs. (45 ml) all purpose flour
2 tsp. (10 ml) regular Cream of Wheat®
6 Tbs. (90 ml) whole or 2% lowfat milk (see Note)
Seeds of 2 to 3 cardamom pods

For the soaking syrup:

1 cup (250 ml) sugar
1½ cups (375 ml) water

4 whole cardamom pods
Vegetable oil for deep-frying
Garnish: toasted slivered almonds or pine nuts (optional); silver leaf (optional; see "A Glossary of Spices and Ingredients")

1. Prepare the cooking syrup: Bring sugar and water to boil in a large pan. Let boil for a few minutes, then reduce heat and keep warm. (This will be a thin syrup.)
2. Prepare the balls: Combine dry milk, flour, and Cream of Wheat® in a small bowl. Gradually mix in the milk. Knead 4 to 5 minutes. Pinch off portions of the dough and roll into cherry-size balls. (They will approximately double in size when cooked in the syrup.) Cup one ball in the palm of your hand, make an indentation with the little finger of the other hand, place a cardamom seed inside, and close it again. Repeat for the remaining milk puffs.
3. Prepare the soaking syrup: Bring sugar, water, and cardamom pods to boil. Boil for 3 to 4 minutes, then remove from heat.
4. Heat oil in a deep-fat fryer or pan to about 350°F (180°C). Fry 3 or 4 balls until evenly browned, 2 or more minutes. Remove with a slotted spoon and drain on paper towels.
5. Bring the cooking syrup back to a simmer. Gently place the cooked balls in the syrup and simmer for 15 minutes; they will start to puff up. Transfer to the soaking syrup with a slotted spoon to make room for the remaining balls as they are fried.
6. Let cool, then refrigerate overnight or up to 3 days. The milk puffs will continue to absorb the syrup and improve in flavor for several days. You can flavor them further by adding rosewater to the cooled soaking syrup.

Makes 18 to 20 puffs.

Serving suggestion: Serve 1 or 2 puffs per person at the end of any meal, with a little syrup drizzled over them and a slivered almond or a pine nut on top of each.

Note: For a splendid taste treat, replace part or all of the milk with whipping cream.

Chaler Payesh
ROYAL RICE PUDDING

The term *payesh* applies to puddinglike desserts in general, and to rice pudding in particular. References to this ancient dessert can be found in texts more than 3,000 years old. It is a must in many ceremonies. For example, when breaking their day-long fast after a religious observance, devotees start with spoonfuls of this rich, nourishing sweet.

Rice pudding is also served on "Brother's Day," the day when a Bengali woman customarily entertains her brother. She dips a finger in sandalwood paste and puts a mark on his forehead while praying for his long life and good health. A leisurely meal follows, typically ending with a small bowl of this dainty dessert—sometimes garnished with rose petals that are not eaten.

8 cups (2 liters) whole or 2% lowfat milk
4 cups (1 liter) half and half (see Note)
1 bay leaf
6 whole cardamom pods
⅓ cup (100 ml) Basmati (preferred) or fine long-grain white rice
¼ cup (60 ml) slivered almonds
2 Tbs. (30 ml) raisins (preferably golden)
¼ tsp. (1 ml) ground cardamom
½ cup plus 1 Tbs. (140 ml) sugar
Flavoring: dash of rosewater or kewra water (optional)
Garnish: chopped unsalted pistachios

1. Lightly oil the bottom and sides of a deep, heavy-bottomed, preferably nonstick pan at least 10 inches (25 cm) in diameter. (See "Sweets Tips" in this chapter.) Bring milk and half and half to boil over medium high heat. Lower heat to medium and stir constantly until the milk subsides.
2. Add bay leaf, cardamom pods, and rice. Cook for 30 minutes, watching carefully and stirring when the milk rises and foams. Scrape the bottom and sides frequently to loosen accumulated milk solids and incorporate them into the liquid. If any skin forms on the surface, stir it into the liquid as well.
3. Add almonds, raisins, and ground cardamom. Cook until the mixture has the consistency of whipping cream, another 25 to 40 minutes.
4. Mix in sugar and remove from heat. Let cool to room temperature, then refrigerate for several hours (the pudding will thicken). Just before serving, sprinkle with a few drops of rosewater and with pistachios.

12 servings.

Serving suggestions: Serve as is, with slices of fresh mango or strawberries on the side, or on mango halves. This delicious payesh goes well with any meal.

Note: For a lower-fat dessert, substitute whole or 2% lowfat milk.

Semair Payesh
RICH VERMICELLI PUDDING

This is a favorite dish of the Moslems, who prepare it during an event of great religious significance, Id-Ul-Fitr. Pullao, Pan-raised Bread, and a mutton dish are other musts of this day. If you have never thought of using pasta in a dessert, this unusual pudding, made with a very thin vermicelli called *semai*, will come as a pleasant surprise. Like most payesh, this dish cooks slowly but is easy to make. It creates a grand finale to any meal, and I serve it often for entertaining.

Bengalis judge the quality of vermicelli by its thinness. "How thin should it be?" asked the apprentice. "The best is as fine as a baby's hair," replied his master.

1 cup (250 ml) very fine vermicelli (see Note)
8 cups (2 liters) whole or 2% lowfat milk
5 whole cardamom pods
2 Tbs. (30 ml) slivered almonds
¼ cup (60 ml) sugar
Flavoring: dash of rosewater or kewra water (optional)

1. If the vermicelli is not already roasted (check the label), roast over low heat in an ungreased griddle or skillet, stirring often, until light brown; do not burn. Remove from the skillet immediately and set aside.
2. Lightly oil the bottom and sides of a deep, preferably nonstick pan at least 10 inches (25 cm) in diameter. (See "Sweets Tips.") Bring milk to boil over medium high heat. Stir constantly until rising and foaming subside, then lower heat to medium.
3. Add the vermicelli, cardamom pods, and almonds. Cook until the mixture has the consistency of thick chowder, about 1 hour (65 minutes if using lowfat milk); it will thicken more as it cools. Watch carefully and stir often to prevent boiling over, scraping the bottom and sides to loosen any accumulated milk solids and incorporate them into the liquid. If any skin forms on the surface, stir it into the liquid as well.
4. Add sugar and mix well. Remove from heat and let cool to room temperature. Sprinkle with rosewater. Serve at room temperature or, better yet, refrigerate and serve chilled.

8 to 9 servings.

Note: For best results, buy the very slender vermicelli (usually already broken into small pieces) sold in Indian stores, not the thicker variety available in Western supermarkets. Angel hair or similar thin pasta will produce acceptable results but is difficult to handle. Break it into short lengths before using.

Narkeler Payesh
COCONUT-SCENTED RICE PUDDING

Rice pudding prepared with milk is more common in Bengal, but this coconut milk version, which is quicker to make, has a fragrant, sweet aroma. Since coconut has an affinity with fish, I often serve this dessert after a seafood meal. Try as is, or arrange slices of fresh ripe papayas, bananas, or mangoes around the pudding.

    This dessert is best enjoyed soon after it's made. If allowed to sit for several hours, it will become dry. If that happens, add a little milk (or coconut milk), reheat, and serve.

¾ cup (175 ml) Basmati (preferred) or other fine long-grain white rice
1½ cups (375 ml) water
2 Tbs. (30 ml) raisins (preferably golden)
2 Tbs. (30 ml) toasted cashews or slivered almonds
1 tsp. (5 ml) ground cardamom
¼ cup plus 1 Tbs. (75 ml) sugar
1¼ cups (300 ml) fresh or unsweetened canned coconut milk, stirred until
    evenly mixed (see Note)
Garnish: chopped raw pistachios

1. Bring rice and water to boil in a pan. Simmer, covered, until all water is absorbed and rice is tender, 20 or so minutes.
2. Add raisins, cashews, and cardamom. Dissolve sugar in the coconut milk and stir into the rice mixture gently, so as not to break the rice kernels. Raise heat slightly and cook uncovered until the mixture thickens, 5 to 10 minutes. Remove from heat. Let cool slightly. Garnish with pistachios and serve.

6 servings.

Note: You can substitute a mixture of ½ cup (125 ml) coconut milk and ¾ cup (175 ml) whole or 2% lowfat milk.

Channer Payesh
TENDER SWEET CHEESE MORSELS IN CREAMY SAUCE

If you crave Milk Balls in Rich Saffron Cream Sauce but don't have the time to prepare them, try this recipe instead. It is quicker but equally tasty. The delicate cheese morsels melt in your mouth while the creamy sauce caresses your palate. Serve chilled, alone or with slices of ripe mango or peach.

For the cheese morsels:

4 cups (1 liter) whole or 2% lowfat milk
1½ to 2 Tbs. (22 to 30 ml) fresh lemon juice
2 Tbs. (30 ml) sugar

For the cream sauce:

4 cups (1 liter) whole or 2% lowfat milk, or half and half
5 whole cardamom pods
1½ Tbs. (22 ml) sugar
¼ tsp. (1 ml) ground cardamom
Flavoring: rosewater or kewra water (optional)

1. Prepare fresh cheese using milk and lemon juice, following the "20-minute" routine. (See "A Glossary of Spices and Ingredients.") The yield will be about ½ cup (125 ml).
2. Add the 2 tablespoons (30 ml) sugar and knead the cheese a few more times. Pinch off tiny pieces of cheese, about the size of chickpeas, and roll into balls (or spread mixture on a small plate to a thickness of ½ inch/1 cm and cut into sugar-cube–size pieces.) Refrigerate until the sauce is ready.
3. To prepare the sauce, follow step 2 of the recipe for Milk Balls in Rich Saffron Cream Sauce. Stir in sugar and ground cardamom. Remove from heat and immediately transfer sauce to a serving bowl. Add the cheese bits to the still-hot sauce and let cool; the sauce will thicken. Refrigerate until chilled. Just before serving, sprinkle with rose or kewra water.

3 to 4 servings.

Serving suggestions: Same as for Milk Balls in Rich Saffron Cream Sauce except, since the cheese morsels are smaller, you can serve several per person.

Misti Doi

SWEET YOGURT "CUSTARD"

Misti doi, which literally means "sweet yogurt," is the customary end to a Bengali meal. During my youth I frequented a sweet shop called Jolojog, known throughout Calcutta for its custard-style curd, just to buy it.

I believe one of the secrets of this establishment was the use of a porous clay pot to make the yogurt. Another was the slow reduction of the milk. After much experimentation I have come up with a recipe for a luscious, nutty yogurt that closely resembles Jolojog's, but can be made in a Western kitchen.

4 cups (1 liter) whole or 2% lowfat milk
3½ Tbs. (52 ml) sugar
3 Tbs. (45 ml) instant dry milk
1 cup (250 ml) plain yogurt, lightly beaten until smooth

1. Lightly oil the bottom and sides of a large pan. (See "Sweets Tips" in this chapter.) Bring milk to boil over medium to medium high heat, stirring constantly until rising and foaming subside. Lower heat to medium and stir in sugar. Gradually sprinkle in dry milk so that no lumps form. Cook until milk is reduced to half its volume and has the consistency of whipping cream, about 15 minutes (20 minutes for lowfat milk). Watch carefully and stir often to prevent boiling over, scraping the bottom and sides to loosen any accumulated milk solids and incorporate them into the liquid. If any skin forms on the surface, gently stir it into the liquid mixture as well.
2. Remove from heat. Transfer milk to a bowl (this will help to cool it faster), and let cool for 10 minutes or until lukewarm to the touch. Add 2 tablespoons (30 ml) of the thickened milk to the yogurt and beat lightly with a spoon until smooth.
3. Preheat oven to 200°F (100°C; gas mark ¼). Pour the yogurt mixture into the thickened milk and stir until thoroughly blended. Pour into 4 individual custard cups or a 7-inch (17.5 cm) baking dish. Set the cups or dish into a larger baking pan and pour very hot water into the larger pan to a depth of about ¼ inch (6 mm).
4. Bake for 20 minutes. The custard will be soft and may not be completely set. Let cool, then cover and refrigerate at least 30 minutes or until custard is completely set. Serve chilled.

4 servings.

Serving suggestions: Serve at the end of a meal with either Silk and Satin Bars or Milk Balls in Rose Syrup. You can also serve this velvety custard with slices of ripe mango or papaya, strawberries or raspberries, or any combination of these.

Sandesh
SILK AND SATIN BARS

The aristocratic sandesh, with its gentle sweetness and soft, refined texture, belies the fact that it's made of only two ingredients: milk and sugar. It can be flavored with mango puree or orange essence, or sweetened with dark, rich, unrefined sugar. It comes in more than 40 varieties and has names such as "Moon's Mate," "One More Piece," and "Star of the Eyes." If you're touring Bengal, don't miss the opportunity to try this famous sweet and its many variations.

The proportion of fresh cheese to sugar determines to which of 12 classic grades the sandesh belongs. The greater the amount of fresh cheese, the better the product. This recipe represents the highest grade.

The word sandesh *literally means "news." Traditionally no good news is celebrated without sharing a platter of sandesh and other sweets with family and friends.*

Instead of shaping sandesh as bars, you can use tiny decorative molds. In Bengal, we use molds with patterns of fish, fruit, or flowers.

Fresh cheese (see "A Glossary of Spices and Ingredients")
¼ cup plus 1 Tbs. (75 ml) powdered sugar
¼ tsp. (1 ml) ground cardamom
Garnish: thinly slivered pistachios

1. Knead the fresh cheese for at least 10 minutes. Combine the cheese, powdered sugar, and cardamom in a bowl and mix thoroughly. Place in a heavy-bottomed pan over very low heat; too much heat will toughen the cheese. Stir constantly to hasten the evaporation of water from the cheese and to make sure that it does not burn at the bottom. When the

mixture begins to look somewhat drier and forms a solid mass, 10 to 15 minutes, remove from heat. (It will firm up as it sits.)

2. Immediately place on an ungreased plate and spread with a spatula into a rectangle ½ to ¾ inch (1 to 2 cm) thick. Smooth the top with your fingertips or the back of a spoon. Sprinkle pistachios over the sandesh and press gently into the surface. Let cool to room temperature, then refrigerate for an hour or more. Cut into 1-inch (2.5 cm) squares.

Makes about 15 pieces.

Serving suggestions: Serve at the end of a meal with Sweet Yogurt "Custard," or plain yogurt lightly sprinkled with sugar. Or serve with a platter of fresh fruits such as kiwi, orange sections, fresh strawberries, and bananas.

Daler Borfi
GOLD BARS

Borfi is the generic name for fudgelike bars that are made with milk and either nuts or legumes. They resemble sandesh, but have a slightly firmer and more crumbly texture. Borfi was originally eaten during Holi, a joyous and colorful celebration of the coming of spring. On this day, everyone wears old clothes and goes out on the streets in a playful mood, splashing each other with colored water carried in buckets.

These legume-based bars have the fragrance of cardamom and a nutlike texture, and are prized for their nutritional value. In Bengal they are usually prepared with split hulled mung beans and a good dose of ghee. I have used yellow split peas, which are faster to cook and more common in the West, and substituted a moderate amount of oil, but find these lighter bars to be equally tasty.

1 cup (250 ml) yellow split peas, soaked in 4 cups (1 liter) water overnight (or soaked in 4 cups/1 liter boiling water for 4 hours)
2 Tbs. (30 ml) vegetable oil
⅔ cup (150 ml) sugar
½ cup (125 ml) water
1 12-oz. (350 ml) can unsweetened evaporated skim milk
1 cup (250 ml) instant dry milk
½ cup (125 ml) raw cashews, ground in a blender to a coarse powder
½ tsp. (2 ml) ground cardamom
Garnish: chopped unsalted raw pistachios; silver leaf (see "A Glossary of Spices and Ingredients")

1. Drain the peas well, reserving the soaking liquid to cook rice, soups, or vegetables if you like. Heat oil in a skillet over medium heat. Fry the peas for 6 to 7 minutes, stirring often; they will absorb the oil quickly, but continue to stir them, as this slow frying will give them a nutty flavor. Grind the split peas in batches in a blender to a smooth paste. Remove and set aside.

2. Combine sugar and water in a large, heavy-bottomed, and preferably nonstick pan over medium low heat and bring to a boil. Add the pea paste. In a few seconds, when all liquid is absorbed, add evaporated milk and heat through. Gradually add dry milk, stirring and mashing any lumps against the sides of the pan with a spoon. Add cashews and cardamom. Cook until most of the moisture has been absorbed and the mixture is thick and doughy, about 20 minutes, stirring often.

3. Spread mixture in an ungreased 8-inch (20 cm) square baking dish, smoothing the top. Sprinkle with pistachios and press gently into the surface. Let cool to room temperature. Decorate the top with silver leaf, if desired. (See "A Glossary of Spices and Ingredients.") When cool, cut into diamond shapes. Serve at room temperature or chilled.

Makes 20 bars.

Serving suggestions: Good for breakfast or as a snack. Serve on a buffet table or as a dessert at the end of a light meal.

Chandrapuli
HARVEST MOON CAKES

In Bengal, these delicious cakes are offered during the autumnal worship of the goddess Durga. Once I watched an elderly Bengali woman prepare them. She carefully scraped the meat of a fresh coconut, not allowing the tiniest shred of its brown skin to fall into the milky flesh. She would occasionally stir the milk that was simmering on a nearby stove. Finally she molded the dough, made with coconut and thickened milk, into half-moon–shaped forms and sprinkled rosewater over them. It was a delightful eating experience.

I serve these luscious cakes on a platter with sliced fresh fruits such as bananas, peaches, and mangoes.

4 cups (1 liter) whole or 2% lowfat milk
¼ cup plus 1 Tbs. (75 ml) sugar (add 1 Tbs./15 ml more sugar if using freshly grated coconut)
¼ cup (60 ml) water

1 cup (250 ml) dried flaked or shredded sweetened coconut, ground in a
   blender to a coarse powder, or freshly grated or shredded coconut
1 Tbs. (15 ml) raisins (preferably golden)
¼ tsp. (1 ml) ground cardamom
Flavoring: rosewater (optional)

1. Use the milk to prepare khoya, or thickened milk. (See "A Glossary of
   Spices and Ingredients.") This amount of milk will take 20 to 30 minutes. Set aside.
2. Bring sugar and water to boil in a 10-inch (25 cm) skillet. Turn heat low
   and cook for about 5 minutes. Add coconut and cook for a few minutes
   until all of the syrup is absorbed. Add the khoya, raisins, and cardamom. Cook until the mixture turns into a solid mass and pulls away
   from the sides of the pan, 10 to 15 minutes, stirring constantly. Remove
   from heat and let cool. Stir in rosewater. Pinch off pieces of the dough
   and roll into balls, about 1 inch (2.5 cm) in diameter. Flatten them
   slightly, then elongate them and shape into crescents.
Makes 15 pieces.

Gokul Pitha
DIVINE DUMPLINGS

Dip this coconut-filled pastry in a sweet syrup and allow its flavors to
explode on your palate. Of the many varieties of pitha, or dumplings, this
version is considered to be the best. Legend says these were Lord Krishna's
favorites when he was a child. "You are as naughty as Lord Krishna," a
Bengali mother says to a child who eats too many of these dumplings.

The traditional way to prepare them is with milk that has been thickened by slow simmering, and which acquires in the process a delicate nutty
flavor. In my shortcut version I use instant dry milk. For a lighter dessert I
poach the dumplings in a creamy sauce instead of deep-frying. The result is
still wonderful.

For the dumplings:

8 cups (2 liters) whole or 2% lowfat milk, made into khoya, or thickened
   milk (see "A Glossary of Spices and Ingredients"), or ¾ cup (175 ml)
   instant dry milk mixed with 3 Tbs. (45 ml) water to form a smooth paste
¾ cup (175 ml) firmly packed dried flaked or shredded sweetened coconut,
   ground in a blender to a coarse powder, or freshly grated or shredded
   coconut
2½ Tbs. (37 ml) sugar (add 1 Tbs./15 ml more sugar if using freshly grated
   or shredded coconut)
¼ tsp. (1 ml) ground cardamom

For the creamy sauce (lowfat version):

1 cup (250 ml) 2% lowfat milk
1 tsp. (5 ml) sugar

For the syrup (optional; if deep-frying):

½ cup (125 ml) sugar
¾ cup (175 ml) water

For the batter (optional; if deep-frying):

¼ cup (60 ml) all purpose flour, sifted
1 Tbs. (15 ml) regular Cream of Wheat®
2 Tbs. (30 ml) vegetable oil
6 Tbs. (90 ml) water
Vegetable oil for deep-frying (optional)
Garnish: chopped raw pistachios (optional)

1. *Prepare the dumplings:* Mix all dumpling ingredients in a pan. Cook over low heat, stirring often, until the mixture forms a solid mass and pulls away from the sides of the pan, 15 to 20 minutes. Let cool. Pinch off pieces of dough and roll into balls about 1 inch (2.5 cm) in diameter. Flatten each into a disc ½ inch (1 cm) thick and 1¾ inches (4 cm) in diameter. Set aside.

2. For the lowfat version, prepare the creamy sauce: Pour milk into a lightly oiled heavy-bottomed pan and bring to boil. Cook over medium heat until milk is reduced to about half its volume, 8 to 10 minutes. Turn heat to low and stir in sugar. Gently place the dumplings in this sauce and cook for 2 minutes. Remove from heat. Serve hot, at room temperature or chilled, garnished with the pistachios.

2. Prepare the syrup (if deep-frying): Bring sugar and water to boil. Simmer uncovered over low heat until the consistency of thin syrup, about 15 minutes. Remove from heat.

3. Prepare the batter (if deep-frying): Mix flour and Cream of Wheat® in a small bowl. Mix in oil. Gradually add water and stir until a smooth batter is formed.

4. Fry the dumplings: Heat oil in a deep-fat fryer or pan to 375°F (190°C). Gently place 3 or 4 dumplings in the batter and deep-fry until both sides are golden brown. Remove with a slotted spoon and drain on paper towels.

5. Return syrup to medium low heat. As soon as it starts to bubble, drop 3 or 4 dumplings into it and cook for 3 to 5 minutes. (They will increase in size slightly.) Remove and transfer to a bowl. When all the dumplings have been cooked, pour the remaining syrup over them and let soak for

15 minutes. If not serving immediately, let the dumplings cool, then chill. Serve at room temperature (preferred) or chilled.
Makes about 15 dumplings.

Serving suggestion: Place 2 dumplings on a plate. Drizzle a little syrup over them and sprinkle pistachios on top.

Narkeler Naru
FESTIVAL ROUNDS

A *naru* or *laddoo* is a sweet ball made of coconut or some form of legume, often served in religious ceremonies. Ganesh, the elephant-headed "Lord of success," is said to be fond of them. The area of Barisal in Bangladesh is known for this naru.

To have laddoos in both hands

—expression heard in Calcutta, meaning
that you are in a win-win situation

In Bengal, we prepare this easy and flavorful treat with fresh coconut and unrefined palm sugar. But even packaged coconut and refined sugar yield good results.

4 cups (1 liter) whole or 2% lowfat milk
2 cups (500 ml) firmly packed dried flaked or shredded sweetened coconut, ground in a blender ½ cup (125 ml) at a time to a coarse powder, or freshly grated or shredded coconut mixed with ½ Tbs. (7 ml) sugar
3 Tbs. (45 ml) sugar

1. Thicken the milk following step 2 of Milk Balls in Rich Saffron Cream Sauce.
2. Add coconut and sugar. Cook until the mixture acquires a thick, doughy consistency, 6 to 8 minutes, stirring frequently. Remove from heat and let cool slightly. While still a little warm, pinch off portions of the dough and roll into balls about 1 inch (2.5 cm) in diameter. Serve at room temperature or chilled. (These tend to harden if left in the refrigerator for several days.)

Makes 18 to 20.

Serving suggestions: Serve on a platter alone or with sliced fresh pineapple, mandarin oranges, or bananas.

Ananda Naru
COCONUT SESAME JOY

The word *ananda* means joy, and these delectable rounds are served on joyous occasions such as weddings, anniversaries, or a child's "first rice" ceremony. They symbolize long life and good health. One traditional pre-wedding custom is to break a fresh coconut and use it in the preparation of these easy-to-make cookies. Ground rice and sesame seeds give the dough a chewy, hearty texture and a pleasantly nutty flavor.

To make a sesame seed into a palm fruit
—Bengali expession that indicates exaggeration

1 cup (250 ml) dried flaked or shredded sweetened coconut, ground in a
　blender to a coarse powder, or freshly grated or shredded coconut
3 Tbs. (45 ml) rice flour
2½ Tbs. (37 ml) sugar (add 1 Tbs./15 ml more sugar if using freshly grated
　or shredded coconut)
2 Tbs. (30 ml) toasted sesame seeds
¼ cup plus 1 Tbs. (75 ml) whole or 2% lowfat milk
½ tsp. (2 ml) ground cardamom
Garnish: powdered sugar (optional)

Combine all ingredients in a pan and place over low heat. Cook until the mixture is dry and pulls away from the sides of the pan, stirring often, about 18 to 20 minutes. Remove from heat. As soon as the dough is cool enough to handle, pinch off portions and roll into balls about 1 inch (2.5 cm) in diameter. Just before serving, roll the balls in powdered sugar if desired. Serve at room temperature or chilled. (These tend to harden slightly if left in the refrigerator for several days, but will still taste good.)
Makes 16.

Serving suggestions: Same as for Festival Rounds.

Aam Kheer

GOLDEN MANGO CREAM

To me a ripe, juicy mango is best eaten fresh—but one exception is this dish, in which mango pulp is folded into thickened milk to form a creamy pudding. It has a beautiful yellowish-orange color and the intense flavor of a tropical fruit that has reached its prime. "Better than ice cream," said a Western college student.

4 cups (1 liter) whole or 2% lowfat milk

2½ Tbs. (37 ml) sugar or 1 Tbs. (15 ml) if using canned sweetened mango (see Note)

2 cups (500 ml) ripe fresh mango pulp (see "A Glossary of Spices and Ingredients"), pureed in a blender, or a 16-oz. (½ kg) can of sweetened mango pulp

1. Thicken the milk following step 2 of Milk Balls in Rich Saffron Cream Sauce.
2. Keep the heat low. Add mango pulp and cook until the mixture thickens, stirring often, 5 to 7 minutes. Add sugar. Remove from heat and let cool to room temperature. Cover and refrigerate for at least 30 minutes. The pudding will thicken further as it sits, but it is softer than most Western puddings. Serve chilled.

4 to 5 servings.

Serving suggestions: Serve at the end of a meal, alone or with additional fresh mango slices.

Note: Since the sweetness of mangoes varies, adjust the amount of sugar according to your taste.

DISHES FOR THE ADVENTUROUS

By now you are familiar with Bengali-style dals, vegetables, and fish and meat dishes. Perhaps it is time to experience a more exotic side of this cuisine.

This chapter deals with recipes that may contain ingredients little known in the West. Or they may be made with specialty items, and have a taste new to the Western palate. These dishes are not unusual by Bengali standards—indeed, most are everyday fare.

For example, bitter melon. It's a slender, pale green vegetable about the size of a zucchini, with a wrinkled skin. You may have come across this vegetable in Chinese restaurants or Asian markets. Bengalis eat this vegetable often, insisting that its gentle bitter taste is good for your health. It is splendid either crisply fried or as a part of *shukto*, the multi-vegetable meal starter.

When I first came to the West I missed banana blossom, the male flower of the banana plant. It's a deep purple, cone-shaped vegetable that bears a marked resemblance to artichoke when cooked. Bengalis are masters at preparing it in a variety of tasty ways. When I returned home to Bengal, I asked my sister to prepare it for me. "Of all the food here, this is what you ask for first?" she laughed, pointing to the homey nature of this vegetable. Later I was grateful to find banana blossom in Asian markets in the West.

Each of the remaining dishes in this chapter has a character of its own. Attempt a recipe or two. If the taste does not appeal to you, don't forsake the remainder. Try another; you may find one that opens a gustatory gateway for you.

Karelar Shukto
BITTER MELON WITH MANY FLAVORS

This is a variation of shukto, described in the Vegetarian Dishes Chapter. In this dish you savor the full range of flavors, from sweet to bitter. Some Westerners do not have a penchant for a bitter taste, but Bengalis consider it a part of the flavor palette and include it in many meals to round out the variety of taste sensations.

2½ Tbs. (37 ml) mustard oil
1 cup (250 ml) unpeeled bitter melon, sliced crosswise into ⅛-inch (3 mm) rounds
1 bay leaf
¼ tsp. (1 ml) five-spice
3½ tsp. (17 ml) sugar
¼ tsp. (1 ml) turmeric
¾ tsp. (3 ml) salt
½ lb. (¼ kg) unpeeled potatoes (about 2 medium), cut into 1-inch (2.5 cm) cubes
1 cup (250 ml) water
1½ cups (375 ml) peeled sweet potato, cut into 1-inch (2.5 cm) cubes
1 cup (250 ml) green beans, cut crosswise into 1-inch (2.5 cm) lengths
1½ cups (375 ml) eggplant, cut into 1-inch (2.5 cm) cubes
½ cup (125 ml) *Boris*, preferably made with urad dal (optional) (See "Dals" chapter)
1 tsp. (5 ml) black mustard seeds, ground to a powder, mixed with 2 tsp. (10 ml) water and allowed to stand for 30 minutes
1½ Tbs. (22 ml) peeled, minced fresh ginger
Garnish: toasted cashews (optional)

1. Heat 1 tablespoon (15 ml) oil in a deep-sided and preferably nonstick pan, at least 10 inches (25 cm) in diameter, over medium heat. Fry bitter melon until lightly browned, 3 to 5 minutes. Remove with a slotted spoon and set aside.
2. Add the remaining 1½ tablespoons (22 ml) oil to the skillet and heat over medium low heat. Fry bay leaf and five-spice until the spices start popping. Add sugar and fry until it darkens, a few seconds. Stir in turmeric and salt. Add potatoes and stir a few times. Add water and bring to boil. Simmer, covered, 5 minutes. Add sweet potato, green beans, and eggplant. Simmer, covered, 5 more minutes.
3. Add the bitter melon and boris and simmer, covered, another 10 minutes. Gently stir in black mustard paste and ginger. Simmer, covered, until the vegetables are tender but still hold their shape, an additional

10 minutes. Remove from heat. With the back of a spoon, mash a few of the potatoes and sweet potatoes to thicken the gravy. Let stand covered for 10 minutes to help develop the flavors. Sprinkle with cashews and cilantro and serve.

4 to 6 servings.

Serving suggestions: I serve this multiflavored stew with a simple dal, such as Onion-fragrant Red Lentils, and a hearty condiment such as Country-style Chunky Tomato Chutney.

Variation: Bengalis sometimes serve a few pieces of deep-fried bitter melon with a meal, especially one with a dal dish. To deep-fry bitter melon, cut it crosswise into very thin slices. Use the batter as described in Crisp Fried Eggplant (see "Vegetarian Dishes" chapter) and follow the same procedure for frying.

Pepe Chingri

GREEN PAPAYA TOSSED WITH TENDER BABY SHRIMPS

In the West, papaya is only eaten when ripe. In Bengal, young green papayas are the star of many a delicious dish, such as this. Here, papaya is happily married to baby shrimps. This dish is simple and yet can be a real conversation piece.

Buy unripe cooking papayas in Asian or Latin American markets. Select those that are green outside and white inside. If the inside flesh is pink, the recipe may not work as well.

2 to 3 Tbs. (30 to 45 ml) vegetable oil
½ lb (¼ kg) peeled potatoes (about 2 medium), cut in ½-inch (1.2 cm) cubes
5 whole cardamom pods
2-inch (5 cm) cinnamon stick
1 Tbs. (15 ml) peeled, finely minced fresh ginger
1 tsp. (5 ml) seeded, chopped fresh green chili (or to taste)
¼ tsp. (1 ml) turmeric
2 tsp. (10 ml) ground cumin
1½ cups (375 ml) peeled, seeded green papayas cut in ½-inch (1.2 cm) cubes
¾ cup (175 ml) water
2 Tbs. (30 ml) white poppyseeds made into a paste (see "A Glossary of Spices and Ingredients")
½ tsp. (2 ml) salt

½ tsp. (2 ml) sugar
½ lb. (¼ kg) bay shrimps, fresh or frozen, thawed
Garnish: thinly sliced green onions

1. Heat 2 tablespoons (30 ml) oil in a skillet over medium heat. Fry potatoes until they turn medium brown, about 5 minutes. Remove potatoes with a slotted spoon and set aside. (Or, fry in 1 tablespoon/ 15 ml oil. See "Brown-frying of potatoes" in "A Glossary of Spices and Ingredients.")
2. Add 1 tablespoon (15 ml) oil to the skillet and heat over medium low heat. Fry cardamom and cinnamon for a few seconds. Add ginger and green chili and stir several times. Add turmeric, cumin, and papayas and stir a few times. Add water. Bring to a boil and simmer, covered, 15 minutes.
3. Add the reserved potatoes, poppyseed paste, salt, and sugar. Simmer covered until potatoes and papayas are tender, 15 to 20 minutes. Add the shrimps. Simmer, covered, 2 to 3 more minutes or until the shrimps are done. (See "Test for doneness" under "Seafood Tips.") Remove from heat. Sprinkle sliced green onions on top and serve.

6 to 7 servings.

Shukrobarer Chingri
FRIDAY NIGHT PRAWNS

If you enjoyed the Prawn Pleasure recipe in the "Seafood" chapter, try this adventuresome variation. Here you cook prawns with their shells intact. When cooked in this manner, they retain their natural juices and make the dish more flavorful. And then there is the added pleasure of delicately extracting the meat from the shells with your fingers as you eat. I like to serve this dish on Friday night, when dining can be leisurely.

Follow the recipe and serving suggestions for Prawn Pleasure except use raw unshelled prawns.

Chingri Bhapa
JUMBO PRAWNS IN BANANA LEAF BOAT

For an even greater adventure, steam the prawns in a banana leaf. For this purpose, buy unshelled prawns with the heads on, if possible. Banana leaves are often sold either fresh or frozen in Southeast Asian markets (particularly Thai and Vietnamese). These leaves impart a musky, smoky scent to the prawns and also make a striking presentation. If they are not available, the dish can still be prepared using aluminum foil. (See "To steam fish or shellfish" in "Basic Cooking Principles" section.)

Banana leaves are also used in Bengal as an esthetically pleasing way of serving food. Since the leaves break easily, you layer several (each about the size of a small placemat) one on top of another, the largest leaf at the bottom. Even a sauced dish can be served on these leaves, provided the sauce is not too thin. Once, in a village, I saw a cow devouring banana leaves discarded after a meal. She cleaned up the "dirty dishes."

1 to 1¼ lb. (½ kg to 675 g) prawns, preferably unshelled

1. Prepare the marinade from any one of the following recipes: Steamed Fish in Chili-Mustard Sauce, Steamed Fish in Chili-Cilantro Sauce, or Fish Braised with Ginger and Roasted Red Chili Puree. Marinate the prawns in the refrigerator for 30 minutes.
2. To steam in a banana leaf boat: Thaw the leaves (if frozen). Wash, pat dry, and cut into 2 or more pieces, each 12 × 12 inches (30 × 30 cm). Lay a 15 × 15-inch (37 × 37 cm) piece of aluminum foil on a cutting board. Center a piece of banana leaf on the foil. Place 4 to 5 marinated prawns in the center of the banana leaf, making sure to leave enough space on all sides to fold over and form a pouch that will completely cover the prawns. (For 1 pound/½ kg of prawns, you will need at least 2 pouches, depending on the size of the prawns.) Bring the edges of the aluminum foil together and seal with a double fold, so that no water can seep into the pouch during steaming. Now follow directions for steaming fish. (See "To steam fish or shellfish" in "Cooking Techniques and Equipment" section.)

Serving suggestions: Follow the serving suggestions for the dish from which the marinade was used.

Danta Chochori
HOT SWEET BROCCOLI STALKS IN
EGGPLANT-MUSTARD SAUCE

Succulent and juicy vegetable stalks, such as those from a pumpkin or squash plant, are never discarded in Bengal. They appear in many dishes, as in this recipe, where they are the primary item. The same varieties are not readily available in the West, but broccoli stalks (the thick stems below the florets) make a good substitute. After you've cooked with broccoli florets and have some stalks left, try this recipe.

2 Tbs. (30 ml) vegetable oil

2 whole dried red chilies

¼ tsp. (1 ml) five-spice

½ lb. (¼ kg) unpeeled potatoes (about 2 medium), cut into 1-inch (2.5 cm) cubes

1 tsp. (5 ml) seeded, chopped fresh green chili, or more to taste (see Note)

½ tsp. (2 ml) turmeric

2 tsp. (10 ml) ground cumin

1 cup (250 ml) unpeeled sweet potato cut into 1-inch (2.5 cm) cubes

3 cups (750 ml) eggplant cut into 1-inch (2.5 cm) cubes

2¼ cups (550 ml) broccoli stalks, tough bottom end removed, and cut into 2½ × ½ × ½-inch (6 × 1 × 1 cm) pieces

½ cup (125 ml) water

½ tsp. (2 ml) salt

1 tsp. (5 ml) sugar

1 tsp. (5 ml) black mustard seeds, ground to a powder, mixed with 2 tsp. (10 ml) water and allowed to stand for 30 minutes

1. Heat oil in a large, deep-sided pan over medium low heat. Fry red chilies until they darken. Add five-spice. As soon as it starts popping, add potatoes and fry for a minute or so, turning often. Stir in green chili, turmeric, and cumin. Add sweet potato, eggplant, and broccoli stalks and stir a few times. Add water, salt, and sugar and bring to boil. Lower heat slightly.
2. Simmer, covered, 20 minutes. Stir in black mustard paste. Simmer, covered, until the vegetables are tender, another 10 to 15 minutes. If the gravy is still thin, mash a few potatoes and sweet potatoes with the back of a spoon to thicken. Remove from heat. Serve piping hot.

5 to 6 servings.

Serving suggestions: I try to balance this complex stew with more subtle tastes, such as those of Fish in Silky-thin Sauce or Onion-Fragrant Red Lentils. Rice (or Pan-raised Bread) will be the only other accompaniment you'll need.

Note: This dish tastes best when slightly chili-hot. So use more chili than usual or incorporate some of the seeds.

Mochar Ghanto

BANANA BLOSSOMS IN COCONUT-GINGER SAUCE

My mother says *mochas*, banana blossoms, are a challenge to the uniniti-ated. Both she and my sister are experts in mocha cooking. These are their secrets: Keep your palms oiled for easy handling; take the leaves off, chop them one at a time, and soak them in water.

Since banana blossoms are difficult to find in the West (they are occasionally available in Asian markets), I use the canned variety, which eases the preparation. This vegetable with a fleshy center somewhat resembles an artichoke in flavor. In fact, artichoke hearts are a good substitute for it.

1½ Tbs. (22 ml) vegetable oil
¼ tsp. (1 ml) five-spice
1 Tbs. (15 ml) peeled fresh ginger, grated or made into a paste
    (see "A Glossary of Spices and Ingredients")
1 tsp. (5 ml) seeded, chopped fresh green chili (or to taste)
½ tsp. (2 ml) turmeric
10-oz. (280 g) can of banana blossoms (drained weight), finely chopped, or
    artichoke hearts from a can or jar
⅛ tsp. (.5 ml) salt
3 Tbs. (45 ml) water
2 Tbs. (30 ml) dried flaked or shredded sweetened coconut, ground in a
    blender to a coarse powder, or freshly grated or shredded coconut mixed
    with ½ tsp. (2 ml) sugar
¼ tsp. (1 ml) garam masala

Heat oil in a skillet over medium low heat. Fry five-spice for a few seconds until it starts crackling. Add ginger, green chili, and turmeric and stir several times. Add banana blossoms, salt, and water. Bring to boil, then lower heat slightly and simmer, covered, 12 to 15 minutes. Stir in coconut. Remove from heat. Blend in garam masala. Let stand covered for 15 minutes to help develop the flavors. Serve piping hot.
4 servings.

Serving suggestions: A favorite home-style meal for me is this fragrant vegetable sauté served with rice and Tart Red Lentils. For a more substantial meal, I add Prawns in a Pot of Gold and Splendid Cilantro Chutney.

Narkel Diyea Sosha
HOT AND COLD POTATO CUCUMBER TOSS

Cucumber is regarded as a salad ingredient in the West, but in Bengal we treat it like other vegetables. This dish, made with few simple ingredients, is one that's hard to forget. "It's like traveling without leaving home," said a Western friend after tasting this dish. The cucumber cubes tend to cool you even when the dish is served hot.

2 Tbs. (30 ml) vegetable oil (mustard oil preferred)
1 whole dried red chili
¼ tsp. (1 ml) five-spice
1 Tbs. (15 ml) peeled, minced fresh ginger
1 tsp. (5 ml) seeded, chopped fresh green chili (or to taste)
¾ tsp. (3 ml) turmeric
3 cups (750 ml) peeled, seeded cucumber cut into ¾-inch (2 cm) cubes
¾ tsp. (3 ml) salt
¼ tsp. (1 ml) sugar
1½ lb. (750 g) peeled, cooked, cubed potatoes (5 medium), cut into ¾-inch
   (2 cm) cubes
3 Tbs. (45 ml) dried flaked or shredded sweetened coconut, ground in a
   blender to a coarse powder, or freshly grated or shredded coconut mixed
   with ½ tsp. (2 ml) sugar
Garnish: chopped fresh mint leaves

1. Heat oil in a 12-inch (30 cm) skillet over medium low heat. Fry red
   chili until it darkens. Add five-spice and fry until it starts crackling. Add
   ginger, green chili, and turmeric and fry for 1 minute, stirring constantly. Add cucumber, salt, and sugar. Keep heat medium low to low
   and cook, covered, until cucumber is tender, 10 to 15 minutes, stirring
   occasionally. (Cucumber will cook in its own juice. If the skillet is too
   dry, add a tablespoon/15 ml or so of water.)
2. Add potatoes and cook 2 to 3 minutes, stirring constantly. Add coconut
   and mix well. Remove from heat. Let stand covered for a few minutes to
   help develop the flavors. Garnish with mint and serve.
4 to 6 servings.

Serving suggestions: Put in lunch boxes, carry along at picnics, or include
as part of a dinner. This homey dish was a hit when I once served it to
company with rice, Steamed Fish in Chili-Cilantro Sauce, and Spinach in
Spiced Yogurt.

Echorer Dalna
YOUNG GREEN JACKFRUIT WITH CHUNKY POTATOES

Jackfruit is a large, pale green fruit with a bumpy skin that occupies a
special position in Bengali cuisine. When ripe, its creamy yellow flesh has a
faintly sweet, musky flavor and is much prized as a fresh fruit. The flesh of
the immature jackfruit, treated as a vegetable, takes on a rich, meaty flavor
when simmered with spices, and has acquired the nickname of "goat in a
tree." Fresh jackfruit is not readily available in the West, but an acceptable
canned version may usually be found in Asian markets.

2 Tbs. (30 ml) vegetable oil
¼ tsp. (1 ml) cumin seeds
¼ tsp. (1 ml) turmeric
2 tsp. (10 ml) ground cumin
2 tsp. (10 ml) ground coriander
Dash ground red chili or cayenne pepper (or to taste)
10-oz. (drained weight) (280 g) can of young green jackfruit (unsweetened,
   water-packed variety), cut into 1-inch (2.5 cm) slices
½ lb (¼ kg) peeled, cooked potatoes (about 2 medium), cut into 1-inch
   (2.5 cm) cubes
¼ tsp. (1 ml) salt
¼ tsp. (1 ml) sugar
½ tsp. (2 ml) garam masala

1. Heat oil in a skillet over medium low heat. Fry cumin seeds for a few
   seconds. Add turmeric, ground cumin, coriander, and red pepper and
   stir a few times. Add jackfruit. Simmer covered 5 to 7 minutes.
2. Add salt, sugar, and potatoes and mix well. Cover and simmer 2 to
   3 more minutes. Remove from heat. Blend in garam masala. Serve
   piping hot.
4 to 5 servings.

MENUS

"ONE HOUR OR LESS" MENU

Steamed Fish in Chili-Mustard Sauce
Splendid Cilantro Chutney
Pronto Potatoes
Plain Boiled Rice

"ONE HOUR OR LESS" MENU—VEGETARIAN

Steamed Spicy Cauliflower
Onion-Fragrant Red Lentils
Tempting Mint Chutney
Plain Boiled Rice

CANDLELIGHT DINNER FOR TWO

Tender Beginning with Many Flavors
Fancy Fish in Cashew-Pistachio Sauce
Smoked Eggplant in Garlic-Poppyseed Sauce
Ginger-Yogurt Chutney
Plain Boiled Rice
Milk Balls in Rich Saffron Cream Sauce

FAMILY DINNER

Vegetables in a Mingling Mood
Savory Sunday Chicken
Ginger-Scented Yogurt Rice
Mellow Tomato Chutney

FAT-FREE LUNCH

Street-Style Tangy Potatoes
Tempting Mint Chutney
Plain Boiled Rice
Baked Papad

SUMMER BANQUET

Pea-Filled Puffed Buns
Smoked Eggplant and Green Onions in Roasted Red Chili Sauce
Fragrant Roasted Mung Bean Stew
Vegetable Pullao
"Queen Pleasing" Meat Croquettes
Lamb Swimmimg in Creamy Green Sauce
Lemon-laced Rice
Splendid Cilantro Chutney
Green and White Coconut Chutney
Sweet Yogurt "Custard"
Silk and Satin Bars
Lime Yogurt Cooler

PICNIC OR BRUNCH BUFFET

Piquant Potato Croquettes
Cauliflower with a Hint of Mustard
Spinach in Spiced Yogurt
Chic Tart Chickpeas
Chicken Roasted with Fragrant Spices
Tempting Mint Chutney
Delicate Lime Drink
Pan-raised Bread
Papad

CHRISTMAS OPEN HOUSE

Coconut Sesame Joy
Festival Rounds
Gold Bars
Enchantment Bars
Rich Vermicelli Pudding
Piquant Potato Croquettes
Hot and Savory Party Mix

CHUTNEY PARTY

Joyous Ginger-Raisin Chutney
Tempting Mint Chutney
Green and White Coconut Chutney
Tender Tamarind Chutney
Pleasing Plum Chutney
A Platter of Raw and Steamed Vegetables
Plain Boiled Rice
Papad

FESTIVE DINNER

Aromatic Rice with Peas and Whole Spices
Crisp Fried Eggplant
Butternut Squash in Mustard Sauce
Prawns in Coconut Cream Sauce
Fragrant Roasted Mung Bean Stew
Mellow Tomato Chutney
Sweet Yogurt "Custard"
Silk and Satin Bars
Milk Balls in Rose Syrup

NAMASHKAR

We have shared much across the pages of this book, walking through the gentle landscape of Bengal, savoring the varied flavors and aromas of its rich cuisine. I hope some of what I have presented here will become a part of your daily life. Now we must say farewell. As in the beginning, so also in the end: *Namashkar*—"I bow to the divine in you." May this be but the debut of a lifelong journey into the joys of Bengali cooking.

WHERE TO BUY BENGALI INGREDIENTS

Indian grocery stores have proliferated in major cities in the U.S. and Canada in recent years. You can mail-order from most of them. Ask that each item be clearly marked in English.

CALIFORNIA
Bazaar of India, 1331 University Avenue, Berkeley 94702.
Bombay Bazaar, 1034 University Avenue, Berkeley 94710.
India Spice House, 6715-H Dublin Blvd., Dublin 94568.
India Bazaar, 3838 W. 102nd St., Inglewood 90303.
Bezjian's Grocery, 4725 Santa Monica Blvd., Los Angeles 90029.
Haig's Delicacies, 642 Clement St., San Francisco 94118.
India Gift & Foods, 907 Post Street, San Francisco 94109.
Spice Plus, 244 Northgate One, San Rafael 94903.
Bharat Bazaar, 3680 El Camino Real, Santa Clara, CA 95051.
Tarver's Delicacies, De Anza Shopping Center, 1338 South Mary Avenue, Sunnyvale 94087.

WASHINGTON, D.C.
Spices and Foods Unlimited, Inc., 2018 A Florida Ave., N.W., Washington, D.C. 20009.

GEORGIA
Raj Enterprises, 881 Peachtree St. S.E., Atlanta 30307.

ILLINOIS
India Gift and Food Store, 1031 Belmont, Chicago 60657.
India Spice Company, 437 South Boulevard, Oak Park 60302.

MASSACHUSETTS
Vinod Shah, 3 Prescott St., North Woburn 01801.

MICHIGAN
Delmar and Co., 501 Monroe Ave., Detroit 48226.
India Food and Gifts, 3729 Cass, Detroit 48201.

MISSOURI
India Food Center, 15–43 McCausland Ave, St. Louis 63117.

NEW YORK
Kalpana Indian Groceries, 4275 Main St., Flushing 11355.
House of Spices, 76–17 Broadway, Jackson Heights 11373.
Annapurna, 127 E. 28th St., New York 11373.
Aphrodisia, 28 Carmine St., New York 10014.
India Food and Gourmet, 110 Lexington Ave., New York 10016.
K. Kalustyan, Orient Export Trading Corp., 123 Lexington Ave., New York
    10016.
Little India Store, 128 E. 29th St., New York 10016.

NEW JERSEY
T. G. Koryn, Inc., 66 Broad St., Carlstad 07072.
Kumar Bros., 536 Bloomfield Ave., Hoboken 07030.
House of Spices, 9 Elm Row, New Brunswick 08901.

OKLAHOMA
Antone's, 2606 Sheridan, Tulsa 74129.

PENNSYLVANIA
House of Spices India, 4101 Walnut St., Philadelphia 19104.
Bombay Emporium, 3343 Forbes Ave., Pittsburgh 15213.
India Super Bazaar, 1401 Walnut St., Philadelphia 19104.
Spice Corner, 904 S. 9th, Philadelphia 19157.

OREGON
Porter's Food Unlimited, 125 W. 11th St., Eugene 97401.

TEXAS
Jung's Oriental Foods, 2519 North Fitzburgh, Dallas 75204.
Yoga and Health Center, 2912 Oaklawn, Dallas 75222.
Jay Store, 4023 Westheimer, Houston 77027.

TENNESSEE
Giant Foods of America, 100 Oaks Shopping Center, Nashville 37204.

WASHINGTON
Singh's International Video & Spices, 15920 N.E. 8th St., #4, Bellevue
    98008.
Laxmi Emporium, Sound View Plaza, 24817 Pacific Highway S., Suite 203,
    Kent 98032.
R & M Videos & Spice Center, 5501 University Way N.E., Seattle 98105.
The Souk: Two locations, 1916 Pike Pl., N., Seattle 98101; 11730 Pine-
    hurst Way N.E., Seattle 98125.

WISCONSIN
International House of Foods, 440 West Gorham St., Madison 53703.
Indian Groceries and Spices, 2527 W. National Ave., Milwaukee 53208.

CANADA
J and B Foods, 6607 Main, Vancouver, B.C.
Michael's Discount Foods, 6635 Main, Vancouver, B.C.
T. Eaton's Co., 190 Yonge St., Toronto, Ontario.
S. Enkin Inc., Imports and Exports, 1201 St. Lawrence, Montreal, Quebec.

FURTHER READING

If this book has aroused in you a desire to know more about the history, geography, literature, or culture of Bengal, the following books will provide many hours of pleasurable and informative reading.

Bandyopadhyaya, Bibhutibhusan, *A Strange Attachment and Other Stories* (New York: Mosaic Press, 1984)

Banerjee, Bibhutibhusan, *Pather Pachali* (*Song of the Road*) (London: George Allen and Unwin Ltd., 1968)

————, *Pather Pachali* Part 2, "Trumpet Call of Childhood Days" (Calcutta: Writer's Workshop, P. Lal, 1973)

Basu, Tara Krishna, *The Bengal Peasant From Time to Time* (Calcutta: Eka Press, 1962)

Chakravarty, Indira, *Saga of Indian Food* (New Delhi: Sterling Publishers Ltd., 1972)

Darian, Steven, *The Ganges in Myth and History* (Honolulu: The University Press of Hawaii, 1978)

Fruzzetti, Linda, *The Gift of a Virgin: Women, Marriage, and Ritual in a Bengali Society* (New Brunswick, N.J: Rutgers University Press, 1982)

Ghosh, J. C., *Bengali Literature* (London: Oxford University Press, 1948)

Greenough, Paul R., *Prosperity and Misery in Modern Bengal: The Famine of 1943–44* (New York: Oxford University Press, 1982)

Hillary, Edmund, *From the Ocean to the Sky* (New York: Viking Press, 1979)

Kabir, Humayun, *Green and Gold: Stories and Poems of Bengal* (New York: New Directions Books, 1958)

Mahindru, S. N., *Spices in Indian Life* (New Delhi: Sultan Chand, 1982)

Marshall, P. J., *East Indian Fortunes: The British in Bengal in the Eighteenth Century* (Oxford: Clarendon Press, 1976)

Morton, William, *A Collection of Proverbs* (Calcutta: Aparna Book Distributors, 1987)

Paul, Promode Lal, *The Early History of Bengal* (Calcutta: The Indian Research Institute, 1939)

Rice, Edward, *The Ganges: A Personal Encounter* (New York: Four Winds Press, 1974)

Tagore, Rabindranath, *Collected Poems and Plays of Rabindranath Tagore* (New York: The Macmillan Company, 1960)

————, *Cycle of Spring* (New York: The Macmillan Company, 1917)

————, *Gitanjali* (London: Macmillan & Co., 1914)

Note that Bandyopadhyaya and Banerjee are the same author; the name is spelled in two different ways in English.

INDEX